GOVERNORS STATE UNIVERSITY LIBRARY

SO-AQI-951
3 1611 00248 8754

FEB 1 3 1985

ADVANCES IN
APPLIED
MICRO-ECONOMICS

Volume 3 · 1984

ADVANCES IN
APPLIED
MICRO-ECONOMICS

A Research Annual

Editors: V. KERRY SMITH
Department of Economics and
Business Administration
Vanderbilt University

ANN DRYDEN WITTE
Department of Economics
University of North Carolina,
Chapel Hill

VOLUME 3 · 1984

UNIVERSITY LIBRARY
GOVERNORS STATE UNIVERSITY
PARK FOREST SOUTH, ILL

 JAI PRESS INC.

Greenwich, Connecticut   *London, England*

Copyright © 1984 JAI PRESS INC.
36 Sherwood Place
Greenwich, Connecticut 06830

JAI PRESS INC.
3 Henrietta Street
London WC2E 8LU
England

All rights reserved. No part of this publication may be reproduced, stored on a retrieval
system, or transmitted in any form or by any means, electronic, mechanical, filming,
photocopying, recording or otherwise without prior permission in writing from the
publisher.

ISBN: 0-89232-398-1

Manufactured in the United States of America

HB
172
.A38
v. 3
1984
c. 1

CONTENTS

LIST OF CONTRIBUTORS   vii

OVERALL INTRODUCTION TO THE VOLUME
V. Kerry Smith   ix

PART I. ISSUES IN MODELING AND VALUING AMENITY RESOURCES

INTRODUCTION TO PART I
V. Kerry Smith   3

AN ANALYSIS OF CONGESTED RECREATION
FACILITIES
Kenneth E. McConnell and Jon G. Sutinen   9

INTRINSIC BENEFITS OF IMPROVED WATER
QUALITY: CONCEPTUAL AND EMPIRICAL
PERSPECTIVES
Ann Fisher and Robert Raucher   37

TRAVEL COST AND CONTINGENT VALUATION:
A COMPARATIVE ANALYSIS
John Duffield   67

AN APPLICATION OF THE HEDONIC TRAVEL
COST FRAMEWORK FOR RECREATION MODELING
TO THE VALUATION OF DEER
Robert Mendelsohn   89

PART II. ECONOMIC IMPACT ANALYSIS AND CLIMATE CHANGE

INTRODUCTION TO PART II
V. Kerry Smith   105

MODELING THE PROSPECTS OF CLIMTE CHANGES:
CURRENT STATE-OF-THE-ART AND IMPLICATIONS
  William W. Kellogg   109

WELFARE ANALYSIS OF INCOMPLETE ADJUSTMENT
TO CLIMATIC CHANGE
  Daniel McFadden   133

INTERACTIONS BETWEEN ECONOMY AND
CLIMATE: A FRAMEWORK FOR POLICY DESIGN
UNDER UNCERTAINTY
  Geoffrey Heal   151

THE HEDONIC PRICE TECHNIQUE AND THE VALUE
OF CLIMATE AS A RESOURCE
  A. Myrick Freeman, III   169

**PART III.   ISSUES IN MODELING PUBLIC PROVISION OF
EDUCATION AND CRIME PROTECTION**

INTRODUCTION TO PART III
  Ann Dryden Witte   189

IMPROVING THE USE OF EMPIRICAL RESEARCH AS
A POLICY TOOL: REPLICATION OF EDUCATIONAL
PRODUCTION FUNCTIONS
  Anita A. Summers and Barbara L. Wolfe   199

CRIME IN SWEDEN: CAUSALITY, CONTROL EFFECTS
AND ECONOMIC EFFICIENCY
  Harold L. Votey, Jr.   229

A DYNAMIC MODEL OF THE PROVISION OF
PUBLIC SAFETY AND JUSTICE
  Llad Phillips   267

LIST OF CONTRIBUTORS

John Duffield

Department of Economics
University of Montana

Ann Fisher

Office of Policy, Planning
and Evaluation
U.S. Environmental Protection
Agency, Washington, D.C.

A. Myrick Freeman, III

Department of Economics
Bowdoin College

Geoffrey Heal

Graduate School of Business
Columbia University

William W. Kellogg

National Center for Atmospheric
Research, Boulder, Colorado

Kenneth E. McConnell

Department of Agricultural and
Resource Economics
University of Maryland

Daniel McFadden

Department of Economics
Massachusetts Institute of
Technology

Robert Mendelsohn

Department of Economics
School of Natural Resources
University of Michigan

Llad Phillips

Department of Economics
University of California,
Santa Barbara

Robert Raucher

Office of Policy, Planning
and Evaluation
U.S. Environmental Protection
Agency, Washington, D.C.

V. Kerry Smith

Department of Economics and
Business Administration
Vanderbilt University

Anita A. Summers

Department of Public Policy
and Management
The Wharton School
University of Pennsylvania

Jon G. Sutinen

Department of Resource
Economics
University of Rhode Island

Harold L. Votey, Jr.

Department of Economics
University of California,
Santa Barbara

Ann Dryden Witte

Department of Economics
University of North Carolina,
Chapel Hill

Barbara L. Wolfe

Department of Economics
University of Wisconsin

OVERALL INTRODUCTION

V. Kerry Smith

This third volume of *Advances in Applied Micro-Economics* expands the range of topics considered in a single volume. Three areas of considerable academic and professional interest among applied micro-economists are treated in this volume.

The first considers the modeling and valuation of amenity resources. Benefit-cost analyses have begun to play an increasingly important role in the design and evaluation of environmental policies. Benefits analysis is now a major preoccupation of environmental economists. Part I assembles a collection of papers that deal with some of the current research issues in this area as they relate to the valuation of the recreational and amenity services provided by environmental resources.

The second part also deals with a timely topic—climate change and the role of economic analysis in evaluating its effects. The contrast between two recent government sponsored reports[1] on the implications of the accumulation of carbon dioxide for climate changes has focused increased attention on this subject. To date, economic analyses of the problems posed by climate change has been limited. Consequently, these authors provide background on the subject and a consideration of some of the conceptual issues associated with using conventional economic methods in this area.

The last part of the volume considers empirical and methodological issues associated with economic models of the public provision of education and crime protection.

Since each part of the volume has rather different topics, separate introductions discussing the relationships between the papers in each have been prepared. Volume 3 of the series also introduces a guest editor of this volume, Ann Dryden Witte of the University of North Carolina at Chapel Hill. Ann was responsible for assembling the papers in Part III of this volume. Her input has enhanced the scope and quality of the papers in the volume and was greatly appreciated.

In an effort to expand the range of topics that can be reflected in the series, I plan to invite guest editors to work with me in the development of sections in future volumes of the series.

NOTE

1. The two reports were:

    Changing Climate, the Report of the Carbon Dioxide Assessment Committee (Washington, D.C.: National Academy of Sciences, 1983)

    and

    Stephen Seidel and Dale Keyes, *Can We Delay a Greenhouse Warming?* Strategic Studies Staff, Office of Policy Analysis, U.S. Environmental Protection Agency, September 1983.

PART I

ISSUES IN MODELING AND VALUING AMENITY RESOURCES

INTRODUCTION TO PART I

V. Kerry Smith

Benefit estimation has become a major preoccupation of environmental economists. Nearly all of the funded research in this area is concerned with some aspect of the valuation of environmental amenities. In many respects this represents a remarkable transformation in the interests of the policymakers who have provided much (but not all) of the support for this research. While it would be inappropriate to attribute all of the impetus for this change to the growing acceptance of benefit-cost analysis as a legitimate component of the information used in the design of environmental policy, *it has played a role*. Indeed, Executive Order 12291, issued by President Reagan in February 1981 can be viewed as a logical step in a process that began during the Ford Administration. These efforts progressively increased the required evaluation of regulations, moving ever closer to detailed analysis of their economic consequences.

Executive Order 12291 requires that all new major regulations be subjected to a benefit-cost analysis.[1] Moreover, it admonishes regulatory agencies to seek to define regulations so as to maximize the aggregate net benefits they realize. Of course, this requirement can only be imposed

Advances in Applied Micro-Economics, Volume 3, pages 3–8.
Copyright © 1984 by JAI Press Inc.
All rights of reproduction in any form reserved.
ISBN: 0-89232-398-1

on those decisions where statutory provisions do not explicitly prohibit the use of benefit-cost analysis.[2]

To the extent some form of these requirements remains in force in the future, and this seems plausible regardless of the politics of the next administration, then attention to problems posed by valuing environmental amenities is unlikely to diminish. The papers in Part I of Volume III of *Advances in Applied Microeconomics* offer an ideal cross-section of the research issues that are likely to occupy a prominent place in that future research agenda.

Environmental quality has many dimensions. When we consider how individuals utilize environmental amenities for recreational purposes, these dimensions are tacitly understood to influence these decisions (especially by those analysts of the recreational activities under study who are themselves participants during their leisure time). Skiing, when there are long lift lines or crowded slopes, is a different experience than under conditions with ready access to the slopes. Similarly, solitude, or more properly the ability to select the group of individuals with whom one interacts, is an important dimension of low density recreation.

McConnell and Sutinen provide a careful and insightful discussion of how congestion and the associated conditions of access to an environmental resource will affect the measurement of the benefits associated with modifying that resource. For example, expansions to the size of a skiing facility or improvements in the water quality of a flat-water recreation site can each have different values depending upon the management practices in effect for each type of facility.

These authors develop their arguments in analytical terms for decisions involving a single site and for two interrelated sites. Their analysis reflects their appreciation and direct involvement in a substantial amount of the empirical research on the effects of congestion in outdoor recreation. It is clear that there are many factors that can serve to affect an individual's willingness to pay for amenity services. Given heterogeneous preferences, we can expect that management practices which influence these characteristics will also implicitly lead to non-price rationing that affects who uses a facility. For example, some individuals will not be willing to incur the costs to visit a recreation site when they expect the recreational experience will have undesirable characteristics. While the McConnell-Sutinen framework assumes homogeneous individuals, it is careful to identify how this assumption would affect their conclusions. Moreover, they acknowledge that perceptions and individuals' expectations about an experience (and how these expectations change over time) are critically important to characterizing the equilibrium conditions in these types of markets. Thus, this paper not only enhances our appreciation of the role of congestion and management practices designed to affect its level for benefit measurements, it also lays the groundwork for the additional research needed to understand how the markets for these types of resources operate in the real world.

The second paper in this section also addresses a difficult and important problem for the benefit analyses associated with modifications to natural and environmental resources. It considers the relationship between the user and the intrinsic (or nonuser) benefits associated with these resources. Since Krutilla's (1967) classic paper "Conservation Reconsidered," economists have recognized that natural and environmental resources provide benefits that extend beyond the direct uses which are made of them. Krutilla identified option, existence, and bequest values as considerations that were likely to be especially important to unique natural environments. Subsequent research has suggested that these values might be important to a variety of environmental amenities.

Unfortunately, the measurement of these values has proved especially difficult. By nature, if we define a motivation for valuing a good or service that is not associated with an act of consumption (as economists have ordinarily defined consumption), it will be difficult to observe actions based on these values. That is, most economic descriptions of individuals' motives for valuing goods and services "tie" that valuation to some form of consumption. Intrinsic values do not necessarily lead to (nor do they require) a tangible act of consumption. Our models of their role in individual decision-making remains at a fairly elementary and crude level. Basically, what is at issue is establishing some basis for judging how the presence of these values might be detected and the magnitude measured.

To date, our empirical estimates have been based on contingent valuation surveys. In these surveys, the researchers have attempted to elicit individuals' valuation of resources and, at the same time, identify the motives for these valuation responses using direct questions. In some cases a total "bid," including user and intrinsic values was requested and a subsequent partitioning was elicited. In others separate components were requested. Fisher and Raucher's paper draws these findings together for the case of water quality improvements. It relates the design of these empirical studies to the theoretical literature providing the basis for the motivations leading to intrinsic values. By considering the relationship between intrinsic and user values across studies and types of resources, this paper provides the first comprehensive review of the empirical research in this area to date. Equally important, this appraisal evaluates the prospects for transferring existing estimates of the intrinsic to user benefits ratio to new areas. This practice has been proposed as one means for estimating intrinsic values for resources where estimates of only the user values are available.

There has been increasing awareness of the need to use survey based or contingent valuation methods in valuing many types of environmental amenities. Often indirect market methods, such as the hedonic property value model, are not available. Nonetheless, contingent valuation methods are viewed with skepticism by many (if not most) economists. As a consequence, recent research has attempted to provide comparative evaluations of contingent valuation and indirect market based estimates of the valuations of particular environmental amenities. Brookshire et al. (1982), provided the first such evaluation, comparing a contingent valuation and hedonic property value model's estimates of the benefits associated with air quality improvements. More recently, Desvousges, Smith, and McGivney (1983) compared the travel cost recreational demand framework with a contingent valuation survey for water quality changes. While both studies indicated the indirect method and the survey approach provided comparable estimates in order of magnitude terms, they also highlighted a number of reasons for varied performance of both approaches to benefit estimation. Accordingly, it is clear that a full understanding of the relationship between the direct (or survey) and the indirect approaches to benefit measurement will require replication of these comparative studies under a wide array of circumstances.

The third paper in this section provides one such replication. In his paper, Duffield reports a comparative analysis of the travel cost and contingent valuation methods for the valuation of a recreational site—the Kootenai Falls in northwestern Montana. Duffield's results are generally consistent with the two earlier comparative analyses. However, by considering the effects of single versus multiple destination trips and the specification of the functional form for the travel cost model, his analysis serves to illustrate some additional potential sources of discrepancy between these methods' benefit estimates.

This section closes with an application of a new methodology to recreation demand analysis—the hedonic travel cost framework originally proposed by Brown and Mendelsohn (1980). In this paper, Mendelsohn illustrates how the method can be applied to provide a recreational demand model consistent with the needs of wildlife management. As we noted in introducing this section, the characteristics of recreational experiences influence an individual's valuation of the resources' providing those experiences. McConnell and Sutinen demonstrated that if we know these relationships and understand management practices we must incorporate *both* in our evaluation of projects intended to modify the resources providing these services. What remains, of course, is to determine how individuals' value the characteristics of the recreational experience. Brown and Mendelsohn's innovation recognizes that we can characterize how individuals might perceive their opportunities in an implicit price function. That is, under the assumption of complete information, an individual faces the prospect of recreating at a number of different sites, each with differing characteristics. These prices and sets of characteristics provide a description of the locus of opportunities, together with implicit marginal prices of each characteristic. In effect, the natural endowment together with knowledge of an individual's actual choices may provide sufficient information to disentangle a complex index number problem.[3] Moreover, with such a resolution, it is possible to value the attributes of recreational experiences in terms that can facilitate management decisions. Mendelsohn's paper illustrates how this can be accomplished for the case of deer hunting to determine the value Pennsylvania hunters place on deer density.

These four papers have identified some of the most important aspects of the research issues facing benefit estimation for environmental resources. They combine analytical insight with empirical results to help document what we do know and what we need to learn. As such, they provide good background for understanding the research needed in environmental benefit analysis.

NOTES

1. For a more detailed discussion of the background for and effects of Executive Order 12291, see Smith (1984).

2. The most prominent example of a prohibition of benefit-cost analysis would arise in the statutory mandates for the primary national ambient air quality standards for criteria pollutants. These standards are to be set to protect sensitive members of the population from health impacts with an adequate margin of safety.

3. It should be acknowledged that there are several theoretical issues associated with the hedonic travel cost framework that require further attention. For the most part they relate to the plausibility of the maintained assumption that the price function, relating travel costs to site attributes, exists. Among the most important of these are: (1) the definition of the relevant sites considered by individuals in each origin zone; and (2) the mechanism that assures a smooth locus relating implicit prices to site attributes.

The encouraging empirical findings with the method to date should provide further stimulus to the research needed to address these issues.

REFERENCES

Brookshire, David S., Ralph C. d'Arge, William D. Schulze and Mark A. Thayer, "Experiments in Valuing Public Goods." In V. K. Smith (ed.), *Advances in Applied Micro-Economics*, Vol. I. Greenwich, CT: JAI Press, 1981.

Brookshire, David S., Mark A. Thayer, William D. Schulze, and Ralph C. d'Arge, "Valuing Public Goods: A Comparison of Survey and Hedonic Approaches." *American Economic Review* 72(March 1982):165–177.

Brown, Gardner M. and Robert Mendelsohn, "The Hedonic Travel Cost Method." Seattle: Institute for Economic Research, University of Washington, 1980.

Desvousges, William H., V. Kerry Smith and Matthew P. McGivney, *A Comparison of Alternative Approaches for Estimating Recreation and Related Benefits of Water Qual-*

ity Improvement, Environmental Benefits Analysis Series. Washington, DC, U.S. Environmental Protection AGency, 1983.

Krutilla, John V., "Conservation Reconsidered." *American Economic Review* 57(September 1967):777–786.

Smith, V. Kerry (ed.), *Environmental Policy Under Reagan's Executive Order: The Role of Benefit-Cost Analysis*. Chapel Hill, NC: University of North Carolina Press, 1984.

AN ANALYSIS OF CONGESTED
RECREATION FACILITIES

Kenneth E. McConnell and Jon G. Sutinen

I.   INTRODUCTION

The forces of economic development have shifted radically the supply of
and demand for outdoor recreation services in twentieth-century America. These shifts have, in turn, altered the quantity, quality, distribution,
and provision of recreational services.

On the demand side, growth in population and per capita income, the
shorter work week, and the change in transportation facilities have increased the demand for outdoor recreation services. The numbers are
substantial. Population increased 2.9 times between 1900 and 1980. Per
capita personal income grew by 134 percent from 1929 to 1978. From 1900
to 1960, the average work week declined from 58.5 to 41 hours. During
the same period, more school and earlier retirements led to a decline in
the percent of years spent in the labor force from 66.6 to 62.2 percent.
The consequence of the shorter work week and the lower proportion of

Advances in Applied Micro-Economics, Volume 3, pages 9–36.
Copyright © 1984 by JAI Press Inc.
All rights of reproduction in any form reserved.
ISBN: 0-89232-398-1

years in the labor force is that the proportion of life spent in the labor
force declined from 34.8 to 24.5 percent. Improved transportation facilities, especially the interstate highway system, have lowered the costs of
reaching many remote recreation sites.[1]

On the supply side, a modern enclosure movement has spread across
the nation's open access resources. Increasing residential and industrial
exploitation of open access land has eliminated a large stock of assets
once informally available for recreational use. Pollution has also contrib-
uted to the reduction in the quantity and quality of assets which are used
in the provision of recreational services. For example, bodies of water
such as Long Island Sound and Delaware Bay, once major water recreation areas, are no longer available for certain water sports because of
water pollution.

Because of the diversity of facilities and the absence of records, it is
not easy to document the changes in demand and supply. Some broad
measures from the public sector are available. For national parks, visits
per acre increased from .035 in 1904 to 3.2 in 1970. Overnight use of state
parks grew from .68 per acre in 1941 to 5.9 in 1970.[2] The reduction in the
stock of private natural resources available on an open access basis is
even harder to document. But it is subject to a dynamic which has resulted
in closing many private lands and beaches to public use. If demand is low
and there are many private landowners, the cost of granting access to the
public is low to each landowner. If some landowners develop their land
and demand increases, the pressure on remaining landowners is inten-
sified, causing additional landowners to convert their lands or close them
to the public. As this process has evolved, private land has become much
less accessible for the public today than it was before World War II.

One consequence of this long-run change has been a growing gap between the supply and demand for natural resource services at going
prices. In a market dominated by the profit motive, this gap would be
closed by supply and demand responses to induced price increases. In
the United States, however, federal, state, and local governments have
historically provided recreational facilities for the public's use at prices
which do not respond to differences in supply and demand. In the informal
market for services of natural resources, there is the possibility of a substantial disequilibrium at going prices. This disequilibrium is eliminated
by increases in the congestion of public facilities and more provision of
private facilities rather than by price increases. Thus, congestion has had,
and will likely continue to have, a significant role in the equilibrating
process for outdoor recreation resources.

The impetus for research in congestion of natural resources, like many
other topics in natural resource economics, stems from Hell's Canyon.

John Krutilla describes the origins:

> Resources for the Future's interest in the problem of defining the optimal capacity
> for low density, wilderness recreation began with the problem Clifford Russell and
> I confronted in attempting to compare the value of the Hell's Canyon reach of the
> Snake River as a source of electricity with its value as a source of amenity services
> incompatible with hydroelectric development (Shechter and Lucas, 1978, Foreword,
> p. xv).

The basic model of congestion at a single site, developed initially by Fisher and Krutilla (1972), was influenced by economists' concerns over the deterioration in the quality of wilderness areas. Thus, in recreation, the impact of congestion is modeled as reducing the economic value of the recreational experience. (See Sandler and Tschirhart, 1980, p. 1509, for a comparison between recreation and transportation.) The Fisher–Krutilla model, now well known, dealt with the congestion of a pristine environment. Users expected to visit the resource infrequently. Dense use created not only congestion but perhaps environmental degradation as well.

The basic model has received a number of theoretical twists. Freeman and Haveman (1977) analyze the importance of heterogeneity among users, arguing that the optimal admissions fee depends on the incidence of congestion costs on users. Anderson and Bonsor (1974) formulate a model of price-taking, profit-maximizing firms producing services in a congested environment. Freeman (1979) uses the basic model to show that the benefits of improvements in site quality are reduced in the presence of congestion.

While congestion-related phenomena have received the greatest attention in wilderness areas, they are also important in high-density recreation areas, where they have received less attention. Many local, state, and federal recreation facilities attain equilibrium induced by congestion. In those areas, the choice of sites by users and the management of sites differ from the choices and problems in wilderness areas. For users, the choice is often made several times per year, and the choice may be made among sites which are relatively similar except for expected congestion levels. For example, in Walsh et al. (1983) the mean annual number of days skied exceeded 20, whereas McConnell's (1977) beach goers also averaged more than 20 days per season. For management, the problems encountered in dealing with congestion are more likely peak load problems and the distributional effects of policies designed to reduce congestion.

The nature of the research on congestion, typified by the literature following in the Fisher–Krutilla tradition, is to investigate the impact of congestion on the quality of the recreational experience. A less-developed aspect of congestion concerns its role in bringing about equilibrium in the market for outdoor recreation services. In this role, congestion provides two functions:

First, congestion induced by differences in supply and demand brings about equilibrium in the public sector. But equilibrium here is not equality of quantity supplied and demanded at the going price. Rather, it involves the equality of expected and realized congestion. The nature of expectations and the revision of expectations must play a prominent role in establishing and restoring equilibria in the public sector. Freeman and Haveman (1977, p. 230, fn. 4) and Cicchetti and Smith (1976, p. 32, fn. 2) touch briefly on the nature of disequilibrium and expectations for congested recreation facilities.

A second role of congestion, even less well investigated, is to signal the private sector to increase supply. In those cases where private enterprise can profitably provide outdoor recreation services, a more congested public sector raises the price at which the private market clears. Examples abound. Cabana clubs develop on crowded beaches. Private tennis courts and golf courses grow in urban areas. Thus congestion is very important in establishing an equilibrium in the provision of recreational services, both in the public and private sectors.

The purpose of this paper is to show the workings of congested recreation facilities. The paper will show how equilibrium is established and how it responds to shifts in exogenous variables. One theme of the paper concerns the role of government in dealing with congestion. It is shown that the measurement of benefits and the estimation of behavioral functions depend on the degree to which congestion is controlled and the tools which are used to control it.

The paper is organized as follows: Section II deals with congestion at a single site; Section III, with congestion at several sites. In Section IV we consider some empirical problems presented by congested recreation sites.

II. CONGESTION AT A SINGLE SITE

The purpose of this section is to develop theoretical results for a single congested site. The analysis will present some well-known results and make formal some results previously available on an intuitive level. The analysis of congested sites involves two relationships: one involves preferences and generally receives the most attention; the second is the technical relationship between the site use and physical aspects of the capacity of the site. This analysis is developed in the context of homogeneous users determining their quantity of use in a given time period.

Congestion at a recreation site develops because of the physical relationship between the size of the site and the level of use of the site. Assume, for simplicity, that congestion can be measured by a single variable, denoted q. The measurement of q will vary with the nature of the facility. For example, q may be the number of bathers per acre of beach or the length of lines at a ski lift. In wilderness recreation, q has typically been measured as the number of encounters with other visitors per day or per trip. More descriptive analysis would require several dimensions of q [for example, encounters on the trail and contacts at the campsite (Cicchetti and Smith, 1976); or, for skiers, density on the slopes and waiting time in lift lines (Walsh et al., 1983)]. Let the capacity be measured by a single physical measure, denoted S, such as the area of a beach, the length of trails in a wilderness area, or the number of lifts at a ski resort. Visits to the site are denoted v, where v is the product of the number of users and trips per user. The congestion relation, analogous to a production function in some ways, is written

$$q = q(v, S),$$

where $\partial q/\partial S \equiv q_S \leq 0$ is the partial effect of site expansion, which reduces congestion, and $\partial q/\partial v \equiv q_v \geq 0$ is the partial effect of visits on congestion. Intraseasonal variation is a significant issue, but, for the present, we assume that users distribute their visits uniformly over the season. Here S is exogenous and initially constant, so that we occasionally suppress S and write $q = q(v)$.

Let z be visits per user and n be the number of identical users. Then $v = nz$ is total visits. The number of users is assumed constant. Each user takes as given prices and congestion at the site. The users behave according to the Marshallian demand function

$$z = f(p, q)$$

when p is the price of entrance to the site. In many cases, p will be zero or nominal. Naturally $f_p < 0$. Congestion is present when "personal contact with other facility users is generally regarded as reducing the quality or value of a visitation" (Freeman and Haveman, 1977, p. 232). Thus, $f_q \leq 0$. The inverse of f(z, q) can be written as

$$p = \pi(z, q),$$

where $\pi_z < 0$ and $\pi_q \leq 0$. The inverse demand function $\pi(z, q)$ indicates the maximum dollars the individual is willing to pay for the zth visit when the congestion level is q. Since users never know ex ante what actual congestion at the site is, the argument in the Marshallian demand function must be expected congestion.

The assumption of homogeneous users is an especially vexing one. For a variety of reasons pertaining to income, physical abilities, and social background, tastes for recreational experiences differ. And especially in cases of non–price regulation, heterogeneity becomes relevant in deriving comparative static results. On behalf of the assumption, the broad spectrum of recreational facilities available suggests that similar individuals may select similar sites, increasing the homogeneity of users at any site.

For an individual facing a price p and congestion level q, individual consumer's surplus is given by the area above p under $f(p, q)$:

$$CS = \int_p^\infty f(p', q) \, dp', \tag{1}$$

where p may be set optimally or at zero. Since the n users are identical, aggregate consumers' surplus is given by

$$nCS = n \int_p^\infty f(p', q) \, dp'. \tag{2}$$

Assume, initially, that there are no travel costs and no costs of operating and maintaining the recreation site. Then revenues collected, pnz, are benefits which, when added to consumers' surplus, give the measure of total benefits as

$$\text{rent} + \text{consumers' surplus} = pnf(p, q) + n \int_p^\infty f(p', q) \, dp' \tag{3}$$

$$= n \int_0^{\bar{z}} \pi(z, q) \, dz, \tag{4}$$

where $\bar{z} = f(p, q)$ and $q = q(\bar{z}n)$. Congestion reduces benefits by shifting back $\pi(\bar{z}, q)$. When site operating and maintenance costs are present, they must be deducted from the right-hand side of (3) or (4) to give an appropriate measure of net benefits.

A. Characteristics of Open Access Equilibrium

Let the equilibrium values for individual visits and the congestion level be denoted by z^0 and q^0, respectively. Under open access, which is generally associated with a nominal or zero price, the equilibrium numbers of visits and level of congestion are determined by

$$\pi(z^0, q^0) = p$$

and

$$(5)$$

$$q^0 = q(nz^0).$$

The equilibrium is characterized by two conditions: First, marginal willingness to pay, evaluated at the expected level of congestion, equals price.

The price is determined by fiat, generally having nothing to do with the equilibrium. Second, expected congestion equals actual congestion. When the price is constant, congestion plays the role of price in the equilibrating process.

Nothing is said here about how the equilibrium is reached. The behavior of a congested market out of equilibrium is a vexing problem made more difficult than a dynamic market equilibrium in practice because it is not possible to post, in advance, the congestion level. It can only be determined ex post. In the equilibrium analysis, we assume that users correctly anticipate the actual level of congestion.

The equilibrium for the individual is depicted in Figure 1. Individual consumer's surplus is the shaded area labeled CS, and per-user revenue is the shaded area labeled R. The curve labeled E is the individual's locus of equilibrium z for all $p \geq 0$, i.e., where $p = \pi(z, q(nz))$. There is an

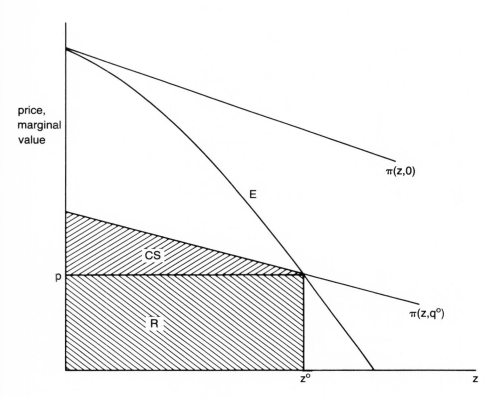

Figure 1.   Individual demand: Trips per period of time

aggregate schedule analogous to E which, at each p on the vertical axis, is nz rather than z on the horizontal axis. Total benefits under open access are simply (3) or (4) evaluated at z^0.

These results for open access equilibrium are often obtained with the use of a marginal cost of congestion schedule (for example, see Cesario, 1980). Freeman and Haveman (1977) explicitly compute the private and social marginal costs of congestion for users making a single visit.[3] Here, we show that when total congestion costs are properly identified, the equality of the marginal value of trips at zero congestion with the marginal costs of congestion determines the open access equilibrium. Define private congestion costs as the individual's benefits foregone because of congestion:

$$\text{private congestion costs} = \int_0^{z^0} [\pi(z, 0) - \pi(z, q^0)] \, dz.$$

Gross individual benefits in this context are defined as the individual's willingness to pay for z^0 visits with no congestion:

$$\int_0^{z^0} \pi(z, 0) \, dz - pz^0.$$

The consumers' surplus equals gross benefits less congestion costs:

$$CS = \int_0^{z^0} \pi(z, 0) \, dz - pz^0 - \int_0^{z^0} [\pi(z, 0) - \pi(z, q^0)] \, dz. \tag{6}$$

The individual chooses z by maximizing (6), which is where

$$\pi(z^0, 0) - [\pi(z^0, 0) - \pi(z, q^0)] - p = 0.$$

Letting the term in brackets be private marginal congestion cost, denoted pmc(z, q), yields the condition

$$\pi(z^0, 0) = pmc(z^0, q) + p. \tag{7}$$

The cost is private because each individual responds at the margin to $\pi(z, 0) - \pi(z, q^0)$ when choosing his number of trips. Equilibrium requires that z^0 satisfy (7) and q satisfy $q = q(nz^0)$. For the same p, this equilibrium condition leads to the same z^0 as condition (5). This result identifies the private cost of congestion as the consumers' surplus foregone by a positive level of congestion.

Some simple comparative statics on (5) help explain the equilibrium conditions. The analysis of changes in the admission fee and site size is straightforward. Rewrite the equilibrium condition for open access as

$$\pi(z^0, q(nz^0)) = p. \tag{8}$$

Totally differentiating with respect to p yields

$$\frac{dz^0}{dp} = \frac{1}{\pi_z + n\pi_q q_v}, \tag{9}$$

which collapses to the slope of the ordinary demand function when the congestion effect is zero ($\pi_q = 0$) or the facility is not congested ($q_v = 0$), because $f_p = 1/\pi_z$. The congestion effect makes the demand curve steeper. In Figure 1, dz/dp is traced along the locus E, which is steeper than the $\pi(z, q)$ schedules. The effect of increasing the number of users, n, is to impart additional steepness to dz/dp.

An increase in site size must reduce congestion and increase attendance, if the increase starts from an equilibrium situation. The initial impact of an increase in site size is to shift out individual demands as congestion drops. But the outward shift increases use, partly affecting the impact of the increase in capacity. Ultimately, there is some more use and less congestion. To show the impact formally, let congestion be an explicit function of site size: $q = q(nz, S)$. Then differentiating (8) with respect to site size yields:

$$\frac{dz^0}{dS} = -\frac{\pi_z q_S}{\pi_z + n\pi_q q_v} \geq 0. \tag{10}$$

Expression (10) shows that, when the congestion effect is not zero, supply (site size), in part, determines demand. The equilibrium impact of capacity expansion on congestion is given by

$$\frac{dq^0}{dS} = \frac{\pi_z q_S}{\pi_z + n\pi_q q_v} \leq 0. \tag{11}$$

Intuitively, capacity expansion must reduce congestion and increase attendance because a simultaneous increase in capacity and congestion and a reduction in attendance is impossible from an equilibrium situation.

B. Equilibrium under Optimal Management

Previously, we have assumed that p is set without regard for congestion and is zero or nominal. This is the typical open access case. It is well known that open access equilibria are not optimal (see, for example, Fisher and Krutilla, 1972). The optimal allocation is achieved by maximizing consumers' surplus:

$$\max_{z^*} nCS = n \int_0^{z^*} \pi(z, q(nz^*))\, dz. \tag{12}$$

The first-order condition for this problem implies

$$\pi(z^*, q^*) = -q_v^* n \int_0^{z^*} \pi_q(z, q^*)\, dz, \tag{13}$$

where $q^* = q(nz^*)$. The left-hand side of (13) is the marginal willingness to pay at the optimum, and the right-hand side is external congestion cost, which is the reduction in all users' willingness to pay to visit the site caused by more congestion.

We can also derive the optimality condition by maximizing the gross consumers' surplus less costs, as in expression (6):

$$\max_{z^*} n \int_0^{z^*} \pi(z, 0)\, dz - n \int_0^{z^*} [\pi(z, 0) - \pi(z, q(nz^*))]\, dz.$$

The first integral gives the total benefits of z^* visits with no congestion; the second integral gives the total costs, or reduction in total benefits, due to congestion when each user takes z^* visits. The first-order condition is

$$\pi(z^*, 0) = [\pi(z^*, 0) - \pi(z^*, q^*)] - n \int_0^{z^*} \pi_q q_v^*\, dz,$$

and π_q is evaluated at q^*. The left-hand side is the marginal willingness to pay for the z^*th trip with no congestion. On the right-hand side, the term in brackets is the individual's private congestion costs (i.e., the reduction in the marginal value of the z^*th trip due to the directly perceived level of congestion q^*). The last term on the right-hand side is the external marginal congestion cost: the reduction in all users' marginal value due to the individual's z^*th visit and not weighed in the individual's calculus.

These results demonstrate that, under open access, too many visits and too much congestion exist at the site. If an admission fee were set equal to the external congestion cost, open access would also be optimal. Using (13) gives

$$p^* = -nq_v(nz^*) \int_0^{z^*} \pi_q(z, q^*)\, dz. \tag{14}$$

A site which is managed optimally will respond differently to changes in exogenous variables from an open access site. This difference has important consequences for measuring the benefits of changes in exogenous variables, such as site size. Cesario (1980, p. 334) has argued that the net benefit is greater under open access than it is under optimal management. To examine the effects of site expansion, we rewrite the consumers' surplus measure with S as an argument in the congestion function:

$$nCS = n \int_0^{\bar{z}} \pi(z, q(n\bar{z}, S))\, dz. \tag{15}$$

Differentiating (15) with respect to S yields

$$\frac{\partial nCS^0}{\partial S} = n \left(q_v n \frac{dz^0}{dS} + q_S \right) \int_0^{z^0} \pi_q(z, q(nz^0, S))\, dz \tag{16}$$

for the open access site and

$$\frac{\partial nCS^*}{\partial S} = nq_S \int_0^{z^*} \pi_q(z, q(nz^*, S)) \, dz \tag{17}$$

for the optimally managed site. To obtain (16), we use first-order conditions (5) with $p = 0$. Comparing (16) with (17) shows that site expansion under open access does not unambiguously yield greater added net benefits than under optimal allocation. Consider the case of a perfectly elastic demand curve. With an open access policy, consumers' surplus is completely eroded away under any site size, implying zero marginal benefits of site size. With optimal allocation, however, site expansioin would yield positive marginal benefits at some site size.

A numerical example can also help establish this case. Suppose that the individual preference function for trips and congestion is given by

$$\pi(z, q) = a_0 + a_1 z + a_2 q,$$

where $a_0 > 0$ and a_1, $a_2 < 0$. The purpose of this numerical example is to show that capacity increases may increase optimal benefits more or less than open access benefits, depending on the parameters.

For simplicity, let the congestion function be a density function:

$$q(nz, S) = nz/S.$$

The open access equilibrium occurs where condition (5) holds, implying

$$z^0 = - \frac{a_0}{a_1 + a_2 n/S} \, .$$

The optimal use level occurs where condition (13) holds, implying

$$z^* = - \frac{a_0}{a_1 + 2a_2 n/S} \, .$$

Table 1 gives some numerical parameters and consumers' surplus in pairs of rows. In case 1, the relative effects of a unit change in trips and congestion are equal: $a_1 = a_2$. In an open access facility, individual surplus increases by .75 with a doubling of site capacity from 400 to 800, while optimal surplus increases by .7. In cases 2 and 3, when the effect of congestion is much higher than the effect of trips, optimal surplus increases more than open access surplus.

These results are especially interesting when viewed in relation to the literature on the size of underpriced facilities (e.g., see Seneca, 1970; Mumy and Hanke, 1975; Porter, 1977). This literature, which analyzes heterogeneous users, demonstrates that the welfare measure used to determine optimal capacity should consider explicitly the method used to

Table 1. Numerical Parameters and Consumers' Surplus

Case*	Parameter Value			Open Access Consumers' Surplus	Optimal Consumers' Surplus
	a_1	a_2	S		
(1)	$-.1$	$-.1$	400	3.20	3.30
	$-.1$	$-.1$	800	3.95	4.00
(2)	$-.01$	$-.8$	400	.11	1.22
	$-.01$	$-.8$	800	.42	2.38
(3)	$-.01$	$-.1$	400	4.07	8.33
	$-.01$	$-.1$	800	9.87	14.29

Note:
* For all cases, $a_0 = 1$ and $n = 100$.

eliminate excess demand. The same results emerge here when homogeneous users are considered. The benefits of site expansion depend on whether use levels are determined optimally or by open access.

C. Enhancing the Quality of a Site

The role of congestion in the measurement of the benefits of environmental improvement is an important topic because many recreation sites which are heavily polluted also have the potential to be highly congested. In the United States, this is especially true of water recreation in the Northeast. In speaking of water recreation sites, Freeman (1979, p. 220) states "the benefits of improving water quality at a site are reduced if congestion is present." We show that this conclusion depends on the kind of management regime in force and does not hold if the site is optimally managed.

Suppose there is an environmental quality variable, denoted α, which is exogenous to the individual user and determines, in part, the marginal value of trips. For example, α could measure the biological oxygen demand (BOD) content of water. It is well known that when α is weakly complementary to trips to the site or when trips to the site are essential to enjoy the quality of the site, the social value to users of changes in α can be calculated by aggregating changes in the area under individual demand curves for trips to the site (see Freeman, 1979; Chap. 4). Let us further suppose that changes in α are of no interest to anyone who does not use the site. Hence, the social value to users captures the whole value of changes in α. Now, we show the impact of congestion on measures of the value of improving the quality of the site.

Let the marginal value of the site be $\pi(z, q, \alpha)$, where, as before, $q = q(nz, S)$. Then the accepted measure of site value is

$$nCS = n \int_0^{\bar{z}} \pi(z, q(n\bar{z}, S), \alpha) \, dz,$$

where $\bar{z} = z^0$ for open access and $\bar{z} = z^*$ for optimal allocation. The change in this value from changing α is

$$\frac{\partial nCS^0}{\partial \alpha} = n^2 q_v \frac{dz^0}{d\alpha} \int_0^{z^0} \pi_q(z, q^0, \alpha) \, dz + n \int_0^{z^0} \pi_\alpha(z, q^0, \alpha) \, dz \quad (18)$$

for open access and

$$\frac{\partial nCS^*}{\partial \alpha} = n \int_0^{z^*} \pi_\alpha(z, q^*, \alpha) \, dz \quad (19)$$

for optimal allocation. The terms in (18) and (19)

$$n \int_0^{\bar{z}} \pi_\alpha(z, \bar{q}, \alpha) \, dz \qquad \text{for} \quad \bar{z} = z^0, z^*$$

are the conventional measure of the social value of changes in α, i.e., the increase in the area under the demand curve. Note, however, that the first term on the right-hand side of (18) is negative. This means that the added benefits of improving the quality of the site are reduced by congestion under open access. If the site is optimally managed, the conventional measure of benefits as the shift in the area under the demand curve holds. While it may seem academic to discuss site improvements under optimal management, rationing is often present, preventing congestion from eating away the enhanced site value.

The incremental benefits from enhanced quality in open access depend on the amount by which congestion shifts the per-user demand curves. Thus, water recreation sites which have poor water quality but are densely used may provide little real increase in benefits if the sites are open access. With a correctly specified and estimated demand function, the conventional measure will give correct information about the value of a change in the quality of an optimally congested site but will overestimate the value of a congested open access site if only the site quality-induced shift is computed.

We should emphasize that quality improvement under optimal management may or may not yield greater benefits than under open access. The similarities between Eqs. (16) and (18) and Eqs. (17) and (19) imply the same ambiguity for benefit changes as in the site expansion case.

These results show that the nature of the management regime has a significant impact on the benefits from site improvement. Nothing is said about how optimal management is achieved, but the results would vary with the instruments used to control congestion. While the optimal site size and congestion are easily defined in concept, their attainment in practice is subject to several barriers. Some approaches to managing congestion promote empirical problems and thus warrant some discussion here.

Economists are likely to recommend the imposition of a price equal to the marginal congestion cost to achieve optimal use. This approach is unlikely to be adopted, in part because of its impact on the income distribution of site users. The most popular approach is rationing use. This approach is deceptively simple. Its success and its impact depend upon how rationing is implemented. For example, suppose that condition (13) were used to determine that nz* was to be the maximum number of trips per season. If rationing were implemented by lottery, with no transaction costs to individuals, management might achieve nz*. However, if use were granted on a first-come, first-served basis, then the uncertainty about whether access to the site would be granted would reduce use (McConnell and Duff, 1976) or perhaps increase time costs of waiting (Porter, 1977). Beach use is often informally rationed by the availability of parking space. This method of rationing effectively makes the recreation problem very much like the transportation problem, as increases in expected time costs incurred in waiting for parking are substituted for the congestion-induced reduction in willingness to pay for the site.

From the work of Seneca (1970), Mumy and Hanke (1975), Freeman and Haveman (1977), and Porter (1977), it is clear that (i) the method used to induce equilibrium is a determinant of the net benefits to the facility, and (ii) the heterogeneity of users will have an impact on the net benefits, especially when the use of the facility is rationed on a first-come, first-served basis. The assumption of the homogeneity of users in this paper is limiting but necessary to achieve analytical results. It is particularly apparent from the literature that the assumption of homogeneity in a heterogeneous world will give a misreading of aggregate benefits when rationing is by a first-come, first-served basis.

Whether the tool is direct rationing or imposing fees, frontal attempts to solve congestion problems have not proven politically popular. Indirect approaches to dealing with congestion implicitly attempt to shift the congestion function q(nz, S) exogenously. If, by management or technical change, q(nz, S) can be reduced, given the site size and number of visits, then benefits can be increased. The congestion function can be influenced in a variety of ways. For car camping, campsites can be separated by vegetation, reducing the number of other campers visible. The timing of river raft trips can be controlled to reduce encounters without reducing the flow of users.

III. CONGESTION AT SEVERAL SITES

In many circumstances, user choices and management strategies involve several congested sites. Choices about activities such as downhill skiing, car camping, and beach going are often made among a group of congested sites. The multiple site problem has been dealt with briefly by Cesario (1980). Here, we treat two sites only, for simplicity. The purpose of this section is to show that comparative statics for two sites involves congestion relations as well as preference relations and to show how external government intervention can influence benefit measurement.

The physical sizes of the sites are represented by S_1 and S_2, and an individual's visits to the sites by z_1 and z_2. Congestion at the site is given by $q_i = q_i(nz_i, S_i)$, for $i = 1, 2$. As in the single-site case, each individual takes as given all prices and the congestion levels at the sites. Each individual maximizes utility subject to an income constraint, resulting in Marshallian inverse demand functions $\pi^1(z_1, z_2, q_1, q_2)$ for site 1 and $\pi^2(z_1, z_2, q_1, q_2)$ for site 2, where

$$\frac{\partial \pi^i}{\partial z_i} = \pi_i^i < 0, \qquad i = 1, 2,$$

and

$$\frac{\partial \pi^i}{\partial q_i} = \pi_{i+2}^i < 0, \qquad i = 1, 2.$$

Thus, π_3^1 and π_4^2 take the place of π_q of the previous section, where π_q is the impact of congestion on the marginal value of trips to the site. In addition, we assume that $\partial \pi^1/\partial z_2 \equiv \pi_2^1 = \partial \pi^2/\partial z_1 \equiv \pi_1^2$. The symmetry of cross-partials on the Marshallian functions implies a homothetic subgroup utility function for visits to the site. This assumption is made to ensure a unique measure of consumers' surplus and, equivalently, path-independent line integrals. It seems likely that this assumption involves small errors. It does require equal income elasticities for goods within the group.

With entrance prices at zero, individual consumer's surplus, CS, is given by the line integral

$$CS(z^0, q^0) = \int_R \pi^1(z_1, z_2, q^0)\, dz_1 + \pi^2(z_1, z_2, q^0)\, dz_2, \qquad (20)$$

where R is the path of integration $(0, 0)$ to (z_1^0, z_2^0) and q^0 is the vector of congestion levels, (q_1^0, q_2^0), taken as given. The symmetry assumption implies that the integral (20) is path independent, allowing it to be written in terms of ordinary integrals:

$$CS(z^0, q^0) = \int_0^{z_1^0} \pi^1(z_1, 0, q^0)\, dz_1 + \int_0^{z_2^0} \pi^2(z_1^0, z_2, q^0)\, dz_2, \quad (21)$$

where the path $(0, 0) \rightarrow (z_1^0, 0) \rightarrow (z_1^0, z_2^0)$ is chosen. Aggregate consumers' surplus is $nCS(z^0, q^0)$:

$$nCS = n \left\{ \int_0^{z_1^0} \pi^1(z_1, 0, q^0)\, dz_1 + \int_0^{z_2^0} \pi^2(z_1^0, z_2, q^0)\, dz_2 \right\}; \quad (22)$$

when there are no costs of operating and maintaining the sites, (22) provides the appropriate measure of social benefits.

A. Open Access Equilibrium

As in the single site case, we initially assume the size of both sites is fixed and suppress the S_i in the $q_i(\cdot)$. Let the equilibrium values for individual visits and congestion levels be denoted by z_i^0 and q_i^0 ($i = 1, 2$). Suppose that nominal prices p_i, for $i = 1, 2$, are charged at each site. Then the individual maximizes

$$CS(z^0, q) = \int_0^{z_1^0} \pi^1(z_1, 0, q)\, dz_1$$

$$+ \int_0^{z_2^0} \pi^2(z_1^0, z_2, q)\, dz_2 - z_1^0 p_1 - z_2^0 p_2,$$

which gives the conditions[4]

$$\pi^i(z_1^0, z_2^0, q) = p_i, \qquad i = 1, 2.$$

As in the single-site case, congestion is determined by individual visits. The equilibrium values of the z_i and q_i under open access are given by [where $z = (z_1, z_2)$ and $q = (q_1, q_2)$]

and
$$\left. \begin{array}{l} \pi^i(z^0, q^0) = p_i \\ q_i^0 = q_i(z_i^0 n) \end{array} \right\} \qquad i = 1, 2. \quad (23)$$

We are interested in how attendance at each site changes when we increase price or capacity at one of the sites. This situation is a plausible theoretical framework for choice among beaches, parks, or ski slopes, where the choice is among sites which are substitutes. We seek these results, in part, because they show how the equilibrium for several sites works and, in part, because they are necessary to show how benefits respond to site expansion under open access.

Assume that a pricing system is implemented which allows open access to all who pay the (perhaps nominal) prices of p_1 and p_2 per site.

To examine the impact of a price change, we differentiate the equilibrium conditions

$$\pi^1(z, q) = p_1 \tag{24}$$

$$\pi^2(z, q) = p_2 \tag{25}$$

$$q_i = q_i(nz_i) \tag{26}$$

with respect to parameters. First, differentiating with respect to p_1 gives the impact of increasing the prices at site 1:

$$\begin{bmatrix} \pi_1^1 + nq_{1v}\pi_3^1 & \pi_2^1 + nq_{2v}\pi_4^1 \\ \pi_1^2 + nq_{2v}\pi_3^2 & \pi_2^2 + nq_{2v}\pi_4^2 \end{bmatrix} \begin{bmatrix} dz_1/dp_1 \\ dz_2/dp_1 \end{bmatrix} = \begin{bmatrix} 1 \\ 0 \end{bmatrix} \tag{27}$$

Solving for dz_1/dp_1 gives

$$\frac{dz_1}{dp_1} = (\pi_2^2 + nq_{2v}\pi_4^2)D^{-1},$$

where D is the determinant of the matrix on the left-hand side of (27); D will be positive if the on-site effects of congestion exceed the cross-effects of congestion in absolute value.[5] The term $\pi_2^2 + nq_{2v}\pi_4^2$ contains the on-site effects of trips and congestion and is negative, and thus dz_1/dp_1 is negative. How it compares with dz_1/dp_1 in the absence of congestion depends on the relative strength of all four congestion effects. The effect on trips at the second site is

$$\frac{dz_2}{dp_1} = -(\pi_1^2 + nq_{1v}\pi_3^2)D^{-1}.$$

For $D > 0$, it will be positive when $(\pi_1^2 + nq_{1v}\pi_3^2) < 0$. Intuition suggests that more expected congestion at the first site will increase the marginal value at the second site, implying $\pi_3^2 > 0$, and more trips at the first site will decrease the marginal value at the second site, implying $\pi_1^2 < 0$. Thus the cross-site price effects depend on the strength of the cross-site substitution and congestion effects.

The effect of site expansion can be analyzed by recognizing the dependence of q_i on S_i and differentiating (24)–(26) with respect to S_i. This yields

$$\hat{D} \begin{bmatrix} dz_1 dS_1 \\ dz_i/dS_1 \end{bmatrix} = -q_{1S} \begin{bmatrix} \pi_3^1 \\ \pi_3^2 \end{bmatrix}, \tag{28}$$

where $\hat{D}$ is the matrix on the left-hand side of (27) and $q_{1S} \equiv \partial q_1(nz_1, S_1)/\partial S_1 < 0$. Thus we have

$$\frac{dz_1}{dS_1} = -q_{1S}[\pi_3^1(\pi_2^2 + nq_{2v}\pi_4^2) - \pi_3^2(\pi_2^1 + nq_{2v}\pi_4^1)]D^{-1}, \tag{29}$$

which for $D > 0$ is positive when own congestion effects outweigh cross-congestion effects. For attendance at site 2,

$$
\frac{dz_2}{dS_1} = -q_{1S}[-\pi_3^1(\pi_1^2 + nq_{1v}\pi_3^2) + \pi_3^2(\pi_1^1 + nq_{1v}\pi_3^1)]D^{-1}
$$

$$
= -q_{1S}[\pi_3^2\pi_1^1 - \pi_3^1\pi_1^2]D^{-1},
$$

(29a)

which will be positive when the cross-congestion effect (π_3^2) is positive and trips to the sites are substitutes $(\pi_1^2 < 0)$. These results provide some insight into the comparative statics of several sites, and they also help in evaluating the benefits of site expansion under open access.

B. Optimal Management of Several Congested Sites

The simultaneous management of congested sites is important in heavily populated areas where sites may be chosen on the basis of congestion. Here we analyze how optimality differs for jointly managed sites, for sites which are managed independently of each other, and for sites which are not managed. The notion of weak complementary with regard to congestion will be invoked here. That is, when z_1 is zero, the user is indifferent to changes in q_1, and when z_2 is zero, the user is indifferent to changes in q_2. Optimal allocation is determined by maximizing aggregate consumers' surplus, i.e.,

$$
\max_{z^*} n \left[\int_0^{z_1^*} \pi^1(z_1, 0, q^*)\, dz_1 + \int_0^{z_2^*} \pi^2(z_1^*, z_2, q^*)\, dz_2 \right],
$$

(30)

where $q^* = (q_1(nz_1^*), q_2(nz_2^*))$. The first-order conditions for z_1^* and z_2^* are[6]

$$
\pi^1(z_1^*, z_2^*, q^*) + nq_{1v} \int_0^{z_1^*} \pi_3^1(z_1, z_2^*, q^*)\, dz_1 = 0
$$

(31)

and

$$
\pi^2(z_1^*, z_2^*, q^*) + nq_{2v} \int_0^{z_2^*} \pi_4^2(z_1^*, z_2, q^*)\, dz_2 = 0.
$$

(32)

The first-order conditions intuitively state that marginal values at each site are set equal to the marginal external congestion cost at that site. When the issue is simply what is the optimal attendance, additional terms for intersite congestion effects are unnecessary for demand and benefit functions which are correctly specified.

Determining the optimal entrance prices for users choosing among several congested sites involves measuring the external costs only at the site at which the price is imposed. In terms of the external costs imposed, the optimal prices are

$$p_1^* = -nq_{1v} \int_0^{z_1^*} \pi_3^1(z_1, z_2^*, q^*) \, dz_1 \tag{33}$$

and

$$p_2^* = -nq_{2v} \int_0^{z_2^*} \pi_4^2(z_1^*, z_2, q^*) \, dz_2. \tag{34}$$

These prices are not different in concept from the single-site price. The differences are empirical and practical. Empirically, these prices require that demand functions be estimated as a function of congestion and trips at both sites, a heady econometric enterprise. The practical difference between the single-site price and the multiple-site price is that when there are several sites the prices are determined simultaneously.

The complexities of comparative statics and the difficulties of managing sites without changing the behavioral functions of users being managed are exacerbated when several sites are involved. The expressions for dz_i/dp_j hold regardless of how the p_j are derived, and hence the open access price results also hold for an optimally managed site.

The magnitude of the shift induced by changing capacity may be greater or less than the magnitude in open access, as given by expression (29). As Cesario (1980) has indicated, the benefits from expansion of capacity at one site may require measuring congestion changes at several sites. Using the basic two-site model, we can show that the benefits of capacity expansion at site 1 are[7]

$$\frac{\partial nCS^*}{\partial S_1} = nq_{1S} \int_0^{z_1^*} \pi_3^1(z_1, z_2^*, q^*) \, dz_1 \tag{35}$$

for an optimally managed site. Here, the increased benefits result from a shift in the demand curve caused by a reduction in congestion times the reduction in congestion. Under optimal management at both sites, there is an optimal adjustment at the second site in response to the reduced congestion brought about by capacity expansion at the first site. Thus, while there is no need for explicit consideration of what happens at the second site (as long as the site's demand function is correctly specified), adjustments at the second site are implicit in the measure of benefits in expression (35). This conclusion differs from that of Cesario, who argues that even under optimal management one must account for changes in costs at the other site (1980, p. 336).

When open access prevails, the benefits of capacity expansion are[8]

$$
\begin{aligned}
\frac{\partial nCS^0}{\partial S_1} = n & \left[q_{1S} + nq_{1v} \frac{dz_1^0}{dS_1} \right] \int_0^{z_1^0} \pi_3^1 (z_1, z_2^0, q^0) \, dz_1 \\
& + \frac{nq_{2v} dz_2^0}{dS_1} \cdot n \int_0^{z_2^0} \pi_4^2(z_1^0, z_2, q^0) \, dz_2.
\end{aligned}
\tag{36}
$$

Under open access, the benefits of site expansion include the external costs imposed on site 1 from an expansion in capacity at site 1 less the external costs of congestion imposed on site 2 when a more capacious site 1 draws some users away from site 2. This assumes that the sites are substitutes and that $\partial z_2/\partial S_1 > 0$ [see Eq. (29a)]. If sites are complements, then the intersite effect is negative and the actual site benefits are less than what they appear. As expression (29a) shows, the cross-site effect depends, in part, on whether the sites are substitutes in a price sense. For optimally managed sites, the complement–substitute issues can be ignored. Whether (35) is greater or less than (36) cannot be determined a priori. But under open access, benefit measurement must account for what is happening at the other sites.

C.   Enhancing the Quality of a Site

In the single-site case, we showed that the benefits of environmental improvements depend on how the site is managed. The benefits of environmental improvements are influenced by congestion in a multiple-site setting to the extent that improvements draw use away from other congested sites.

Suppose that an environmental improvement to one of the sites is possible, for example, improved water quality. Let this quality be measured by α, and let $\pi^1(z, q, \alpha)$ and $\pi^2(z, q, \alpha)$ be the marginal value functions. Let α be weakly complementary to z_2, so that the individual is indifferent to the level of α when z_2 is zero. As before, we assume that nonusers do not benefit from changes in α. Intuitively α is the quality of site 2. Benefits from access to both sites are given by

$$
nCS = n \int_0^{\bar{z}_1} \pi^1(z_1, 0, \bar{q}, \alpha) \, dz_1 + n \int_0^{\bar{z}_2} \pi^2(\bar{z}_1, z_2, \bar{q}, \alpha) \, dz_2, \tag{37}
$$

where the $\bar{z}_i$'s may be optimal or open access quantities.

When the site is optimally managed, the marginal benefits of environment improvement are[9]

$$
\frac{\partial nCS^*}{\partial \alpha} = n \int_0^{z_2^*} \pi^2(z_1^*, z_2, q^*, \alpha) \, dz_2. \tag{38}
$$

As in the case of capacity expansion, an environmental improvement at one site need only consider the outward shift in that site's demand curve to capture the benefits of site improvement. Expression (38) is the accepted measure of the benefits of environmental improvement (see Freeman, 1979, Chap. 4).

Suppose the site is available on an open access basis. Then an increase in quality at site 2 increases benefits by

$$
\frac{\partial nCS^0}{\partial \alpha} = n \int_0^{z_2^0} \pi^2(z_1^0, z_2, q^0, \alpha) \, dz_2
$$

$$
+ n \left[\frac{\partial z_1}{\partial \alpha} n \cdot q_{1v} \int_0^{z_1^0} \pi_3^1(z_1, z_2^0, q^0, \alpha) \, dz \right. \tag{39}
$$

$$
\left. + \frac{\partial z_2}{\partial \alpha} n \cdot q_{2v} \int_0^{z_2^0} \pi_4^2(z_1^0, z_2, q^0, \alpha) \, dz_2 \right].
$$

Expression (39) has two terms in addition to the accepted measure of benefits as the shift in the area under the demand curve. The first term in brackets increases benefits because the first site becomes less crowded as the quality of the second site is improved. The second term in the brackets reduces benefits because better environmental quality brings more people to the site, increasing congestion and shifting back the demand curve. It is possible that the congestion effects will make the benefits under congestion greater than simply the increase in the area behind the demand curve at the improved site. For example, suppose that two sites— one congested and clean, and the other uncongested and dirty—were located near each other. Then, if the relatively uncongested site were made clean, not only would we get benefits from cleaning up that site, but we would also get the benefits from reduced congestion at the crowded site, assuming the sites were freely accessible.

In this and the preceding sections, we have developed the analytics of congested sites, assuming that preference functions are known. The next sections deals with some empirical issues created by congestion.

IV. EMPIRICAL ISSUES

Among economists, there appears to be agreement about the basic hypothesis of this paper: at some level of densities, sites become congested and users are willing to pay to reduce congestion.[10] The contribution of of economics to the management of congested facilities depends on its ability to marshal evidence of the conceptual relationships discussed in the previous sections. Here, we review the nature of the evidence collected by economists.

There are two approaches to estimating the demand for and value of outdoor recreation sites. The travel cost method uses individual responses or per capita responses of political or geographic aggregates to travel costs to estimate demand curves. The contingent valuation approach attempts to elicit willingness to pay directly from individuals by inducing them to respond to hypothetical questions. The statistical evidence about the effect of congestion on site benefits comes exclusively from contingent valuation approaches.

The initial study of the economic cost of congestion was performed by Cicchetti and Smith (1973, 1976). They use mail questionnaires to evaluate the responses of backpackers to trail and camp encounters with other backpackers. The variation in congestion is obtained by hypothetically varying the encounters and having the subjects give their willingness to pay at different levels of congestion. They give fairly clear evidence of the negative impact of trail and camp encounters on the willingness to pay for the experience.

A different approach was pursued by McConnell (1977). In a study of Rhode Island beaches, actual densities measured as bathers per acre are used as congestion variables. In this study, contingent valuation estimates of the value of access to the site are then shown to be a statistical function of congestion as actually measured at the time of the interview. It is also shown that responses to congestion, while significant, vary substantially from beach to beach.

Other statistical evidence on the economic costs of congestion follows primarily the Cicchetti–Smith (1973) precedent. Menz and Mullen (1981) use a mail survey to gather data on distance traveled to recreate and expected congestion levels for winter recreationists in the Adirondacks. They show a strong relationship between the expected congestion level and willingness to travel. Allen and Stevens (1979) show that campers in western Massachusetts are willing to pay to avoid congestion. By hypothetically varying the proportion of campsites filled and recording contingent valuation responses, they establish a significant relationship between willingness to pay and congestion.

Walsh et al. (1983) use contingent valuation to measure the responses of willingness to pay by skiers on Colorado slopes to avoid two kinds of congestion: waiting in the lift line and density on the slopes. Their congestion coefficients show exceptional statistical validity, in part because skiers are especially attuned to congestion. By developing statistical relationships between lift line waits and skiers per day and slope density and skiers per day, they convert their congestion variables to a single dimension, skiers per day. This conversion allows them to analyze questions of optimal density, as is done by Cicchetti and Smith (1973), McConnell (1977), and Allen and Stevens (1979).

The contingent valuation is flexible enough to create or to manage variations in congestion and to estimate recreationists' responses to them. The same is not true for the travel cost method. To date, there has been no successful attempt to measure congestion effects in a travel cost framework, although Deyak and Smith (1978) are able to measure the effects of congestion in a reduced form model. Rather, the significant empirical issue concerns the impact of ignoring congestion on travel cost coefficients.

Two separate issues arise in the use of the travel cost method on congested sites. The first issue, the subject of a rash of recent papers, is whether there is any information about congestion embedded in the demand function which relates trips to travel costs. The conclusions of a series of papers by Wetzel (1977, 1981), Anderson (1980), McConnell (1981), Allen and Stevens (1979), and Smith (1981) is that, because the travel cost approach is based on a statistical method in which variations in congestion are uncorrelated to variations in individual travel cost, no error is imparted by the presence of congestion. The same would not be true if, instead of travel costs, we used variations in entrance fees, which would be correlated with congestion.

A second issue in the use of the travel cost method is created by substantial seasonal variations in congestion. This variation creates the possibility that the demand function for congested sites is different from the demand for uncongested sites, as is modeled in Smith (1981). Then a travel cost model which is based on use aggregated over congested and uncongested days will produce coefficients which accurately reflect aggregate demand for the site. However, such analysis will not enable one to analyze the impact of pricing policy on peak or off-peak demand, nor will it allow the correct calculation of consumers' surplus, because the substitution between peak and off-peak demand will not be revealed. When peak and off-peak demands are different, then one must treat a single site as if it were two sites, as in the previous section.

V. CONCLUSIONS

In this paper, we set out to explore some aspects of congested recreation sites. Open access equilibrium and optimal management conditions for one and two sites are analyzed to show the effects of changing environmental quality, site size, and entrance prices. Our basic thesis is that the impact of changes in exogenous variables depends on the management regime in effect. The benefits of expanding site size and of improving environmental quality under open access may be greater or less than the benefits under optimal management. Another dimension of the results emerges in the two-site problem. In that case, under optimality, a correct computation of benefits can be made using shifts of the demand curves at one site only. However, under open access, shifts in both demand curves must be computed to account for all of the benefit changes.

The paper concludes with a discussion of two empirical issues. First, the statistical evidence of the impact of congestion is reviewed. Second, some difficulties in using travel cost models to obtain information about the response to congestion are noted.

This paper did not deal with an important research issue: How are expectations about congestion formed and how do users adjust their expectations to increased density? This topic is important because in the public sector, where price changes are not induced by supply–demand differences, congestion helps bring about equilibria. The study of this topic could be a rewarding avenue for research.

ACKNOWLEDGMENTS

We appreciate the constructive comments of Nancy Bockstael, Virginia McConnell, Virgil Norton, Richard Walsh, and a referee. We owe special thanks to V. Kerry Smith for a thorough and helpful review. We of course accept sole responsibility for any remaining errors.

NOTES

1.   The figures on the availability of leisure time are from Owen (1970, p. 11). The figures do not account for substantial increases in vacation time, which have been substituted for lower hours per week in collective bargaining since World War II. While these figures are for U.S. males, it seems unlikely that the increased labor force participation which has occurred for females is the consequence of substituting out of outdoor recreation.

2.   The figures on densities are from the *Historical Statistics of the United States: Colonial Times to 1970*, Part 1, pp. 396 and 398 (U.S. Department of Commerce, 1975).

3.   Freeman and Haveman deal in discrete numbers of trips and users, while our analysis is continuous. They define congestion costs as the difference in willingness to pay for the actual level of congestion rather than the level of congestion of one user. While it is clear that decisions are made in discrete units, little realism is lost and much mathematical ease is gained by assuming that trips and congestion are continuous.

4.   This derivation follows from symmetry. The derivative of the criterion with respect to z_1^0 is

$$\pi^1(z_1^0, 0, q) + \int_0^{z_2^0} \pi_1^2(z_1^0, z_2, q)\, dz_2 - p_1 = 0.$$

By symmetry, $\pi_1^2 = \pi_2^1$ and so the integral becomes

$$\int^{z_2^0} \pi_2^1(z_1^0, z_1, q)\, dz_2 = \pi^1(z_1^0, z_2^0, q) - \pi^1(z_1^0, 0, q).$$

Substituting into the first-order conditions gives the result in the text.

5. Here,

$$D = [(\pi_1^1 + nq_{1v}\pi_3^1)(\pi_2^2 + nq_{2v}\pi_4^2) - (\pi_2^1 + nq_{2v}\pi_4^1)(\pi_1^2 + nq_{1v}\pi_3^2)]$$

$$= [(\pi_1^1\pi_2^2 - \pi_2^1\pi_1^2) \quad + nq_{2v}\pi_4^2\pi_1^1 + nq_{1v}\pi_3^1\pi_2^2 + n^2q_{1v}q_{2v}\pi_4^2\pi_3^1$$

$$- nq_{2v}\pi_4^1\pi_1^2 - nq_{1v}\pi_3^2\pi_2^1 - n^2q_{1v}q_{2v}\pi_4^1\pi_3^2].$$

The term in parenthesis inside the brackets will be positive if the preference function is convex. Pairwise comparison of the remaining six terms will show that their algebraic sum will be positive if $|\partial\pi^i/\partial\omega_j| < |\partial\pi^j/\partial\omega_j|$ for $i = 1, j = 2$, and $j = 1, i = 2$, where $\omega = q$ and x. Necessary conditions are far weaker. Of course, stability would require that D be positive.

6. The first-order conditions may seem obvious, but their derivation is not. The derivatives of the objective function (30) are

$$\pi^1(z_1^*, 0, q^*) + \int_0^{z_1^\dagger} \pi_3^1(z_1, 0, q^*) \, dz_1 nq_{1v}$$

$$+ \int_0^{z_2^\ddagger} \pi_1^2(z_1^*, z_2, q^*) \, dz_2 + \int_0^{z_2^\ddagger} \pi_3^2(z_1^*, z_2, q^*) \, dz_2 nq_{1v} = 0 \tag{i}$$

and

$$\int_0^{z_1^\dagger} \pi_4^1(z_1, 0, q^*) \, dz_1 nq_{2v} + \pi^2(z_1^*, z_2^*, q^*)$$

$$+ \int_0^{z_2^\ddagger} \pi_4^2(z_1^*, z_2, q^*) \, dz_2 nq_{2v} = 0. \tag{ii}$$

A careful evaluation of these integrals gives the first-order conditions in the text. First, consider the first integral in (ii). Since a unique potential function CS(z, q) is impied by our analysis, it holds that $\pi_4^1 = \pi_1^4$. Making this substitution and integrating over z_1 yields

$$\pi^4(z_1^*, 0, q^*) - \pi^4(0, 0, q^*) = \int_0^{z_1^\dagger} \pi_1^4(z_1, 0, q^*) \, dz_1. \tag{iii}$$

From the notation, $\pi^4 = \partial CS/\partial q_2$. But the left-hand side of (iii) evaluates the change in consumer's surplus from a change in congestion at site 2 when attendance at site 2 is zero. By weak complementarity between z_2 and q_2, this value should be zero. Therefore, the integral of (iii) is zero and the first-order condition for z_2^* is Eq. (32) in the text. Now consider expression (i). First, because $\pi_1^2 = \pi_2^1$, the second integral gives

$$\int_0^{z_2^\ddagger} \pi_1^2(z_1^*, z_2, q^*) \, dz_2 = \int_0^{z_2^\ddagger} \pi_2^1(z_1^*, z_2, q^*) \, dz_2$$

$$= \pi^1(z_1^*, z_2^*, q^*) - \pi^1(z_1^*, 0, q^*). \tag{iv}$$

The first and the third integrals of (i) are written

$$nq_{1v} \left[\int_0^{z_1^\dagger} \pi_3^1(z_1, 0, q^*) \, dz_1 + \int_0^{z_2^\ddagger} \pi_3^2(z_1^*, z_2, q^*) \, dz_2 \right]$$

$$= nq_{1v} \left[\int_0^{z_1^\dagger} \pi_1^3(z_1, 0, q^*) \, dz_1 + \int_0^{z_2^\ddagger} \pi_2^3(z_1^*, z_2, q^*) \, dz_2 \right]$$

$$= nq_{1v}[\pi^3(z_1^*, 0, q^*) - \pi^3(0, 0, q^*)$$

$$+ \pi^3(z_1^*, z_2^*, q^*) - \pi^3(z_1^*, 0, q^*)],$$

which collapses to $nq_{1v}[\pi^3(z_1^*, z_2^*, q^*) - \pi^3(0, 0, q^*)$ and to

$$nq_{1v}\pi^3(z_1^*, z_2^*, q^*)$$

and

$$nq_{1v} \int_0^{z_1^*} \pi_3^1(z_1, z_2^*, q^*)\, dz_1 \qquad (v)$$

under the assumption of weak complementarity between z_1 and q_1. Therefore, using (iv) and (v), the first-order conditions for optimal z_1^* becomes eq. (31) in the text.

7. Equation (35) is derived from differentiating the objective function with respect to S_1 and invoking weak complementarity between z_i and q_i, and the first-order conditions (31) and (32). Alternatively, one can differentiate $CS(z_1, z_2, q_1, q_2)$, observing the implicit dependence of z_i on S_1 and q_i on z_i. Then using weak complementarity and the first-order conditions will also give (35).

8. Equation (36) is derived exactly as (35) except that the open access conditions (20) and (21) are invoked rather than the optimal conditions.

9. Expressions (38) and (39) come from differentiating (37) with respect to α and invoking weak complementarity. The $\bar{z}, \bar{q}$ satisfy

$$\pi^i(\bar{z}, \bar{q}, \alpha) = 0, \qquad i = 1, 2,$$

for the open access site and

$$\pi^1(\bar{z}, \bar{q}, \alpha) + nq_{1v} \int_0^{\bar{z}_1} \pi_3^1(z_1, \bar{z}_2, \bar{q}, \alpha)\, dz_1 = 0$$

and

$$\pi^2(\bar{z}, \bar{q}, \alpha) + nq_{2v} \int_0^{\bar{z}_2} \pi_4^2(\bar{z}_1, z_2, \bar{q}, \alpha)\, dz_2 = 0$$

for the optimally managed site. Then

$$\partial nCS/\partial\alpha = n \left[\pi^1(\bar{z}, \bar{q}, \alpha) + nq_{1v} \int_0^{\bar{z}_1} \pi_3^1(z_1, 0, \bar{q}, \alpha)\, dz_1 \right.$$

$$+ nq_{1v} \int_0^{\bar{z}_2} \pi_3^2(\bar{z}_1, z_2, \bar{q}, \alpha)\, dz_2 \bigg] \frac{\partial \bar{z}_1}{\partial\alpha}$$

$$+ n \left[\pi^2(\bar{z}, \bar{q}, \alpha) + nq_{2v} \int_0^{\bar{z}_1} \pi_4^1(z_1, 0, \bar{q}, \alpha)\, dz_1 \right.$$

$$+ nq_{2v} \int_0^{\bar{z}_2} \pi_4^2(\bar{z}_1, z_2, \bar{q}, \alpha)\, dz_2 \bigg] \frac{\partial \bar{z}_2}{\partial\alpha}$$

$$+ \int_0^{\bar{z}_1} \pi_\alpha^1(z_1, 0, \bar{q}, \alpha)\, dz_1 + \int_0^{\bar{z}_2} \pi_\alpha^2(\bar{z}_1, z_2, \bar{q}, \alpha)\, dz_2.$$

For an optimally managed site, the first two terms in brackets disappear, while weak complementarity implies that

$$\int_0^{\bar{z}_1} \pi_\alpha^1(z_1, 0, \bar{q}, \alpha)\, dz_1$$

is zero. Thus, optimal management and weak complementarity together imply that

$$\frac{\partial nCS}{\partial\alpha} = n \int_0^{\bar{z}_2} \pi_\alpha^2(\bar{z}_1, z_2, \bar{q}, \alpha)\, dz_2,$$

which is (38) in the text. Expression (39) in the text follows because of weak complementarity and because under open access $\pi^1 = \pi^2 = 0$.

10.   Sociologists studying the wilderness congestion phenomenon have been skeptical about the relationship between congestion and user satisfaction. For example, Shelby (1980, p. 53) argues, from a study of raft trips on the Colorado, that "we fail to observe the consistent negative effects of higher densities."

REFERENCES

Allen, P. G. and T. H. Stevens, "The Economics of Outdoor Recreation Congestion: A Case Study of Camping." *Journal of Northeastern Agricultural Economics Council* 8(April 1979):13–16.

Anderson, F. J. and N. C. Bonsor, "Allocation, Congestion, and the Valuation of Recreational Resources." *Land Economics* 50(Feb. 1974):51–57.

Anderson, L. G., "Estimating the Benefits of Recreation under Conditions of Congestion: Comments and Extension." *Journal of Environmental Economics and Management* 7(Dec. 1980):401–406.

Cesario, F. J., "Congestion and the Valuation of Recreation Benefits." *Land Economics* 56(Aug. 1980):329–338.

Cicchetti, C. J. and V. K. Smith, "Congestion, Quality Deterioration and Optimal Use: Wilderness Recreation in the Spanish Peaks Primitive Area." *Social Science Research* 2(March 1973):15–30.

————, *The Costs of Congestion.* Cambridge, Mass.: Ballinger Publishing Company, 1976.

Deyak, T. A. and V. K. Smith, "Congestion and Participation in Outdoor Recreation: A Household Production Function Approach." *Journal of Environmental Economics and Management* 5(March 1978):63–80.

Fisher, A. C. and J. V. Krutilla, "Determination of Optimal Capacity of Resource-Based Recreation Facilities." *Natural Resources Journal* 12(July 1972):417–444.

Freeman, A. Myrick III, *The Benefits of Environmental Improvement.* Baltimore: Johns Hopkins Press (1979).

Freeman, A. M. and R. H. Haveman, "Congestion, Quality Deterioration and Heterogeneous Tastes." *Journal of Public Economics* 8(Oct. 1977):225–232.

McConnell, K. E., "Congestion and Willingness to Pay: A Study of Beach Use." *Land Economics* 53(May 1977):185–195.

McConnell, K. E., "Valuing Congested Recreation Sites." *Journal of Environmental Economics and Management* 7(Dec. 1980):389–394.

McConnell, K. E. and V. A. Duff, "Estimating Benefits of Recreation under Conditions of Excess Demand." *Journal of Environmental Economics and Management* 2(June 1976):224–230.

Menz, F. C. and J. K. Mullen, "Expected Encounters and the Demand for Outdoor Recreation." *Land Economics* 57(Feb. 1981):33–40.

Mumy, Gene E. and Steve H. Hanke, "Public Investment Criteria for Underpriced Public Investment." *American Economic Review* 65(Sept. 1975):712–720.

Owen, John D., *The Price of Leisure.* Montreal: McGill–Queen's University Press, 1970.

Porter, Richard C., "On the Optimal Size of Underpriced Facilities." *American Economic Review* 67(Sept. 1977):753–760.

Sandler, Todd and John T. Tschirhart, "The Economic Theory of Clubs: An Evaluation Survey." *Journal of Economic Literature* 18(Dec. 1980):1481–1521.

Seneca, Joseph J., "The Welfare Effects of Zero Pricing of Public Goods." *Public Choice* 8(Spring 1970):101–110.

Shechter, Mordechai and Robert C. Lucas, *Simulation of Recreational Use for Park and Wilderness Management.* Baltimore: Johns Hopkins Press, 1978.

Shelby, Bo, "Crowding Models for Backcountry Recreation." *Land Economics* 56(Feb. 1980):43–55.

Smith, V. K., "Congestion, Travel Cost Recreational Demand Models and Bebefit Evaluation." *Journal of Environmental Economics and Management* 8(March 1981):92–96.

Smith, V. Kerry and John V. Krutilla, *Structure and Properties of a Wilderness Travel Simulator*. Baltimore: Johns Hopkins Press (1976).

Stevens, Thomas H. and P. Geoffrey Allen, "Estimating the Benefits of Recreation under Conditions of Congestion." *Journal of Environmental Economics and Management* 7(Dec. 1980):395–400.

U.S. Department of Commerce, Bureau of the Census, *Historical Statistics of the United States: Colonial Times to 1970*. Washington, D.C., 1975.

Walsh, Richard F., Nicole P. Miller, and Lynde O. Gilliam, "Congestion and Willingness to Pay for Expansion of Skiing Capacity." *Land Economics* 59(May 1983):195–210.

Wetzel, J. N., "Congestion and Economic Valuation: A Reconsideration." *Journal of Environmental Economics and Management* 8(June 1981):192–195.

Wetzel, J. N., "Estimating the Benefits of Recreation under Conditions of Congestion." *Journal of Environmental Economics and Management* 4(Sept. 1977):239–248.

INTRINSIC BENEFITS OF IMPROVED WATER QUALITY:

CONCEPTUAL AND EMPIRICAL PERSPECTIVES

Ann Fisher and Robert Raucher

I. INTRODUCTION

The benefits of improved water quality can be classified as use benefits or intrinsic benefits. Use benefits are tied to actually using the water for such purposes as public water supplies, recreation, irrigation, industrial processes, and commercial fishing. Intrinsic benefits account for all remaining benefits and are often categorized as the sum of option values, aesthetics, existence values, and bequest values (Krutilla, 1967). While the distinction between use benefits and intrinsic benefits frequently is not clear-cut, there is substantial agreement that intrinsic benefits may account for a sizable portion of society's valuation of improved water quality.[1] More specific information on the size of intrinsic benefits will

Advances in Applied Micro-Economics, Volume 3, pages 37–66.
Copyright © 1984 by JAI Press Inc.
All rights of reproduction in any form reserved.
ISBN: 0-89232-398-1

lead to better estimates in benefit–cost analyses of proposed policies that will affect water quality.

In this paper, we briefly discuss theoretical considerations related to measuring intrinsic benefits. We review prior studies' estimates of intrinsic benefits and their relation to recreation use benefits from water quality improvements. We then compare the methodologies and empirical results of two recent studies that estimated both recreation use benefits and intrinsic benefits. These studies were designed to permit comparison of results across methodologies. The results of these studies are consistent with the hypothesis that intrinsic benefits are large in relation to recreation use benefits. Hence, relying on direct use values alone would significantly understate the total benefits of water quality improvements. The studies also indicate a remarkable similarity in the magnitudes of per capita intrinsic benefits from improved water quality, even though different methodologies and data bases were employed.

II. INTRINSIC BENEFITS DEFINED

Basically, we are interested in determining the total value of an environmental improvement (TWTP):

$$TWTP \approx E(CS) + OV + E + A, \tag{1}$$

where $E(CS)$ is the expected consumer surplus from current and (anticipated) future use; OV is option value; E is existence value; and A is aesthetic value. In this paper, the primary focus is on intrinsic values (IV) where

$$IV = TWTP - E(CS) \approx OV + E + A. \tag{2}$$

The relationships are depicted as approximate because some of these benefit components may not be independent. For example, CS, OV, and E all may be influenced by A, as discussed below. Among other things, this means that the distinction between use values and intrinsic values is not always clear.

Figure 1 illustrates one categorization of water quality benefits into current use benefits and intrinsic benefits. Under the current use category, we concentrate on recreation and related use benefits. This is because most prior estimates of intrinsic benefits have been derived in association with recreation (and, occasionally, related) uses.

The definition of recreation use benefits that result from improved water quality is reasonably straightforward. Use values arise from recreation on or near the water, including such activities as swimming, boating, fishing, or picnicking and hiking along a river or lake. Use values are

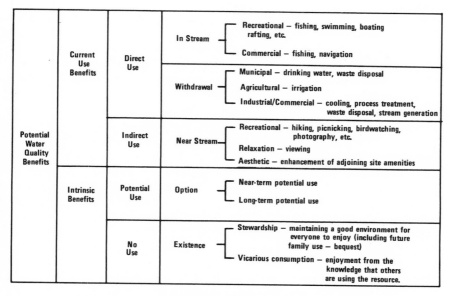

Figure 1. A Spectrum of Water Quality Benefits.

Source: Adapted from Desvousges, Smith, and McGivney (1983).

measured as the willingness to pay for the water quality levels necessary to permit these recreation uses.

As indicated above, intrinsic benefits are the residual benefits after use benefits are subtracted from the total willingness to pay for a particular improvement in environmental quality.[2] Depending on how use benefits are specified, intrinsic benefits can be defined in terms of preserving the potential for use by the individuals whose current demand is being examined and in terms of benefits not at all related to current or future use by those people. For example, people who will never use a particular water body still may value its water quality because they know others can enjoy its use or because they value the preservation of ecological diversity. The next three subsections examine three components of intrinsic benefits: option value, existence value, and aesthetics.

A. Option Value

Weisbrod (1964) was the first to argue that when uncertainty is present, a person's maximum willingness to pay to ensure access to an environmental resource may exceed the expected value of consumer surplus. Then, *option price* can be defined as the maximum amount that the consumer would be willing to pay now for an option to use the services of a public good at some designated future date. It is the sum of the expected value of consumer surplus from using the resource plus an option value or risk premium that accounts for uncertainty in demand or in supply.[3] *Option value* is thus the amount (above any use value) that an individual would be willing to pay to ensure that he (or she) could use the water resource in the future, regardless of whether he is a current user, because of uncertainty regarding future income or tastes (i.e., demand uncertainty) or future availability of suitable water quality at the site (i.e., supply uncertainty).

The distinction between the use value and option value components of option price is complicated and vague. This is because it is not clear where the dividing line should be drawn between use benefits (including current and *expected* future use) and the option value component that accounts for uncertainty in future demand or supply. Long (1967) pointed out the potential double-counting problem and concluded that option value is zero. Zeckhauser (1970), Cicchetti and Freeman (1971), Krutilla and Fisher (1975), and Fisher (1981) examined the effects of uncertainty about the future demand for the services of a resource, with some mention of the effects of supply uncertainty. They found that a risk-averse individual will be willing to pay a premium above his expected consumer surplus to ensure his access to a particular public good. Thus, risk-averse behavior implies a positive option value.[4]

On the other hand, Schmalensee (1972) argued that option value for a risk-averse person could be positive, negative, or zero when uncertainty in future demand results from uncertainties in preferences or income.[5] If negative, then use value (i.e., expected consumer surplus) would overstate actual benefits whenever the negative option value more than offsets other intrinsic benefits such as existence value. Similarly, Hartman and Plummer (1982) have developed a model where uncertainties with respect to future preferences lead to negative option values for a normal good when incomes are uncertain and people are risk averse. If future prices are unknown, the sign of option value in their model is ambiguous, since it depends on how both consumer surplus and the marginal utility of income vary with the uncertain price. This ambiguity is eliminated if relative risk aversion is assumed to be constant and if preferences have constant elasticity of substitution. However, Hartman and Plummer believe these parameters are likely to vary across individuals, making it difficult to generalize about the probable sign of option value.

Graham (1981) also shows that option price is distinct from expected consumer surplus and that option value may be positive, negative, or zero for a risk-averse individual, depending on the shape of his "willingness-to-pay locus."[6] However, Graham argues that whether or not option price exceeds expected consumer surplus is somewhat irrelevant because different measures of benefit are appropriate under alternative conditions. Specifically, where individuals are similar (so that the initial distribution of risk is optimal), contingent claims markets exist, and the resource costs of removing the risks (e.g., of building a dam) are certain, then option price is the appropriate willingness-to-pay measure when the risk is borne collectively (e.g., each local farmer faces the same drought/flood conditions in the absence of the dam). If the risks are borne individually (e.g., each person faces uncertainty as to whether he would desire future visits to the scenic valley that would be submerged if the dam were to be built), then the expected willingness to pay, defined by Graham as the expected value of the "fair bet," is appropriate. The fair bet is the point on the willingness-to-pay locus that has the largest expected value, given the probabilities assigned to the alternate states. Accordingly, expected willingness to pay will be no less than either option price or expected consumer surplus. In the more realistic case when contingent claims markets are not available, Graham regards option price as the "second best" measure of benefits.

Graham's findings have interesting implications for applied benefit–cost analysis. They appear to aggravate the analytical complications since expected consumer surplus may either exceed or understate option price.[7] Still, Graham's results clarify several important issues. First, insofar as collective risks are associated only with uncertainty regarding future supply, option value is positive (Bishop, 1982) and the use of expected consumer surplus will understate the appropriate measure of benefits (i.e., option price). Second, where risks are borne individually and/or contingent markets do not exist, the use of either expected consumer surplus or option price will tend to understate the true level of benefits. This is because the "fair bet point" (the appropriate measure) is defined to be at least as great as either of the other measures. Hence, Graham concludes that the greater of expected consumer surplus and option price should be used as a lower bound estimate of the fair bet, and he acknowledges that Krutilla et al. (1972) were correct in their suspicions that expected consumer surplus would understate the true level of benefits.

In another attempt to reduce the ambiguity surrounding the sign of option value, Bishop (1982) examined the effects of uncertainty in the supply of a public good. His model shows that with demand certainty and supply uncertainty, option value is always positive. Since the net effect of the indeterminacy of the sign of demand-side option value combined with the positive supply-side option value can be resolved only with empirical work, Bishop concurs with Bohm (1975), Graham (1981), and Smith

(1983) in suggesting that option price is the correct measure of consumer welfare when there is substantial uncertainty.

From a practical point of view, this does not make the problem of the sign of option value irrelevant, since it frequently is difficult to measure each person's option price—particularly for nonusers. Although expected use benefits can be estimated more readily, empirical work related to the specific type of commodity and its potential users would be needed to justify the presumption that use benefits (expected consumer surplus) understate total benefits (option price).[8]

On the other hand, the sign of option value is relatively unimportant if option values are so small that they are unlikely to affect the outcome of a benefit–cost analysis. Freeman (1983) develops a model where option value may be positive or negative for an individual, depending on the source of his uncertainty about demand. To represent the case of most relevance to environmental quality issues, Freeman extends the work of Hartman and Plummer (1982), who assumed that preferences are independent of the specific state of the world that actually occurs. In addition to being related to prices of substitutes or complements as in the Hartman–Plummer model, Freeman allows a shift parameter in the utility function to be influenced by factors related to enjoying the resource— such as weather, congestion, or the scheduling of a vacation. By assuming that the utility function is strongly separable in income and the shift variable, Freeman derives a positive option value.[9] He then shows, through hypothetical examples using three functional forms for utility and assigning parameter values as required, that option value with such state-dependent utility functions will be small relative to expected consumer surplus unless the person is unusually risk averse, has a small probability of wanting to visit the site, and has consumer surplus from the visit that would amount to a large share of income. This implies that unless these special conditions are met and/or Freeman's hypothetical calculations fail to reflect the real world, option value will be a trivially small fraction of expected consumer surplus. Then, estimates of expected consumer surplus would be a close enough approximation to option price that they could be used with some confidence in benefit–cost analysis.

Freeman's theoretical analysis would lead one to question the substantial intrinsic value amounts found in empirical studies such as those reviewed below. If these amounts primarily reflect option values, they are inconsistent with his results unless it can be shown that people tend to have a low probability of demand, large expected consumer surplus, and strong risk aversion—or unless the utility functions and parameter values he has chosen are not representative of many consumers. Freeman recognizes that his conclusions may have to be modified if the separability assumption does not hold, i.e., if the marginal utility of income schedule varies across states. Smith and Desvousges (1982) point out that in reality it may be that the marginal utility of income does change with variations in access to the site (e.g., with changes in states of nature, or with changes in water quality). Perhaps some light can be shed on this issue in future studies by identifying the nature and sources of demand uncertainty for environmentally related commodities. Until there is some compelling reason for choosing either separable or nonseparable utility functions, the a priori magnitude of option value must remain ambiguous, along with its sign.

In summary, option price is distinct from expected consumer surplus, and it is not clear a priori as to which is greater and by what magnitude. When the uncertainty is related only to supply, option value is positive (Bishop, 1982). For the source of demand uncertainty that seems most relevant for water-quality–related analyses, option price will exceed expected consumer surplus (Freeman, 1983). Further, either of these measures would understate the true benefit where contingent claims markets do not operate (Graham, 1981), as is generally the case. Therefore, while theoretical issues regarding the size and sign of option value are far from being fully resolved, the conceptual foundations do suggest that measures of expected consumer surplus will understate option price for the scenarios of interest. And either of these values will understate the true expected willingness to pay when there is uncertainty about the future availability of or demand for an environmental commodity at a given level of quality. This would be true even if option value were the only component of intrinsic benefits.

B. Existence Value

Existence value can be defined as the willingness to pay for the knowledge that a particular good exists, regardless of a person's present or anticipated use. For example, people may be willing to pay to know that a particular river is clean, even if they are sure they will never recreate near it, just because they get satisfaction from knowing that it is available for others (vicarious consumption) or from knowing that ecological diversity is being preserved (stewardship).

The distinction between option value and existence value is somewhat clouded by bequest value, which is defined as the willingness to pay for the satisfaction associated with endowing future generations with the resource. Sometimes bequest value is placed in a separate intrinsic value category; sometimes it is treated as part of existence value; and sometimes it is considered in option value. For example, Freeman (1981) includes the utility of the expectation of future use by one's own descendants as a bequest form of vicarious existence benefits. However, since the bequest motive also can be considered as long-term potential use where there may be uncertainties in future demand or supply, this concept can be treated as part of option value. For instance, Mitchell and Carson (1981) divide option value into current (intragenerational) and bequest (intergenerational) categories, with existence value treated separately. Walsh et al. (1978) also separate bequest from existence value.

For the current discussion, existence value is defined as the willingness to pay for the knowledge that a particular environmental quality exists, regardless of any present or anticipated use by the individual, as in Figure 1. Thus, existence value includes any bequest value. Even this restriction does not clearly delineate the existence value category, however. For example, under option value, Krutilla and Fisher (1975) include the demand by people who are not current or prospective users but who value the existence of biological diversity and natural landscape variety. Similarly, the preservation value concept can include option (and bequest) value and existence value.

C. Aesthetics

Another type of benefit sometimes categorized under intrinsic benefits is aesthetics. Given the above definitions, both use benefits and intrinsic benefits have an aesthetic component. For example, improved water quality will enhance the aesthetic values of expected in-stream uses (such as fishing, boating, swimming, and wading) and expected near-stream uses (such as running and picnicking). People also may value aesthetics for vicarious consumption, stewardship, and bequest motives, and because they may have future demand for the resource. Since these latter aesthetic benefits are intrinsic values, it is clear that aesthetics apply to both use and intrinsic benefit categories.

D. Policy Implications of the Conceptual Treatments

It is not completely clear on a conceptual level as to whether intrinsic benefits are positive. As we have seen, the option value component of intrinsic values will have a positive sign if the only uncertainty is with respect to future supply of a particular water quality. If there is some uncertainty with respect to future demand, then the sign of option value cannot always be unambiguously determined in advance. If there are other positive intrinsic values such as existence values, then it becomes likely that use values will understate the actual benefits of a specific water quality improvement. Empirical work can test this hypothesis, and below we shall offer evidence that suggests intrinsic values are positive and nontrivial.

III. DIFFICULTIES IN MEASURING INTRINSIC VALUES

Since environmental services usually are not traded in markets, estimating the demand for these services is more difficult than for ordinary market goods.[10] Nevertheless, there are various indirect and direct methods for such estimation.[11]

A. Indirect Methods

Indirect methods rely on ties between an environmental commodity and good(s) purchased in the market. Information about the demand for the market good is used to infer the demand for the related environmental good.

The most common of the indirect approaches relies on Maler's (1974) assumption of weak complementarity. This condition implies that people who have zero demand for the related market good also have zero marginal willingness to pay for the environmental commodity. Thus, people who do not use a particular lake would have zero willingness to pay for water quality in that lake.[12] This restriction would preclude measuring intrinsic benefits from improved water quality for nonusers of the water body, since the change in water quality leaves no traces on their market transactions.[13]

An example of the indirect approach is the widely used *travel cost* method that can measure users' values of a particular resource (and its environmental quality) but not nonusers' values. This implies that benefit estimates based on weak complementarity will understate actual benefits when nonusers have positive intrinsic benefits. Further examination of direct methods for estimating benefits of environmental quality may establish a relationship between use benefits and the intrinsic benefits for nonusers and users, so that a broader benefit estimate—closer to actual benefits—can be extrapolated from measures relying on the weak complementarity assumption.

The *hedonic* technique relies on a two-step procedure. It first determines the implicit prices of the characteristics of commodities in a product class (such as the implicit price of environmental quality as related to housing) and then regresses these implicit prices against observed quantities to estimate the demand function. The main disadvantage of this technique is that property values do not reflect benefits to users or nonusers who do not own property near the water. Empirical work also is limited by the requirement for variations in water quality within a single market area. Although the hedonic technique could yield information on intrinsic values, the few existing hedonic estimates related to water quality (e.g., Epp and Al-Ani, 1979; Dornbusch and Falcke, 1974; David, 1968;

Brown and Pollakowski, 1977) do not distinguish between use values and intrinsic values.[14]

B.   Direct Methods

Given the above limitations for measuring intrinsic values based on market interactions between public and private goods, the discussion now turns to the remaining alternative: the direct approach of surveying people and asking them about their willingness to pay for improved environmental quality in hypothetical circumstances.[15] This *contingent valuation* approach imposes relatively few restrictions on the form of the utility function and can be applied to both users and nonusers of an environmental good.[16]

Despite these advantages, different types of bias (summarized by Schulze et al., 1981) may affect the benefit estimates. These include: (1) *strategic bias,* where the respondent tries to influence the outcome; (2) *information bias,* where results are affected by the types and amounts of information available to each respondent; (3) *hypothetical bias,* where results are influenced by the interviewees not responding as they would in an actual market situation; (4) *instrument bias,* particularly for the payment vehicle used and for the starting points chosen to initiate bidding; and (5) *sampling, interviewer,* or *nonrespondent bias.*

Evidence on the importance of these biases is mixed, but most writers have found strategic bias to be small.[17] Information bias can be minimized by ensuring that all respondents have access to the same relevant information. Hypothetical bias is reduced if the contingent situation is realistic.[18] This is particularly important in the definition and presentation of the hypothesized changes in environmental quality. Payment vehicle bias is reduced if the chosen vehicle seems appropriate to respondents. There is evidence of starting point bias for the bidding game type of contingent valuation survey. Tests are available for this bias, and it may be smaller for a direct question format, especially when aided by a payment card. Sampling bias can be minimized by designing the sample to reflect the target population, and interviewer bias can be minimized by training and using professional interviewers. Finally, nonrespondent bias is reduced as the response rate rises.

Another difficulty in contingent valuation studies stems from assumed property rights for the particular commodity. Demand theory implies that maximum willingness to pay and minimum willingness to accept compensation for a commodity will be equal except for the income effect. Then, if income has a small effect on the decision of whether to buy (or sell) a commodity, estimates from willingness-to-pay questions or willingness-to-sell questions should be approximately the same. However,

Bishop et al. (1983) found quite different estimates for these two approaches, even with evidence of a negligible income effect. It may be that the importance of such divergences can be reduced by careful determination, before choosing a bidding method, of whether respondents own the property rights to the commodity. Attempts to reduce the artificality of the hypothetical market are likely to reduce this problem as well as those discussed earlier.

The usefulness of each contingent valuation study can be evaluated in terms of the above considerations. Although both indirect market techniques and direct methods have shortcomings, the most helpful information for intrinsic benefit measures is likely to come from carefully designed contingent valuation studies.

IV.   INFERRING INTRINSIC BENEFITS FROM USE VALUES: EVIDENCE FROM A REVIEW OF THE LITERATURE

As we can see, practitioners of benefit-cost analysis face considerable difficulty in determining both what to include within the category of intrinsic (or nonuse) benefits and how to measure such values. We shall now review the empirical evidence on the magnitude of use and intrinsic benefits of water quality improvements, highlighting the inferences that have been drawn regarding quantitative relationships between the two categories. In particular, we investigate the use of a proportional relationship by which some researchers have calculated intrinsic benefits as a fixed positive fraction of certain recreation values.

Abel et al. (1975) appear to have been the first to use a proportional relationship for inferring intrinsic benefits from user values. They observed that in a willingness-to-pay survey conducted in the Fraser River Basin in British Columbia, Canada, Meyer (1974) had obtained "preservation value" bids that were approximately 54 percent of the mean recreation value stated by the users and potential users of the salmon fishery. They argued that such a proportional relationship was further supported by Horvath's (1974) study on the value of wildlife in the southeastern United States. Horvath surveyed more than 12,000 households and obtained values of fishing resources to "nonparticipants" that were 56 percent of the average value stated by users. Accordingly, Abel et al. asserted that the national aesthetic and ecological benefits of water pollution control would approximate 54 percent of aggregate recreational fishing benefits; they estimated the latter and then inferred the value of the former.[19]

The proportional relationship used by Abel et al. is not in the least robust. First, Meyer's estimate of recreation value pertains to the salmon fishery and its attendant benefits, and not to recreational fishing per se. On the other hand, his use estimates include related recreational activities (such as boating) and aesthetic benefits. Option values were to be determined by an explicit question that was dropped from the survey after it was found to confuse respondents. As a result, the intrinsic values obtained by Meyer pertain only to existence value. Hence, Meyer's use values are broadly defined (general recreation plus aesthetics), while his estimates of intrinsic benefits incorporate only one portion (existence value) of such benefits. This indicates that intrinsic benefits are greater relative to recreation use values than was reported by Meyer (1974), and this is supported by Meyer's 1978 update in which intrinsic values were found to exceed recreation benefits (see Table 1, below). In the Horvath study, the distinction between user and nonuser is poorly conceived,[20] and the survey instrument has several shortcomings. Therefore, Horvath's findings cannot be viewed with confidence.

Unger (1976) also inferred nonuse benefits from recreational benefits, but with a different proportional relationship. First, Unger derived three estimates of the combined benefits (recreation and intrinsic) of water quality improvements. He used two property value studies and an oversimplified extrapolation from Radosevich's study (1975) of voting behavior on a California bond issue for abating water pollution. He then apportioned these estimates to use and nonuse categories by using the results of a survey of property owners conducted by Dornbusch and Falcke (1974). In the survey, property owners had been asked to weight the attributes of improved water quality according to relative importance by allocating 100 "votes" among appearance and attractiveness (aesthetics), support of fish and other wildlife (ecology), and ability to offer recreational opportunities. The following subjective valuations were obtained: 33 percent for recreation and 67 percent for aesthetics and ecology (the latter two categories were weighted individually at 24 and 43 percent, respectively). Hence, Unger projected total intrinsic benefits to be twice recreation benefits.[21]

In his review and synthesis of the estimates of pollution control benefits, Freeman (1979b) also resorted to inferring the level of nonuse benefits by using a proportional relationship with certain user benefits. Specifically, Freeman assumed that aesthetic and ecological benefits were 50 percent of the value of recreational fishing. This was based on the Meyer (1974) and Horvath (1974) studies cited earlier, as well as on research by Walsh et al. (1978) in which users and nonusers provided willingness-to-pay bids for cleaning up the South Platte River in Colorado. In Walsh and associates' study, nonusers offered bids that were on average 53 percent of the option prices obtained from actual and potential recreationists. Freeman's discomfort with the proportional inference of intrinsic values is evident from his observation that "this is a very tenuous empirical basis from which to estimate national nonuser benefits" (p. 162).

Additional evidence on the relationship between recreation and intrinsic benefit levels has been supplied by research recently conducted by Mitchell and Carson (1981). They applied contingent valuation surveys to a representative national sample of users and nonusers to obtain willingness-to-pay estimates for various levels of water quality. In this national survey, the results are not linked to changes at a particular site but rather to the quality of all the nation's waterways. Users were defined according to whether they had participated in any direct contact (i.e., in-stream) activities within the past two years. For water of "fishable" quality, the average bid for nonusers was 47 percent of the mean total bid obtained from users. This result lends more weight to the hypothesis that the intrinsic benefits of improved water quality may be systematically related to recreation values.

A summary of the studies for which these use and nonuse values have been compared is provided in Table 1. While this evidence does suggest that the intrinsic benefits of water quality improvements are roughly half (or more) of the recreational fishing value, several points must be emphasized. Each of the studies is based on survey techniques and as such is subject to a number of potential biases (as we have already detailed). Further, one must be aware of differences in the definitions of use and nonuse benefits employed in the various efforts. Therefore, while on the surface the results of the studies portrayed in Table 1 are remarkably consistent, closer scrutiny is required. Nonetheless, the review suggests that intrinsic benefits are substantial and that by estimating intrinsic benefits as half of recreational fishing values one may be fairly confident that they are not grossly overstated and, in fact, may be significantly understated.[22]

V. NEW EVIDENCE RELATING RECREATION USE AND INTRINSIC BENEFITS

Two recent Environmental Protection Agency (EPA) studies shed additional light on the magnitude of the intrinsic benefits of improved water quality and the relationship between intrinsic benefits and recreation use benefits. These studies examined the Monongahela and Potomac Rivers.

A. Monongahela River Project

In the first study, Desvousges, Smith and McGivney (1983) interviewed 301 households (for an 80-percent response rate) in a single-stage, stratified cluster sample of all households in the five Pennsylvania counties

Table 1. Use and Intrinsic Values from Prior Studies

Study	Site	Estimation Technique	Estimates ($1981/household/year)[a]		Ratio of Nonuse to Use	Comments
			Use	Nonuse		
Meyer (1974)	Fraser River, British Columbia	Residents surveyed regarding recreation and preservation values of salmon population.	928[b]	502	.54	• Use values include aesthetic benefits for near-stream activities. • Option value omitted from both categories.
Horvath (1974)	Southeastern United States	Residents surveyed as to value of wildlife attributes.	2824[c]	1574[c]	.56	• Nonusers defined as "those who would have liked to but for some reason did not participate in the study year." • Values presented are averages for fishing.
Dornbusch and Falcke (1974)	Communities along seven U.S. water bodies	Property owners surveyed as to relative importance of water quality improvement attributes.	—	—	.75–2.03	• Lower value ratio based on inclusion of aesthetic values in use benefits. • Higher value ratio based on inclusion of aesthetic values in nonuse benefits.

Study	Location	Description				Comments
Meyer (1978)	Fraser River, British Columbia	Update of Meyer (1974) employing improved sampling and survey instrument.	287[b]	360[b]	1.26	• Same as Meyer (1974).
Walsh et al. (1978)	South Platte River, Colorado	Residents surveyed via bidding game on value of improved water quality.	126	66	.53	• Use value is option price, the sum of recreation and (quasi-) option values to users. • Nonuse value is sum of existence and bequest value to those not expecting to use basin for recreation.
Mitchell and Carson (1981)	U.S. National	National survey of users (recreators) and nonusers of surface water resources.	258	121	.47	• Values presented are for attaining "fishable" level of water quality. • Use value equals the total bid of recreators (use plus intrinsic values for users). • Nonusers defined as nonparticipants in in-stream activities within past two years.

Notes:
[a] Estimates updated by Consumer Price Index.
[b] Estimates presented are averages weighted by population.
[c] Derived by multiplying daily values times annual average household participation as obtained by Horvath.

51

of the Monongahela River watershed. Four alternative contingent valuation questionnaires were used to estimate the willingness to pay for
various water quality levels in the Monongahela River.

While previous studies (Oster, 1977; Gramlich, 1977; Blomquist, 1979;
Binkley and Hanemann, 1978) have used surveys to measure the benefits
of water quality improvements, this study is the first one applied to a
river basin using valid sampling procedures. This study also reduced the
zero-bid problems encountered by Mitchell and Carson (1981). Respondents who gave zero bids were questioned to determine whether the particular water quality level was of no worth to them or whether the zero
bid was a protest to the hypothetical question (because they think environmental commodities are priceless, or, should not be valued). Protest
bids were excluded from the willingness-to-pay estimates. The questionnaires' design also incorporated major improvements for determining the
option and existence values of changes in water quality.

Before asking the willingness-to-pay questions, the interviewer explained the concepts of use value, option value, and existence value as
shown to the respondents on a value card (Desvousges, Smith and
McGivney, 1983, page 4–14). Each of the four versions of the contingent
value questions solicited an option price. The interviewer then asked each
respondent what amount of that option price he associated with his present
and expected future use. By interpreting the use amount as expected
consumer surplus, the remaining portion of the option price can be identified as option value (in response to demand uncertainty).

Depending on the type of contingent valuation question, the annual
mean bids for a household's option *value* of avoiding water quality deterioration (that would cause complete loss of the area for recreation—
the change from D to E in Table 2) ranged from $14 to $58. The differences
between means for users and nonusers are not significant.[23] Since users'
option *price* for preventing this loss ranged from $27 to $95, not only is
option *value* positive but it is also a substantial fraction of users' option
price and generally larger than use value.

Similar results follow for water quality improvements. For the move
from present "boatable" conditions to "swimmable" water quality (i.e.,
the movement from D to B in Table 2), option *value* for both users and
nonusers ranged from $20 to $51, while users' option *price* ranged from
$32 to $100. Although substantial, the option value for this water quality
improvement was not as large a proportion of users' option price (28–67
percent for users; 38–68 percent for nonusers) as in the case of loss of
the area for recreation (57–76 percent for users; 31–113 percent for nonusers). However, the figures in Table 2 imply that the rule of thumb of
adding 50 percent of recreation use values to account for intrinsic values

Table 2. Option Price and Option Value for Users and Nonusers of the Monongahela River[a]

Change in Water Quality	Users' Option Price ($)	Nonusers' Option Price = Option Value ($)	Users' Option Value ($)	User Option Value ÷ User Option Price (%)	Nonuser Option Value ÷ User Option Price (%)
1. Iterative bidding framework: starting point = $25					
Loss[b] (D to E)	27.4	29.7	20.8	76	108
Swimmable[b] (D to B)	32.1	21.7	21.6	67	68
2. Iterative bidding framework: starting point = $125					
Loss (D to E)	94.7	38.8	58.4	62	41
Swimmable (D to B)	99.7	40.5	50.9	51	41
3. Direct question framework:					
Loss (D to E)	45.3	14.2	25.6	57	31
Swimmable (D to B)	52.9	20.3	21.8	41	38
4. Direct question framework: payment card					
Loss (D to E)	46.8	53.0	27.1	58	113
Swimmable (D to B)	71.2	29.9	20.0	28	42

Notes:

[a] Columns 1–3 from Desvousges, Smith and McGivney (1983), Tables 4–9 and 5–4. Users are those engaged in recreation along the Monongahela or who gave positive use values.

[b] "Loss" refers to avoiding complete loss of the resource for recreation uses. "Swimmable" refers to a water quality enhancement that improves conditions from boatable to swimmable.

53

may be a serious underestimate (particularly since the above percentages, as well as most of those summarized in Table 1, take option price as the base, rather than the smaller use value figure).[24] This result is even more striking in view of the fact that the respondents were aware of good nearby substitutes.

The above estimates assume that demand is uncertain but that access to the site is guaranteed. Although Bishop (1982) has shown that supply uncertainty with certain demand will lead to a positive option value, previous work has not permitted examination of the magnitude of this effect. The Monongahela River survey instrument did consider the effect of uncertainty in the supply of water quality. (The question formats are summarized in Desvousges, Smith and McGivney, 1983, Table 5-3.) Respondents were asked to report how their option price (to prevent deterioration plus ensure cleanup to a swimmable level) would change if pollution precluded access on some weekends. Nonusers' bids would decrease about $6, regardless of the number of weekends affected.[25] However, these adjustments are not significantly different from zero. Users' bids would decrease about $15 if access were prohibited on one-fourth of the weekends and $27 when three-fourths of the weekends were affected. Although significantly different from zero, the differences in mean adjustments with increases in supply uncertainty are not significant. However, these results support the hypothesis that supply uncertainty affects option value: a reduction in supply uncertainty has a positive option value.

Desvousges, Smith and McGivney also examined existence values by querying respondents as to their willingness to pay to prevent the deterioration of water quality from boatable conditions to the point where recreation could not take place along the river. It was specified that these amounts did not relate to their potential use of the river. Although bids for both users ($66) and nonusers ($42) were significantly different from zero, there is some indication that respondents had difficulty conceptualizing this question. Since several simply repeated their option price bids, and since the theoretical issues associated with separating use and existence values are unresolved, these results should be interpreted with caution.

On balance, the Monongahela project shows sizable intrinsic benefits, defined as option value plus existence value. Even if existence values are omitted, option values often are larger than the use value component of users' option price. In addition, option values for nonusers are somewhat larger than for users. Hence, the study of Desvousges, Smith and McGivney provides strong support for the argument that benefits of water quality improvements will be understated if they include only option price for users, and even more understated if they rely solely on use values.

B.   Potomac River Study

The second recent attempt to shed light on the relationship between intrinsic benefits and recreation use values relies on a much larger data set (Cronin, 1982). In the fall of 1973, 1529 usable responses were obtained from personal interviews along the Washington, D.C., reaches of the Potomac River.[26] The Cronin study was designed to compare users' and nonusers' willingness to pay for water quality improvements, although the option price for users cannot be decomposed into use value and intrinsic value components.[27]

Given the empirical results reviewed above, it seems safe to conclude that users' option price gives an upper bound on use value, since it may contain some intrinsic values. Because present nonusers could have some expected consumer surplus from using the Potomac River under cleaner conditions (as was found in the Monongahela study), we must also conclude that nonusers' option price gives an upper bound on their intrinsic benefits. On the other hand, users are defined in this study as those who engage in water-related recreational activities, regardless of location.[28] This broad definition makes it less plausible that cleaning up of one water resource would induce many nonusers to become users, since substitute sites are abundant in a global setting. Thus, the option price for nonusers may not seriously overstate intrinsic benefits for this group in the Potomac study.[29]

Table 3 shows option prices for users and nonusers in the Potomac study. For comparison with the Monongahela results, these figures have been converted from 1973 dollars, the year in which the Potomac survey was conducted, to 1981 dollars. In Table 3, WTP1 roughly corresponds to the change in water quality from unusable for recreation to suitable for the (primarily boating) recreation activities existing at that time (i.e., D to E in Table 2) and WTP2–4 corresponds to enhancement of the area from a boatable to a swimmable condition (i.e., D to B in Table 2). Annual willingness to pay for improved water quality ranged from $105 to $162 per household for users and $66 to $98 for nonusers. These figures are somewhat larger than the corresponding results for the Monongahela River: $32 to $100 for users and $20 to $40 for nonusers. The lower Monongahela figures may reflect a difference in preferences across space and time. They also may reflect the generally lower income and education levels and higher age distribution for the Monongahela response group compared with those of the Washington, D.C., response group (and the nation as a whole).

Nonusers' option price can be interpreted as intrinsic benefits in the Potomac study, so the final column in Table 3 underestimates how in-

Table 3.   Option Price for Users[a] and Nonusers in the Potomac River
Study[b]

	Users' Option Price ($)	Nonusers' Option Price ($)	Nonuser Option Value ÷ User Option Price (%)
1. Pay, no information framework:			
WTP1 (Loss)[c]	33.51	—[d]	—[d]
WTP2–4 (Swimmable)	105.48	65.87	62
2. No pay, no information framework:			
WTP1 (Loss)	50.08	26.70	53
WTP2–4 (Swimmable)	161.56	98.43	61
3. Pay, information framework:			
WTP1 (Loss)	39.15	31.25	80
WTP2–4 (Swimmable)	109.50	76.01	69
4. No pay, information framework:			
WTP1 (Loss)	47.33	34.42	73
WTP2–4 (Swimmable)	117.87	93.89	80

Notes:
[a] Users are those who engage in any water-based recreation.
[b] Calculated from significant coefficients in Table 6.1 in Cronin (1982), assuming a 1973 household income of $20,000 and converting to 1981 dollars.
[c] "Loss" refers to avoiding complete loss of the resource for recreation uses. "Swimmable" means improvement from boatable to swimmable.
[d] Not significant.

trinsic benefits compare to use benefits (since users' option price probably has an intrinsic component). However, this table provides figures for a consistent comparison with the studies summarized in Table 1 and with the Monongahela study's results in Table 2. For an improvement in the Potomac River's water quality, nonusers' intrinsic benefits amount to 61–80 percent of the users' option price, compared with 38–68 percent in the Monongahela study.

Yet another interesting comparison is permitted by looking at the mean values from the Potomac River study (Cronin, forthcoming). The information can be segmented into users of the Potomac River, conditional nonusers (respondents not presently using the river who stated they would use it "if it were as clean as [they] would like it to be") and unconditional nonusers (who would not use it under any conditions). In this case, the option price for the 35 percent of the sample who are unconditional nonusers would not contain any use value. If all of the conditional nonusers' option price is assumed to be use value (which is unlikely, given the earlier arguments), then option value for unconditional nonusers divided by he mean option price for users and conditional nonusers would give a lower bound on the ratio of intrinsic values to recreation use values.

As shown in Table 4, unconditional nonusers' option values for avoiding complete loss of the Potomac River for recreation ranged from 41 to 122 percent of the mean option price for users plus conditional nonusers. Similarly, unconditional nonusers' option values for improving the conditions to swimmable ranged from 30 to 57 percent of the mean option price for users plus conditional nonusers. These compare with ranges of 53–80 percent and 61–80 percent, respectively, for comparable water quality changes in Table 3, where the nonuser class contains conditional nonusers.

Thus, even the most restrictive empirical work implies intrinsic benefits of preventing the loss of a recreation area to equal at least 41 percent of the benefit values obtained from users. The same restrictive definition implies intrinsic benefits for enhancing the area of at least 30 percent of the users' values. Both the Monongahela and the Potomac studies also suggest that intrinsic values may be substantially larger.

C.   Comparison with Earlier Studies

Table 5 summarizes the results of the recent studies for comparison with the prior studies shown in Table 1. The figures in Table 5 represent average bids, assuming no statistical differences among question formats within a study. At best, the evidence on this point is mixed. For example, in the Monongahela study, there is more difference between results for some of the question formats than between results for users and nonusers. On balance, however, the differences that are masked by this averaging probably are less than those that are obscured in Table 1.

Table 5 shows a narrower range of ratios of nonuse to use values (.44–.80) compared with the earlier studies (.47–2.03), even though the range for the recent studies is consistent with those in Table 1. This additional evidence supports the hypothesis that intrinsic benefits of improved water quality are not only positive but substantial.

Since these two recent studies focused on specific water bodies, it could be argued that nonusers' values may overstate intrinsic values if they decrease with distance from the recreation site. However, the Mitchell and Carson study (1981) asked about national water quality rather than values for specific sites. Although there is some question about whether respondents' keyed their answers to nearby sites, the Mitchell–Carson ratio of nonuse to use values is consistent wih the range in Table 5.

Table 4. Option Price for Users, Conditional Nonusers, and Unconditional Nonusers in the Potomac River Study[a]

	Users' Option Price ($)	Conditional Nonusers' Option Price ($)	Users' plus Conditional Nonusers' Mean Option Price ($)	Unconditional Nonusers' Option Price = Option Value ($)	Unconditional Nonusers' OV ÷ Users' plus Conditional Nonusers' Mean Option Price (%)
1. Pay, no information framework:					
WTP1	40.14	35.61	37.73	15.35	41
WTP2–4	132.94	91.65	111.08	53.69	48
2. No pay, no information framework:					
WTP1	35.98	61.61	51.99	46.14	89
WTP2–4	169.96	165.16	166.97	86.66	52
3. Pay, information framework:					
WTP1	36.44	41.35	39.19	31.03	79
WTP2–4	152.67	97.24	121.44	36.22	30
4. No pay, information framework:					
WTP1	44.20	48.58	46.56	56.98	122
WTP2–4	140.43	151.29	146.27	82.96	57

Note:
[a] Calculated from Tables IV and V in Cronin (forthcoming) and converted to 1981 dollars. The mean values for users' option price here are not directly comparable to the regression results presented in Table 3.

58

Table 5. Use and Intrinsic Values from New Studies

Study	Site	Estimation Technique	Estimate (1981 $/household/year)[a]		Ratio of Nonuse to Use	Comments
			Use	Nonuse		
Desvousges, Smith and McGivney (1983)	Monongahela River	Residents surveyed via bidding game, direct question, and question with payment card on value of water quality	Prevent loss: 52 Improvement: 62	Prevent loss: 34 Improvement: 28	.65 .44	Summary measure may mask differences among question formats. Use values include intrinsic values for users. Nonuse values may include expected use values.
Cronin (1982)	Potomac River	Residents surveyed via direct question approach, for value of water quality	Prevent loss: 42 Improvement: 125	Prevent loss: 30 Improvement: 84	.71 .67	Same as above.
Cronin (forthcoming)	Potomac River	Same as Cronin (1982)	Prevent loss: 44 Improvement: 137	Prevent loss: 35 Improvement: 66	.80 .48	Same as above. Nonusers are defined as those who would not use the Potomac, even if it were as clean as they would like it to be. Users are present users and those who would use a cleaned-up river.

Note:
[a] Cronin estimates updated by Consumer Price Index.

VI. CONCLUSION: THE NEED TO INCLUDE INTRINSIC VALUES IN BENEFIT–COST ANALYSES

The intrinsic, or nonuse-related, benefits of water quality improvements are difficult to define precisely. Their estimation may be even more elusive. An extensive body of literature has proposed alternate definitions and subcategorizations, and has aired conceptual debates regarding such topics as the sign and size of option value and the role of irreversibility. Despite the professional controversies and some unsettled points, empirical efforts to measure intrinsic benefits consistently show these nonuse values to be positive and nontrivial.

The empirical evidence provided by several existing studies and as supported by two more recent EPA works indicates that excluding intrinsic benefits would understate the total benefits of water quality improvements.[30] Each study cited here must be interpreted with some caution, and the implications across different sites are uncertain. Still, the existing evidence indicates that nonuse benefits generally are at least half as great as recreational use benefits. Hence, in those cases in which the costs of a project or regulation exceed expected use benefits, benefit–cost analyses that fail to include intrinsic values may lead to significant misallocations of resources.

The importance of intrinsic benefits in the economic assessment of water-quality–related policies, coupled with the conceptual and empirical difficulties associated with their estimation, illustrate the need for continued research in this area. Since contingent valuation techniques represent the likely path of new empirical evidence, efforts to clarify several potential generic problems with the approach will be of great importance. Some of the issues deserving attention include the accurate depiction of the environmental commodity to the valued, continued vigilance with regard to potential biases, and further inquiries into the issue of how property rights are assigned (i.e., willingness to pay versus willingness to accept compensation). Additional concerns meriting future attention include the importance of the uniqueness of the site(s) to be valued and, if substitute commodities exist, the impact on respondent bids of the ordering (or aggregation) of the commodities (as in Randall et al., 1982). Also worthy of examination are the underlying motives behind the values offered by nonusers as compared to users. For example, can one employ values obtained from nonusers to infer the use and intrinsic components of a recreator's total bid? These are the types of issues that future research may help to clarify. In the meanwhile, the interpretation and transfer of existing findings must be conducted with caution, though evidence does indicate that when intrinsic values are omitted from an analysis the benefits probably will be understated significantly.

ACKNOWLEDGMENTS

An earlier version of this paper was presented at the American Economic Association conference in New York City, December 28–30, 1982. Helpful comments were received from V. Kerry Smith, William H. Desvousges, Timothy Doe-Kwong Hau, Richard C. Bishop, Robert D. Rowe, and Joan O'Callaghan. The views presented are the authors' alone and do not represent the views of EPA.

NOTES

1.   The emphasis here will be on recreation and intrinsic benefits, since these would form most of the benefits from additional water quality improvements. This ignores potential health effects associated with toxic substances that may be discovered to be significant when more information becomes available. The concentration on recreation and related benefits is consistent with a frequently cited study of nationwide benefits of water regulations (Freeman, 1979b).

2.   Alternatively, intrinsic benefits can be defined as the premium added to the expected consumer surplus from use, to yield total willingness to pay.

3.   This risk premium is assumed to be constant, regardless of whether the person actually uses the services in the future.

4.   Arrow and Fisher (1974) examine a situation where there is uncertainty about the benefits of an irreversible project. If the future will reveal new information about the benefits of the irreversible action, then deferring a decision allows the new information to be taken into account. Under these circumstances, Arrow and Fisher argue that the aggregate expected value of benefits of the project should be adjusted to reflect the loss of options (if the decision is to be made in the initial period). They show that this "quasi-option value" must be positive. According to Conrad (1980), this quasi-option value equals the expected value of information. The irreversibility aspect is not pursued here, since water quality changes generally would be reversible, given a reasonable time period. Exceptions would occur if allowing pollution would eliminate a species that was restricted to the few areas that were to become more polluted.

5.   Bohm (1975) and Smith (1983) point out that Schmalensee's analysis is a bit misleading due to an unusual definition of risk aversion and to the choice of an incorrect point for one of his evaluations of the sign of option value. However, when these difficulties are corrected, both the above authors agree with Schmalensee's conclusion (and that of Byerlee, 1971) that option value may be positive, negative, or zero, depending on the relationship between the marginal utilities of income across the uncertain states of the individual's preference structure. In particular, Anderson (1981) shows that the difference between the Cicchetti and Freeman (1971) finding of a nonnegative option value and Schmalensee's results depends on two additional restrictive assumptions (which imply that the utilities in all states of nature are equal) adopted by Cicchetti and Freeman. Anderson argues that most analysts would avoid such strong assumptions, so that the sign of option value cannot be unambiguously specified in advance for practical applications.

6.   The willingness to pay locus is the locus of alternative sets of contingent payments $(C_1, \ldots, C_n)$ that yield the same expected utility as the set of consumer surplus values enjoyed in each of n possible states of nature. The point on the locus at which the contingent payments are equal across states represents option price $(OP = C_1 = C_2 = \cdots = C_n)$.

7.   To further complicate the matter, Graham (1982) also has shown that, with state-dependent utility functions, having measures of an individual's consumer surplus under alternate states is not sufficient to generate either upper or lower bounds on his option price.

8. For now, this ignores any existence or other intrinsic values, which are considered in the next sections.

9. Freeman also shows that when demand uncertainty is caused by uncertainty about future income, rather than uncertainty about future preferences, option value is negative for risk-averse individuals whose preferences are state (here, income) dependent. Under such conditions, expected consumer surplus could substantially overstate option price. Where demand uncertainty arises from uncertainty about future prices of substitutes or complements of the good to be evaluated, and where preferences are state dependent with respect to those prices, then no clear relationship between option price and expected consumer surplus is evident unless several very restrictive assumptions are made.

10. Freeman (1979) summarizes the techniques that can be used to estimate consumers' demand for environmental commodities. Improvements in environmental quality that affect the production processes for market goods can be measured through their market influence on output prices, factor prices, and profits. These *supply* considerations are not considered further in this paper (see Freeman, 1979a).

11. A third approach, using a public referendum, would be impractical for each major regulation. Hence, this technique is not explored here. It should be noted, however, that the public hearing process accompanying regulatory development provides a forum for a nonmarket expression of demand.

12. For our purposes, the individual gains utility from a site only by visiting it:

$$U_i = U(X, V_i, Q),$$

where X = a vector of other commodities;
          V_i = visits by individual i;
          Q = a measure of water quality at the site;

and where $\partial U_i/\partial Q = 0$ when $V_i = 0$.

13. Of course, if water quality is strongly separable in the utility function, not even use benefits can be measured.

14. A method with some potential for future application to water quality issues is the hedonic travel cost approach. This generalization of the travel cost method can value many sites and variations in the characteristics (such as water quality) of a specific site. Brown and Mendelsohn (1981) have applied this model to fishing, and Charbonneau and Hay (1978) have used a similar approach to value hunting and fishing. At this point, water quality has not been one of the characteristics included in the hedonic travel cost model.

15. Estimates from these nonmarket techniques also can provide a check on the consistency of the estimating procedures used for market-related benefit measures. See Desvousges, Smith and Fisher (1983) or Bishop et al. (1983).

16. Indirect methods have restrictions on the nature of individual preferences or rely on observed technical relations in the delivery of commodities. Direct methods avoid these assumptions but require the establishment of a hypothetical market for the contingent transactions.

17. Recent exceptions may be Cronin (1982) and Bohm (1979). However, their results also might reflect hypothetical bias.

18. Freeman (1979a) noted that attempts to reduce strategic bias by decoupling the interviewee's response from any actual payment or outcome may reduce the incentives for an accurate response. Since an inaccurate response would be inconsistent with how the individual would react if the situation actually occurred, this attempt to reduce strategic bias may instead introduce hypothetical bias.

19. Heintz et al. (1976) also applied Meyer's .54 ratio of aesthetic and ecological benefits to recreational fishing benefits to their estimate of the value of national recreational fishing, thereby obtaining a value for the intrinsic worth of water quality improvements.

20. Nonusers were defined as "those who would have liked to but for some reason did not participate during the study year." Thus, Horvath's (1974) findings represent values to past and/or expected future users, and not intrinsic values.

21. In Dornbusch and Falcke (1974), if aesthetics were considered as a portion of use benefits, then intrinsic (ecology) values would amount to .75 of total use (recreation plus aesthetic) values.

22. The willingness-to-pay ratio of intrinsic to recreation use benefits may be higher for unique sites. This is supported by the work of Schulze et al. (1980) who conducted interviews in four cities across the United States to measure user and "existence" values for visibility in the Grand Canyon. Using a direct question format in a contingent valuation survey, they found user values to be negligible compared with existence values. At this time, no studies are available to assess the relative size of the intrinsic value to use value ratios from water quality improvements for "unique," compared with "ordinary," water recreation sites.

23. However, regression analysis using survey respondents' economic and demographic characteristics showed that users have somewhat lower option values than nonusers for most changes in water quality. This lends even more weight to the argument that estimates of the benefits of improved water quality should not be based solely on recreators' use values.

24. Option values for improving water quality in the area would be 39–207 percent of the smaller use value figure; and for preventing loss of the area, 72–450 percent of use value.

25. The figures in this paragraph are from Table 5-7 in Desvousges, Smith and McGivney (1983).

26. This figure represents a 75 percent response rate. Both Davis (1980) and Cronin (1982) conclude that the sample is representative of the metropolitan Washington area.

27. Davis examined the data with respect to the impact on recreation participation along the river as water quality improved. However, his analysis did not distinguish between users and nonusers.

28. Under this definition, 80 percent of the Potomac study respondents are users.

29. For purposes of comparison, it should be mentioned that the Monongahela study definition of users is narrower, referring to those who reported use of sites along the Monongahela River or who gave positive use values when asked to partition their option price for water quality in the Monongahela River. (Substitute sites also are abundant in this area.) Under this definition, 23 percent of the Monongahela study respondents are users. Given these differences in classification, we would expect the option value estimates from the Monongahela study to be more precise.

30. Bishop et al. (1983) found willingness-to-pay measures from contingent valuation surveys understated willingness-to-sell measures for goose hunting permits. If the same is true for water quality, this gives even more weight to the argument that (recreation) use benefits measured in terms of willingness to pay are insufficient as the sole basis for evaluating improved water quality insofar as property rights to such attributes belong to the general public.

REFERENCES

Abel, Fred H., Dennis P. Tihansky, and Richard G. Walsh, *The National Benefits of Water Pollution Control*. Washington, D.C.: U.S. Environmental Protection Agency, 1975.

Anderson, Robert J., "A Note on Option Value and the Expected Value of Consumer's Surplus." *Journal of Environmental Economics and Management* 8(June 1981):187–191.

Arrow, Kenneth, and Anthony C. Fisher, "Environmental Preservation, Uncertainty, and Irreversibility." *Quarterly Journal of Economics* (May 1974):312–319.

Binkley, C. S., and W. M. Hanemann, *The Recreation Benefits of Water Quality Improvements: Analysis of Day Trips in an Urban Setting*. Washington, D.C.: U.S. Environmental Protection Agency, 1978.

Bishop, Richard C., "Option Value: An Exposition and Extension." *Land Economics* 58(February 1982):1–15.

Bishop, Richard C., Thomas A. Heberlein, and Mary Jo Kealy, "Contingent Valuation of Environmental Assets: Comparisons with a Simulated Market." *Natural Resources Journal* (July 1983):619–633.

Blomquist, G., "Measuring the Recreational and Aesthetic Benefits of Cleaner Water." Unpublished manuscript, 1979.

Bohm, Peter, "Option Demand and Consumer's Surplus: Comment." *American Economic Review* 65(September 1975):733–736.

———, "Estimating Willingness to Pay: Why and How?" *Scandanavian Journal of Economics* 81(No. 2, 1979).

Brown, Gardner M., and Henry O. Pollakowski, "Economic Valuation of Shoreline." *Review of Economics and Statistics* 59(August 1977):272–278.

Brown, Gardner, M., Jr., and Robert Mendelsohn, "The Hedonic Travel-Cost Method." University of Washington mimeo, March 1981.

Byerlee, D. R., "Option Demand and Consumer Surplus: Comment." *Quarterly Journal of Economics* (August 1971):523–527.

Charbonneau, J. John, and Michael J. Hay, "Determinants and Economic Values of Hunting and Fishing." Paper presented at the 43rd North American Wildlife and Natural Resources Conference, Washington, D.C., published in *Transactions,* Wildlife Management Institute, 1978, pp. 391–403.

Cicchetti, Charles J., and A. M. Freeman III, "Option Demand and Consumer's Surplus: Further Comment." *Quarterly Journal of Economics* (August 1971):528–539.

Conrad, Jon, M., "Quasi-Option Value and the Expected Value of Information." *Quarterly Journal of Economics* (June 1980):813–820.

Cronin, Francis J., *Valuing Nonmarket Goods through Contingent Markets*. Richland, Washington: Pacific Northwest Laboratory, PNL-4255, September 1982.

———, "Estimating the Use, Option, and Existence Values for Improved Water Quality." Richland Washington: Pacific Northwest Laboratory, forthcoming.

David, Elizabeth, L., "Lake Shore Property Values: A Guide to Public Investment in Recreation." *Water Resources Research* 4(August 1968):697–707.

Davis, Robert K., "Analysis of the Survey to Determine the Effects of Water Quality on Participation in Recreation." U.S. Department of Interior memorandum to John Parsons, July 28, 1980.

Desvousges, William H., V. Kerry Smith, and Ann Fisher, "A Comparison of Direct and Indirect Methods for Valuing Public Goods." University of North Carolina at Chapel Hill mimeo, April 1983.

Desvousges, William H., V. Kerry Smith, and Matthew P. McGivney, *A Comparison of Alternative Approaches for Estimating Recreation and Related Benefits of Water Quality Improvements*. Washington, D.C.: U.S. Environmental Protection Agency, 1983.

Dornbusch, David M., and Caj O. Falcke, *A Generic Methodology to Forecast Benefits from Urban Water Projects*. Washington, D.C.: U.S. Department of the Interior, 1974.

Epp, D. J., and K. S. Al-Ani, "The Effect of Water Quality on Rural Nonfarm Residential Property Values." *American Journal of Agricultural Economics* (August 1979):529–534.

Fisher, Anthony C., *Resource and Environmental Economics*. New York: Cambridge University Press, 1981.

Freeman, A. Myrick III, *The Benefits of Environmental Improvement*. Baltimore: The John Hopkins University Press for Resources for the Future, 1979.

———, "Approaches to Measuring Public Goods Demands." *American Journal of Agricultural Economics* 61(December 1979a):915–920.

———, *The Benefits of Air and Water Pollution Control: A Review and Synthesis of Recent Estimates.* Washington, D.C.: Council on Environmental Quality, December 1979b.

———, "Notes on Defining and Measuring Existence Values." Bowdoin College mimeo, June 1981.

———, "The Size and Sign of Option Value." Bowdoin College mimeo, 1983.

Graham, Daniel A., "Cost-Benefit Analysis Under Uncertainty." *American Economic Review* 71(September 1981):715–725.

———, "Estimating the 'State Dependent' Utility Function." Preliminary draft, presented at the Allied Social Science Association meetings, December 1982.

Gramlich, Frederick W., "The Demand Curve for Clean Water: The Case of the Charles River." *National Tax Journal* (June 1977):183–194.

Greenley, Douglas A., Richard G. Walsh, and Robert A. Young, "Option Value: Empirical Evidence from a Case Study of Recreation and Water Quality." *Quarterly Journal of Economics* (November 1981):657–673.

Hartman, Richard, and Mark L. Plummer, "Option Value Under Income and Price Uncertainty." University of Washington mimeo, March 1982.

Heintz, H. T., A. Hershaft, and G. Horak, *The National Damages of Air and Water Pollution.* Washington, D.C.: U.S. Environmental Protection Agency, 1976.

Horvath, Joseph C., "Economic Survey of Southeastern Wildlife and Wildlife-Oriented Recreation." Paper presented at the Thirty-ninth North American Wildlife and National Resources Conference, Washington, D.C.; published in *Transactions,* Wildlife Management Institute, March 1974.

Krutilla, John V., "Conservation Reconsidered." *American Economic Review* (September 1967):777–786.

Krutilla, John V. and Anthony C. Fisher, *The Economics of Natural Environments.* Baltimore: The Johns Hopkins University Press for Resources for the Future, 1975.

Krutilla, John V., et al., "Observations on the Economics of Irreplaceable Assets." In Allen V. Kneese and Blair T. Bower (eds.), *Environmental Quality Analysis: Theory and Method in Social Sciences.* Baltimore: The Johns Hopkins University Press for Resources for the Future, 1972.

Long, Millard F., "Collective Consumption Services of Individual Consumption Goods: Comment." *Quarterly Journal of Economics* 81(May 1967):351–352.

Maler, Karl-Goran, *Environmental Economics: A Theoretical Inquiry.* Baltimore: The Johns Hopkins University Press for Resources for the Future, 1974.

Meyer, Philip A., *Recreation and Preservation Values Associated with the Salmon of the Fraser River.* Information Report Series, No. PAC/N-74-1, Vancouver, B.C., Canada: Fisheries and Marine Service, 1974.

———, *Updated Estimates for Recreation and Preservation Values Associated with the Salmon and Steelhead of the Fraser River.* Vancouver, B.C., Canada: Fisheries and Marine Service, March 1978.

Mitchell, Robert C., and Richard T. Carson, *An Experiment in Determining Willingness to Pay for National Water Quality Improvements.* U.S. Environmental Protection Agency, June 1981 Draft Report, Grant No. R806906010.

Oster, Sharon, "Survey Results on the Benefits of Water Pollution Abatement in the Merrimack River Basin." *Water Resources Research* (1977):882–884.

Radosevich, Ted C., "Clean Water Bond Study." Project report, University of California Berkley, Institute of Government Studies, 1975.

Randall, Alan, John P. Hoehn, and David S. Brookshire, "Contingent Valuation Surveys for Evaluating Environmental Assets." Presented at the Allied Social Sciences Association meetings, December 1982.

Schmalensee, Richard, "Option Demand and Consumer's Surplus: Valuing Price Changes Under Uncertainty." *American Economic Review* 62(December 1972):813–824.

Schulze, W. D., D. S. Brookshire, E. G. Walther, K. Kelley, M. A. Thayer, R. L. Whitworth, S. Ben-David, W. Malm, and J. Molenar, *The Benefits of Preserving Visibility in the National Parks of the Southwest.* Final report to the U.S. Environmental Protection Agency, Contract No. R8069772010, August 1980.

Schulze, William D., Ralph C. d'Arge, and David S. Brookshire, "Valuing Environmental Commodities: Some Recent Experiments." *Land Economics* (May 1981):151–172.

Smith, V. Kerry, "Option Value: A Conceptual Overview." *Southern Economic Journal* (January 1983):654–668.

Smith, V. Kerry, and William H. Desvousges, Letter responding to A. Myrick Freeman's comments on *A Comparison of Alternative Approaches for Estimation Recreation and Related Benefits of Water Quality Improvements,* September 8, 1982.

Unger, Samuel G., *National Benefits of Achieving the 1977, 1983, and 1985 Water Quality Goals.* Washington, D.C.: U.S. Environmental Protection Agency, 1976.

Walsh, Richard G., Douglas A. Greenley, Robert A. Young, John R. McKean, and Anthony A. Prato, *Option Values and Recreational Benefits of Improved Water Quality: A Case Study of the South Platte River Basin, Colorado.* U.S. Environmental Protection Agency, Research Triangle Park, EPA-600/5-78-001, January 1978.

Weisbrod, Burton A., "Collective-Consumption Services of Individual-Consumption Goods." *Quarterly Journal of Economics* (August 1964):471–477.

Zeckhauser, Richard J., "Uncertainty and the Need for Collective Action." In R. Haveman and J. Margolis (ed.), *Public Expenditure and Policy Analysis.* Chicago: Markham Publishing, 1970.

TRAVEL COST AND CONTINGENT VALUATION:

A COMPARATIVE ANALYSIS

John Duffield

I. INTRODUCTION

This paper provides a comparative analysis of the two most widely used
approaches for estimating recreational demand: the travel cost method
and contingent valuation. The travel cost approach estimates demand
functions for a given site from observed visit rates corresponding to the
supply prices (travel costs) from origins surrounding the site. The method
has a long history and has been widely applied. In the contingent valuation
approach individuals are directly surveyed as to their willingness to pay
for the services of a given resource contingent on the existence of a hypothetical market situation. Because responses are not based on observed
behavior, they may be biased or even meaningless. It may safely be said
that there is a considerable difference of opinion within the economics

Advances in Applied Micro-Economics, Volume 3, pages 67–87.
Copyright © 1984 by JAI Press Inc.
All rights of reproduction in any form reserved.
ISBN: 0-89232-398-1

profession as to the preferred methodology. While travel cost is derived from an observable visit rate, the perceived supply price particularly with regard to the value of travel time must be inferred. In application considerable judgment is involved in the selection of this parameter. In addition, typical data limitations generally require additional assumptions regarding visitor and visit homogeneity. Thus both methods face limitations.

One approach to evaluating these two benefit estimation methods is to compare their respective estimates for a given resource decision. Our specific application relates to a proposed hydroelectric site at Kootenai Falls in northwestern Montana. The site is on a major tributary of the Columbia River and has been described as the last major undeveloped waterfall in the Pacific Northwest. Because the site is unique, it provides an opportunity for a relatively simple single-site application of the travel cost model for comparative purposes. In addition to the comparative analysis, our results include a direct survey estimate of the value of travel time and an exploratory estimate of a travel demand model for multisite visits. We also examine the implications of payment vehicles, starting bids, and information levels for contingent valuation estimates. Consumer surplus estimates derived from the two methods are compared with regard to theoretically expected differences.

II. LITERATURE REVIEW

There have been comparatively few side-by-side applications of contingent valuation and the travel cost method. The first such study by Knetsch and Davis (1966) was in fact derived from Davis's (1963) seminal application of the survey method. More recently, several other such comparisons[1] have been undertaken by Bishop and Heberlin (1980) and Desvousges et al. (1982). To review these studies, it is necessary to provide a brief review of the conceptual framework for each of the methods.

A.   The Travel Cost Method

Two different travel cost models have evolved. In the zonal model, originally developed by Clawson (1959) and Knetsch (1963), recreational trips arising at equal distances from the site are aggregated to derive visits per capita by distance zone. This procedure necessitates additional assumptions regarding visitor homogeneity within zones and, as generally applied, constant unit costs of travel across zones. A more recently developed model (Brown and Nawas, 1973; Gum and Martin, 1975) uses individual observations of visit frequency and travel costs. The latter is more appealing on theoretical grounds, but it is difficult to apply if typical behavior is to visit no more than once a year (Freeman, 1979).

To justify consumer surplus estimates with either model, it is usually stated that one must assume that recreationists will view travel cost increases as being equivalent to a fee increase for a site visit. The most critical problems in application have been market definition and the measurement of the price variable.

As McConnell (1975) has pointed out, the appropriate measure of recreational use for the travel cost model is visits. However, limiting the data set to a market for homogeneous visits (or trips) is often problematic. On-site visits may vary by length of stay, purpose, and activity. The critical characteristic for trips is purpose. Inclusion of multiple-destination trips in a model ascribing travel costs to a single destination can lead to very badly overestimated demand functions (Smith, 1975). Disaggregation of the data is an obvious solution, but Smith and Kopp (1980) have also suggested a statistical technique for defining the spatial market limits. The latter is not exclusively associated with multiple-destination problems.

The travel cost method has a special measurement problem in that the visitor's perceived price is not directly observed. This parameter is often heavily judgmental. In many applications it is based on no more than the estimated cost of a round trip to the site and published national estimates of the variable costs of automobile transportation. Even with on-site survey evidence of the costs of travel, there is considerable variability across studies as to which travel or on-site expenditures are included. In addition, as was noted in even some of the earliest studies (Knetsch, 1963), the omission of the value of time can bias valuation estimates downward. A considerable literature has addressed the issue of how much time involved is costly and the appropriate value to place on this time (Cesario and Knetsch, 1970; Cesario, 1976; McConnell, 1975).

Aggregation in the zonal model results in strong collinearity between distance and travel time (not to mention that the latter is often not independently observed). As a result, the convention (following Cesario, 1976) has been to value travel time at 25–50 percent of the wage rate. The empirical basis for applying these values to any given recreational site is weak, since the estimates are derived from the transportation literature on urban commuters. Where the individual model can be applied, average cost and travel time (or distance) can be included as separate regressors. The estimated parameters should be unbiased, but the poor overall explanatory power of the reported estimates (Brown and Nawas, 1973; Gum and Martin, 1975) is not encouraging. The evidence on what the value of recreational time might be is limited. McConnell and Strand (1981) used the individual model and the assumption that response to monetary and travel time costs should be the same. They derived an estimate of the value of travel time at 60 percent of the wage rate for a sample of sport fishermen. Desvousges et al. (1983) tested both the hypothesis that opportunity costs of time are equal to the full wage rate and the Cesario hypothesis that costs are one-third the wage rate. For a sample of 22 sites, the full-cost and Cesario hypothesis were rejected with about the same frequency (about one-third of the cases). Desvousges et al. also made direct estimates of opportunity cost as an approximate constant multiple of the wage rate (following McConnell and Strand, 1981; most of these were either negative or greater than unity. In general, their findings appeared to be limited by the available data.

The basic conclusion here is that the travel cost method is appealing on theoretical grounds. However, and all other problems aside, judgmental parameters relating to travel costs and multisite visits can lead to order-of-magnitude differences in consumer surplus estimates.

B.   The Direct Survey Method

The obvious criticism of the direct survey method is that responses may have little or no correspondence to true willingness to pay. Rowe et al. (1980) have noted three main types of potential bias: strategic, informational, and hypothetical. The first of these could result from a respondent trying to strategically influence results to favor his preferred outcome. The second is the possibility that results are being affected by the test instrument, the interviewer, or the interview process. The third is the problem of the basic working assumption: that the hypothetical market institutions described to the respondent are not sufficiently real to generate valid responses.

The general approach to strategic and information bias has been to put sufficient variation in the survey instrument to test for these potential problems (Brookshire et al., 1976). The general finding of such studies has been that strategic behavior does not appear to be a problem: respondents appear to be answering honestly (Thayer, 1981). However, responses have often shown considerable variation across payment vehicle, information level, and starting bid.

The presence or absence of hypothetical bias is not easily identified. Most studies, including Davis's (1963) seminal paper, have examined internal consistency in responses and the theoretically expected correlation with explanatory variables. The results have been generally encouraging, and there is also some evidence that results may be replicable across different studies (Rowe et al., 1980). However, a result of these direct survey studies that has been consistently at odds with accepted theory (Willig, 1976; Randall and Stoll, 1980) is the unexpected divergence of willingness to pay and compensation (or willingness to sell) measures. Meyer (1979) reviewed a series of recreational studies that all showed a considerable difference between the two measures ranging from 3 : 1 to

20:1. These findings have led some analysts to suggest that survey estimates are unreliable (Dwyer and Bowes, 1978). However, cash transaction experiments reported by Knetsch and Sinden (forthcoming) have showed similar divergences.

It may be that we have expected both too much and too little from the survey method. It is perhaps too much to expect that significant variations in property rights, payment vehicles, and information levels will result in the same response. Sensitivity to these characteristics is in fact a feature of real markets. Some of what has been labeled as bias may instead be an indication that the working assumption is basically valid. Nonetheless, the differences with respect to accepted theory have yet to be resolved.

C. Analytical Basis for Comparison

Aside from the problems peculiar to each methodology, there are several theoretical reasons for expecting differences between contingent valuation and travel cost estimates. The travel cost approach measures ordinary (Marshallian) consumer surplus. However, contingent valuation implicitly measures welfare changes with respect to compensated demand functions. Following the usual definitions (Currie et al., 1971), quantity reductions in unpriced resources are measured by direct survey as compensating variation for willingness to sell and equivalent variation for willingness to pay. The converse holds for gains. The standard result for losses is that ordinary consumer surplus estimates will be greater than equivalent variation (or surplus for these cases) and less than compensating variation, and conversely for gains (Freeman, 1979). As noted, the expectation is that these differences will be small (Willig, 1976).

The other basic reason for expecting travel cost and contingent valuation estimates to diverge is that the former is limited to the value of direct use of the resource whereas the latter may include indirect benefits such as option, existence, and bequest (Krutilla, 1967). Following Bohm (1975), several studies have attempted to disaggregate contingent valuation responses into user and indirect value categories using a simple follow-up question. Direct use shares for recreational resources have been estimated at as much as 50 percent to as little as 10 percent (Sutherland, 1982); Walsh et al., 1982). As one would expect, the higher direct percent estimates appear to occur when current users are well represented in a given household sample.

D. Comparisons of Travel Cost and Contingent Valuation

Partial findings for the three previous studies that have compared travel cost and direct survey results in side-by-side applications are summarized in Table 1. The theoretical expectation that travel cost estimates of or-

Table 1. Comparison of Mean Travel Cost and Survey Estimates (dollars)

	Travel Cost		Direct Survey (Consistent)[a]		
Study	Monetary Only	Includes Time	WTD	WTP	WTA
Knetsch and Davis (1966):	6.72		6.16 (yes)	6.92 (no)	
Bishop and Heberlin (1980):					
	8.51			21	101
		32.21		(no)	(yes)
				(yes)	(yes)
Devousges et al. (1982):					
Direct question		82.65		19.71 (yes)	
Payment card				19.71 (yes)	
Iterative bid (25)				6.58 (yes)	
Iterative bid (125)				36.25 (yes)	

Note:

[a] Consistant with theory as to direction of differences with respect to the travel cost estimates. Here WTD, WTP, and WTA denote willingness to drive, willingness to pay, and willingness to accept (compensation) estimates, respectively.

dinary consumer surplus for site loss[2] will exceed the equivalent variation measure is supported only for estimates that include the time cost of travel (Table 1). The one compensating variation measure reported (Bishop and Heberlin, 1980) is consistent both with regard to travel cost (with and without travel time) and also with regard to the relevant willingness to pay estimate (Table 1). The Desvousges et al. (1982) estimates are based on a household survey and are corrected to exclude indirect values (following Bohm, 1975). The other surveys may also provide a comparison for direct values only, given that the users were sampled for visits under particular conditions.

While the conventional theory predicts the direction of differences between the measures, it also suggests that the differences should generally be quite small. The Bishop and Heberlin (1980) study of surveyed willingness to pay and willingness to sell for goose-hunting permits in Wisconsin resulted in the usual large difference between the two measures (5:1 in this case). They also report an experiment in which cash offers varying from $1 to $200 were mailed to a separate sample of hunters. The surveyed compensation measure was not significantly different from the cash offer acceptance rate for offers up to $40. Beyond that level the survey response diverged to the extent that the mean cash offer accepted was $63 compared to the survey estimate of $101. With respect to travel cost, small differences were reported only for the Knetsch and Davis (1966) study of the Pittston area in Maine. The remarkable similarity in their results across methods (Table 1) is sensitive to the cents-per-mile basis for transforming miles into a monetary measure. In this case the valuation of additional miles was not independently determined, but instead was derived from the estimated relationship of the willingness to pay and willingness to drive responses, with an apparent slope coefficient of 5 cents per mile. This value was also used in the travel cost analysis. The authors also note that calculations were in terms of one-way mileage costs. This seems contrary to logic and the current practice.

Near equivalence of the travel cost estimate in Knetsch and Davis (1966) also included the ad hoc addition of multiple destination visitors at half-weight. In fact evaluation of any of the comparisons in Table 1 is complicated by judgmental treatment of the cost of travel and multiple-destination visits. The latter problem is not explicitly discussed by Bishop and Heberlin (1980) and may not be a problem for their case. Desvousges et al. (1982) note data limitations. The alternative approaches taken for estimating the costs of travel can be briefly summarized and compared. For travel time, a range representative of the existing literature is present: from zero, to Cesario's (1976) recommended 50 percent of the wage rate, to the full wage rate (Table 1). For Bishop and Heberlin's methodology, including travel time at 50 percent of the wage rate quadruples the average consumer surplus from $8 to $32 per hunter.

For the monetary costs of travel, there are at least two models which can be considered in deciding on the appropriate travel cost per mile. One describes decisions on a household basis and assumes the travel party is the household. In this approach, taken by Knetsch and Davis, the costs per mile are on a vehicle or group basis. The other approach focuses on the individual and requires a measured or assumed number of individuals per vehicle. Both Desvousges et al. and Bishop and Heberlin defined travel costs as the variable costs of operating an automobile, based on national estimates for 1976 of gas, oil, maintenance, and parts per vehicle-mile (around 8–10 cents). While both studies appear to be on an individual basis, it is not clear that vehicle costs were changed to a per-passenger-mile basis. The latter adjustment can be significant. For example, Suth-erland (1982) also used a vehicle-mile cost of about 8 cents (1976 dollars), but he used a cost per individual of about 3 cents per mile based on his sample of 2.7 passengers per vehicle. These are merely accounting prob-lems; a more fundamental difficulty is that there is no basis for excluding other costs of travel such as vehicle depreciation and lodging. Such costs have been included in some other studies (e.g., Burt and Brewer, 1971) and can result in per-mile travel costs that are up to four times higher than those limited to vehicle operating costs.[3]

The main conclusion of this review is that difficult-to-avoid judgmental factors in the application of the travel cost method can cloud any clear comparison with direct survey measures. In addition, these comparative studies provide evidence on the variation between willingness to pay and compensation and also across method that is similar to data provided by other direct survey studies reviewed above.

III.   ANALYSIS OF THE TRAVEL COST APPROACH

A.   Methodology

The conventional travel cost model is site oriented and presumes that the only choice variable is the number of visits to each destination. An al-ternative view is that travelers choose among trips or routes which differ in regard to having different combinations of possible destinations or stops. Travel in itself, aside from stops, can generate recreational ser-vices. In this context, Freeman (1979) and Wilman (1980) have previously developed a utility maximization framework that admits of the possibility of utility to travel. A basic result from their first-order conditions is that the marginal utility of a given visit is a function of monetary costs, one-site time, and the costs of travel time net of the marginal (dis)utility of travel. Wilman (1980) suggests that the latter, which she calls the value of time saved, can be directly estimated by the use of survey techniques. The central assumption is that travelers can conceptually distinguish the services and joint costs of travel and site.

As an approximation, we might assume that the value of travel time can be identified as a parameter. Then solving the conditions for a utility maximization yields the usual general function result that the demand for visits is a function of income, own price, and the price of related goods. Using the zonal model, two alternative specifications of the per capita visit function were examined—semilog and log-linear:

$$\ln V_i = B_0 + B_1 D_1 + B_2 S_i + B_3 Y_i + E_i \tag{1}$$

and

$$\ln V_i = B_0 + B_1 \ln D_i + B_2 \ln S_i + B_3 \ln Y_i + E_i, \tag{2}$$

where V_i is per capita visits from zone i;
D_i is distance from i to the site;
Y_i is mean income for zone i;
B_j are parameters to be estimated (j = 1, 2, 3);
S_i is the substitute measure;
E_i is the error term.

These functions can be directly intergrated for estimates of consumer surplus by zone, where the upper limit of integration is the greatest zone distance in the sample (D_n). Then sample aggregate consumer surplus estimates (CS_k) for the two specifications are given by

$$CS_1 = \frac{(v + t/H)e^{B_0}}{B_1} \sum_{i=1}^{n-1} P_i e^{B_2 S + B_3 Y}(e^{B_1 D_n} - e^{B_1 D_i}) \tag{3}$$

and

$$CS_2 = \frac{(v + t/H)e^{B_0}}{1 + B_1} \sum_{i=1}^{n-1} P_i S_i^{B_2} Y_i^{B_3}(D_n^{B_1+1} - D_i^{B_1+1}), \tag{4}$$

where P_i is population of zone i;
D_i is the travel distance in zone i;
Y_i is per capita income in zone i;
v is the estimated variable expenses of travel;
t is the survey cost of travel time;
H is the average velocity of travel.

The specific formulation here was necessitated by the fact that travel time was not independently observed, which is a limitation of the study. This specification also assumes that visits are homogeneous, including the dimension of time on site. If the sample is representative of the user population, annual consumer surplus (A_k) associated with the site is given by sample size (r) relative to estimated visits per year (N) or

$$A_k = \frac{CS_k N}{r} . \tag{5}$$

The preceding formulation is appropriate for single destination trips. For multiple destination trips, the approach taken here was to assume that such visitors were on fairly homogeneous "western tours." Then the zonal model outlined above can provide an estimate of the consumer surplus for the entire trip. Visitors were surveyed as to the percentage of their travel expenses that could be allocated to this site. Consumer surplus for the site was then estimated based on the perceived allocation of joint costs. This approach is not conceptually rigorous; however, such an exploratory analysis can indicate the relative error involved in the conventional assumption that no multiple-destination visits are present in the sample.

B.   Travel Cost Estimates

The basic data for the travel cost analysis was collected during June–September of 1981. A short questionnaire established the basic origin/destination and cost of travel information for a sample of 181 users. A somewhat more detailed set of questions were used for a separate sample of 281 users. Of the total sample of 462 users, only 86 (or 20 percent) responded that Kootenai Falls was the main destination of their trip. All but two of these 86 also said that 99 or 100 percent of the cost of their travel was on account of their visit to the falls. For the other 80 percent of respondents, the falls was not the main destination and the relative share of total trip expenses averaged 7 percent. Accordingly, the main- and multiple-destination groups were analyzed separately to help ensure homogeneity. Based on the two sets of sampled visits, origin zones were defined in such a way that no origin zone had zero visits and zones of approximately equal distances away were of similar geographic size. The sample was such that the main destination subgroup had 10 zones and the multiple destination group 69.

Measures of substitutes were based on visitor perceptions. A pure substitute price approach for each substitute was obviously not possible because of degrees of freedom constraints. Respondents were asked if there was a place near their home that was comparable to the falls (yes/no) and were asked to rank this area on a 1 to 5 "much less" to "much more" interesting scale. They also were asked to name the substitute and estimate its distance from their home. Several alternative "attractiveness" weighted price measures were constructed from these responses and aggregated by zone (Table 2).

Average household income for each zone was based on published sources. Map highway distances were used to derive average mileage to the site by zone. Ordinary least squares estimates of the per capita visit functions are reported in Table 2. Distance (as the travel cost proxy) is always negative and highly significant. Unlike many studies, the income variable was significantly correlated to the visit rate; unfortunately, the correlation was strongly negative. The result is undoubtedly due to the fact that the further you live from Libby, Montana (near Kootonai Falls), the richer you are likely to be. The income variable had a simple correlation coefficient of .7 to .8 with distance. Because of this strong multicollinearity, income was excluded from the estimates, at the risk of understating the negative effect of distance. The substitute variables consistently had the correct sign (negative), and one or the other provided a significant correlation for all but the log-linear multiple estimate.

The overall explanatory power of the estimates was generally high for both functional forms. However, the relatively small sample for the main-destination subgroup results in more sensitivity to the functional form. No formal tests were undertaken, but based on the adjusted R^2 the log-linear estimate appeared to provide a better fit for this group. Unlike the application reported by Bowes and Loomis (1980), the best measured observations are probably for low-population nearby zones. Integration of the visit functions [Eqs. (1) and (2)] yields consumer surplus estimates

Table 2. Estimated Travel Cost Visit Functions

Category	Estimated Parameters[a]			Adjusted R-Square
	Intercept	Distance	Substitute	
Main-destination subgroup:				
Log-linear	+1.77	−2.66	−2.91[b]	.966
		(16.00)	(2.96)	
Semilog	−5.65	−.008	−1.52[c]	.679
		(3.54)	(1.23)	
Multiple-destination subgroup:				
Log-linear	−.234	−1.68		.755
		(14.5)		
Semilog	−7.95	−.003	−.335[c]	.792
		(16.1)	(2.41)	

Note:
[a] Parenthesis indicate t-statistic.
[b] Substitute variable defined as (yes, substitute exists)/all responses).
[c] Substitute variable defined as (miles/gallon)/(comparison to falls) (miles to substitute).

in distance units (Table 3). These measures are for the consumer surplus
loss associated with eliminating the site (i.e., the triangle bounded by the
demand curve and the implicit price for each zone).[4] The log-linear estimate is about one-third of the semilog for the main destination subsample,
but the two approaches yield nearly identical estimates for the multiple
destination group.[5]

Variable costs of travel were estimated by regressing reported trip expenses (per passenger) on estimated distance. Both travel group samples
had very significant slope coefficients, with the main-destination estimate
at .140 and the multiple-destination estimate at .066. However, distance
explained only about 30 percent of the variation in multiple-destination
expenses, compared to 93 percent for those of the main-destination
subgroup. This may be due both to more time-dependent costs entering
the longer trips (e.g., lodging as a function of days rather than of miles)
and a downward bias on the estimated coefficient due to measurement
error. Comparison of average costs for the two subsamples indicated that
the variables costs for the multiple-destination group were also probably
at least 14 cents per mile and that measurement and specification error
were masking this result. This estimate is based on all surveyed variable
costs of travel and is several times higher than the conventional estimate
that would result from limiting costs to vehicle expenses.

An estimate of the value of travel time was derived from responses to
two questions similar to those suggested by Wilman (1980). Visitors were

Table 3.   Travel Cost Estimates for Annual Value of Kootenai Falls
Recreation (1981 dollars)

Demand Category	Total One-way Miles[a]	Percent Expenses For Falls	Dollar per One-way Mile	Total Value[b]
Main-destination subgroup:				
Log-linear	7439.0	100.0	.28	80,200
Semilog	24027.4	100.0	.28	259,100
Multiple-destination subgroups:				
Log-linear	546302	3.88	.28	163,100
Semilog	538921	3.88	.28	160,800
Totals				
Log-linear				243,300
Semilog				419,900

Note:
[a] These estimates are for the sample.
[b] Estimates are limited to the .711 estimated proportion adults and are inflated by sample fractions of
.01846 for the main-destination subgroup and .02588 for the multiple-destination subgroups.

asked if the time they spent traveling to Kootenai Falls was enjoyable or not, based on a five-category scale. Ninety-nine percent of responses fell in the *very enjoyable* and *enjoyable* categories. The second inquiry was an open-ended contingent valuation question: "If you could cut travel time to this area by one hour by spending more money to get here, how much more would you be willing to spend?" To ensure plausibility, visitors from destinations less than two hours away were asked a similar question for the option of halving travel time. The mean bids were $1.52 and $0.76 per hour for the main- and multiple-destination groups, respectively. However, there were only 32 nonzero responses out of 265 individuals that answered the question. Based on the dominant response, the value of travel time saved can be conservatively taken as zero. These limited findings may be contrasted to the conventional application that takes the value of travel time at 25–50 percent of the wage rate.

Taking the estimated unit costs of travel at 14 cents per passenger mile, aggregate consumer surplus[6] for the site is derived in Table 3. The main-destination estimate is $80,000 to $260,000 for the two functional forms. Multiple-destination visits in annual terms are valued at about $160,000 for either specification. The latter are derived assuming that the perceived allocation of joint costs to the site is a reasonable basis for allocating consumer surplus. An estimate of 3.88 percent was derived by weighting zone average percent expenses by the zone's contribution to total consumer surplus for the log-linear estimate. Alternatively, if travel time was valued at the full wage rate (and assuming an average velocity of travel of around 45 miles per hour), the estimates would be approximately doubled.

IV. ANALYSIS OF THE CONTINGENT VALUATION APPROACH

A. The Direct Survey Method

The contingent valuation approach used in this study was the iterative bidding game. The basic methodology is similar to that developed for estimating the impacts associated with new power plants in the Southwest (Brookshire et al., 1976; Rowe et al., 1980). In an attempt to minimize hypothetical bias and nonresponse, all samples were taken on site in personal interviews. Following the literature, the features of the hypothetical market institution posed to respondents were varied by payment vehicle, starting bid, and implicit property right assignment [willingness to pay (WTP) and compensation]. The payment vehicles examined were day-use entrance fees, monthly utility bills, and incremental mileage to the site [willingness to drive (WTD)]. The first two vehicles were chosen on the assumption that they were plausible market institutions for the site resource. The WTD vehicle was designed to allow a direct comparison to the travel cost consumer surplus measure of incremental mileage. Of the three payment vehicles, only the utility bill approach was a logical possibility for the compensation measure.

Starting bid levels were systematically varied across the payment vehicles at $0.50 to $1.50 to $3.00 for the money vehicles and at 10, 25, and 50 incremental round-trip miles for willingness to drive. Also, within each payment vehicle set, respondents were provided differing amounts of information on the extent and impact of development of the falls. A separate compensation estimate in 1982 increased the starting bid range to $0.50–$20.00 and investigated other potential sources of information bias, including response to different visualizations (artists sketches) of the project. A follow-up question to this sample was designed to distinguish direct and indirect use values associated with the site. The questionnaires also collected information on socioeconomic and use-related characteristics of the respondents. Each questionnnaire also contained a feedback section to, in part, separate true zero-bid responses from protest responses.

B.   Direct Survey Findings

Two contingent valuation surveys were undertaken, one in 1981 and one in 1982. In the initial survey, a high priority was placed on getting samples of over 100 for each of the WTP estimates, which were expected to be more conservative. As a result of time and budget constraints, only 65 individuals were asked the compensation bid question in 1981, and 40 cash bids were obtained. Because of the preliminary findings, a second compensation sample of 486 visitors was taken in the summer of 1982. As noted previously, this survey also addressed in greater detail several issues of verification and interpretation. The actual questions were nearly identical in the two samples, but greater variation in the lead-in project descriptions was introduced in 1982. A statistical analysis of the two samples in terms of standard socioeconomic variables indicated that they were generally comparable.

In the first sampling period, June–September 1981, the contingent valuation survey was completed for 281 individuals. For the subsample responding to a question about how much their monthly utility bill would have to decrease to compensate for loss of Kootenai Falls, the mean bid was $22.09. However, based on a subsample of 95 respondents, the average individual was willing to pay only $3.48 per month to protect the falls based on this vehicle. This substantial divergence between willingness to pay and compensation (a 6:1 ratio here) is consistent with the differences reported in the literature. These mean bids are for total yearly use of the falls. Aggregation to an associated annual site valuation requires the assumption that the sample is representative of the user population. The estimates in Table 4 are derived based on mean visits per year (1.89), estimated total visitation (63,700), and the proportion of adults in the sample (.711).

As in other studies, the response was also sensitive to the payment vehicle. The average entrance fee that surveyed individuals (106 observations) were willing to pay was $2.00 per adult visit. This results in an annual value estimate that is one-tenth the WTP utility bill vehicle (Table 4). As suggested earlier, these findings may be evidence that the hypothetical market institutions being posed are taken seriously. Specifically, the hypothesized entrance fee situation corresponds to the actual collection of nominal fees at a variety of public recreation sites. It is likely that the response here is dominated by expectations of reasonable fees at other sites.

The 1982 survey was limited to the compensation bid; the main finding was that basically the 1981 results were replicated. One 1982 bid for $300 was excluded from the analysis as it was over 10 standard deviations from the mean and because other information limited its credibility. Otherwise the range and distribution of bids in the two sample years were quite similar. The means at $22.09 and $18.35 were not significantly different

Table 4. Comparison of Survey and Travel Cost Estimates for the Recreational Value of Kootenai Falls (1981 dollars)

		Consistent with Respect to Travel Costs	
Category	*Annual Value*	*Log-linear*	*Semilog*
Travel cost estimate:			
Log-linear	243,300		
Semilog	419,900		
Willingness to pay survey:			
Entrance fee	90,600	yes	yes
Utility bill	1,001,800	no	no
Willingness to drive survey			
	536,300	no	no
Compensation survey estimate:			
1981	6,359,300	yes	yes
1982	4,995,200	yes	yes
Compensation survey: direct only:			
1981	699,500	yes	yes
1982	549,500	yes	yes

at the 90-percent level. Since there were some changes in question format and because a different interviewer was used in each year, these findings indicate that the estimate is fairly robust.

The unsettling aspect of the 1982 response was that the proportion of respondents offering cash bids dropped considerably from 62 percent (40 of 65) to only 29 percent (141 of 486). Essentially all respondents otherwise participated in the interview process and were not "nonrespondents" per se. The reasons for this substantial change are not altogether clear. The most likely explanation is the differing ability of the two interviewers to elicit responses to a difficult question.

The basic result of the follow-up question relating to direct and indirect values was that respondents attributed only 11 percent of their compensation bid to direct use. These findings are on the same order as results from previously noted household surveys (Sutherland, 1982; Walsh et al., 1982) relating to the Flathead Lake area of Montana (11 percent) and the Colorado wilderness (U.S. sample, 14 percent) but are perhaps surprisingly low for a user population. The validity of these responses is difficult to establish.

For the WTD survey, the mean bids in incremental miles are 121 for the main-destination subsample and 68 for the multiple-destination subsample. Converting these to mileage at the same rate as in the travel cost analysis results in a total annual value estimate of about $500,000 (Table 4).

These and the other contingent valuation bids were evaluated for information and starting bid bias, and to identify correlation to socioeconomic or use-related characteristics of respondents. There was generally no significant correlation between the varying information levels embodied in the questionnaires and the bid response. Starting bid was a significant factor only for the entrance fee bids. However, a consistent and interesting finding was that when bids were sorted by "up" and "down" bidding from the starting bid, the correlations generally became significant and were always higher for "down" bidding. There is evidently a greater reluctance of bidders to move down from the initial suggestion if their desired bid lies in that range than if it is up. In the case at hand, the bias for the entrance fee case may have to do with the relatively high range of the starting bids relative to the mean.

V.   COMPARISON OF ESTIMATES

The WTD responses provide the most direct comparison to travel cost, as responses are in the same metric as the travel cost visit functions. Based on the number of estimated main-destination (19,900) and multiple-destination (43,850) visitors in 1981, a mean willingness to travel can be derived from the travel cost consumer surplus estimates presented in Table 3. The basic finding is that the WTD survey mean response of 80 miles is quite similar to the semilog travel cost estimate at 95 miles but about double the loglinear estimate of 38. Disaggregated by main and multiple destination, the WTD mean mileages are 121 and 68, respectively, versus 131 and 37 for the semilog and 41 and 37 for the log-linear estimate. Given the quite different assumptions and methodologies of the two approaches, the similarity of results is perhaps encouraging. Certainly the most questionable aspect of the travel cost analysis is the valuation of multiple-destination visits based on respondent-reported share of travel expenses. For both specifications, this exploratory approach is half the direct survey estimate.

A comparison of the travel cost estimate to the full range of survey measures is summarized in Table 4. Theory would suggest that the estimates should be fairly similar. Our findings indicate that for all of the WTP measures except for the entrance fee vehicle this holds true. Moreover, as discussed earlier, there are a priori reasons for expecting that the latter may not have elicited reservation prices and may therefore not be comparable measure. As in most other studies, the compensation estimates are substantially higher than the travel cost and other WTP measures. The direction of differences between travel cost and the other measures (Table 4) is consistent with theoretical expectations for the compensation estimate, but only for the entrance fee measure under a WTP approach. Even including travel time at the full wage rate would not change these conclusions.

Several possible interpretations can be noted that could indicate somewhat greater consistancy among the estimates. The travel cost, WTD, and entrance fee estimates are limited to direct use, while the other survey measures could plausibly include indirect values. As noted, the share allocable to direct use was directly estimated for the compensation measure at 11 percent. This ratio results in a compensation direct use estimate (Table 4) that is on the same order ($600,000 to $700,000) as the WTD and high travel cost estimates. It is conceivable that the divergence of the utility bill vehicle estimate (at about $1 million) from the other WTP responses could also be due to indirect values.

Another issue that affects the comparison of results is whether responses are to be interpreted on an individual basis or as outcomes of a group decision implying group responsibility. Some effort was made in survey design to elicit responses that could be clearly interpreted on an individual basis. However, the monthly utility bill vehicle perhaps implies a household group and may have been more realistic for eliciting a group decision. Such an interpretation would reduce the utility bill bid responses by a factor of 2 to 3. For the travel cost measure, response to a question in the 1982 survey indicated that more than 85 percent of visitors would be willing to bear the costs of travel even if traveling alone. This suggests that using travel costs on a passenger-mile basis results in an underestimate for the WTD measure and also possibly for the travel cost approach.

VI. CONCLUSIONS

Prudence requires a cautious attitude in generalizing from our empirical findings. As in most other studies, the travel cost application reported here required assumptions and judgments that can easily be criticized. A tentative finding is that the cost of travel time may be less than is commonly assumed. Further research is called for on this issue as the open-ended question format may not be the most appropriate for eliciting these values. The findings also provide some indication of the relative magnitude of values associated with multiple-destination visits. Variable costs of travel based on survey response were found here to be considerably greater than automobile operating costs.

The contingent valuation application seems to provide further evidence on the reliability of this technique. Sample means were shown to be relatively stable across sample years, and good internal consistancy was found with respect to user characteristics. Strategic and information bias were not found to be significant problems. It appears that a case can be made for a general strategy of low starting bids relative to expected means. However, the cash bid response rate for compensation was found to be quite variable, indicating the sensitivity of some result to interviewer or interview procedure.

The comparison of travel cost with contingent valuation is encouraging with respect to indicating the possible consistency of the two approaches. However, results are found to be sensitive to the allocation of survey values between direct and indirect uses. In general it appears that contingent valuation has a relatively unexploited potential for exploring the many assumptions entailed in travel cost analysis. One priority might be the analysis of individual WTP observations with respect to the relative virtues of the zonal and individual models.

In the context of previous studies, the results here provide further evidence that contingent valuation responses are sensitive to payment vehicle and implied property right assignment. These findings have generally been the main basis for questioning the overall reliability of the survey method. We have been perhaps too simplistic in characterizing hypothetical situations and in interpreting the complex responses that are generated. There would appear to be possibilities for the use of contingent valuation techniques in areas beyond the usual nonmarket good valuations. The interesting work ahead is in learning to adjust the instrument for the problem at hand: closely specifying the hypothetical institution that is appropriate for a given issue.

ACKNOWLEDGMENTS

The design and implementation of the recreational survey described here was a collaborative effort with Stewart Allen of the Montana Department of Natural Resources and Conservation. I am grateful to Don Loftsgaarden and Rudy Gideon of the Mathematics Department, University of Montana, for their help with the data analysis. This paper has also benefited substantially from the editor's comments. The above-named individuals are of course absolved from responsibility for any remaining errors.

NOTES

1. Capel and Pandey (1973) and Sutherland (1982) have also reported side-by-side applications of the two methods. However, the former is difficult to interpret because of the aggregation method, and the latter does not provide an explicit comparison.

2. The Desvousges et al. (1982) study is also somewhat more ambitious in attempting to use travel cost to evaluate changes in water quality, rather than simply site valuation. They also report results for gains. For water quality improvement on the Monongahela River, only the iterative bidding method with a low ($25) starting bid was theoretically consistent. The other WTP measures of compensating variation (direct question, payment card, and iterative bid starting at $125) were some two to three times higher than the ordinary consumer surplus estimate.

3. Clawson and Knetsch (1966) report that based on 19 surveys, transportation averages only 25 percent of the cost of travel.

4. It is assumed here that construction of the proposed dam would amount to elimination of the site. The proposed hydroelectric project would have the effect of reducing the flow over the falls to approximately 10 percent of its current volume. A reservoir upstream would inundate the main fishing areas. In addition, response to bidding questions indicated a very low value would be placed on visits with a dam in place.

5. Since distance is scaled by a constant in each of these models (with the constant reflecting the appropriate per-mile travel cost), we would expect that the parameter for the implicit price (i.e., travel cost or distance) in the double-log model will not change at all. The effect will simply be to change the intercept in the estimated model. By contrast, in the semilog model, we would expect a change in this estimated coefficient. Consequently, comparing the parameter estimates across the two models can be misleading.

6. A problem here is that consumer surplus estimates from a log-linear or semilog specification are subject to bias. They are good estimates of the conditional median of the consumer surplus statistic, but not of the conditional mean. Goldberger (1968) spells out the difficulties associated with estimating predictions from models that involve logarithms.

REFERENCES

Bishop, Richard C. and T. A. Heberlin, "Simulated Markets, Hypothetical Markets, and Travel Cost Analysis: Alternative Methods of Estimating Outdoor Recreation Demand." Agricultural Economics Staff Paper Series, No. 187, Department of Agricultural Economics, University of Wisconsin, Madison, 1980.

Bohm, P., "Option Demand and Consumer Surplus: Comment." *American Economic Review* 65(September 1975):733–736.

Bowes, M. D. and J. B. Loomis, "A Note on the Use of Travel Cost Models with Heterogeneous Zonal Populations." *Land Economics* 56(November 1980):465–470.

Brookshire, D., B. Ives, and W. Schulze, "The Valuation of Aesthetic Preferences." *Journal of Environmental Economics and Management* 3(December 1976):325–346.

Brown, William G. and Farid Nawas, "Impact of Aggregation on the Estimation of Outdoor Recreation Demand Functions." *American Journal of Agricultural Economics* 55(May 1973):246–249.

Burt, O. R. and D. Brewer, "Estimation of Net Social Benefits from Outdoor Recreation." *Econometrica* 39(October 1971):813–827.

Capel, R. E. and R. K. Pandey, "Evaluating Demand for Deer Hunting: Comparison of Methods." *Canadian Journal of Agricultural Economics* 21(1973):6–14.

Cesario, Frank J., "Value of Time in Recreation Benefit Studies." *Land Economics* 52(February 1976):32–41.

Cesario, Frank J. and Jack L. Knetsch, "Time Bias in Recreation Benefit Estimates." *Water Resources Research* 6(June 1970):700–704.

Clawson, M., "Methods of Measuring the Demand for and Value of Outdoor Recreation." Reprint No. 10, Washington, D.C.: Resources for the Future, 1959.

Clawson, M. and Jack L. Knetsch, *Economics of Outdoor Recreation.* Washington, D.C.: Resources for the Future, 1966.

Currie, John M., John A. Murphy and Andrew Schmitz, "The Concept of Economic Surplus." *Economic Journal* 81(December 1971):741–799.

Davis, Robert K., "The Value of Outdoor Recreation: An Economic Study of the Maine Woods." Unpublished Ph.D. Dissertation, Harvard University, 1963.

Desvousges, William H., V. Kerry Smith and Matthew P. McGivney, "A Comparison of Alternative Approaches for Estimating Recreation and Related Benefits of Water Quality Improvement. Draft." Washington, D.C.: U.S. Environmental Protection Agency, 1982.

———, "The Opportunity Cost of Travel Time in Recreation Demand Models." *Land Economics* 59(August 1983):259–278.

Dwyer, J. F. and M. D. Bowes, "Concepts of Value for Marine Recreational Fishing." *American Journal of Agricultural Economics* 60(December 1978):1008–1012.

Freeman, A. Myrick, III, *Benefits of Environmental Improvement.* Baltimore: Johns Hopkins, 1979.

Goldberger, Arthur S., "The Interpretation and Estimation of Cobb–Douglas Functions." *Econometrica* 35(July–October 1968):464–472.

Gum, R. and W. E. Martin, "Problems and Solutions in Estimating the Demand for the Value of Rural Outdoor Recreation." *American Journal of Agricultural Economics* 57(November 1975):558–566.

Knetsch, Jack L., "Outdoor Recreation Demands and Benefits." *Land Economics* 37(1963):387–396.

Knetsch, Jack L. and Robert K. Davis, "Comparison of Methods for Recreation Evaluation." In Allen V. Kneese and S. C. Smith (eds.), *Water Research.* Baltimore: Johns Hopkins, 1966.

Knetsch, Jack L. and J. A. Sinden, "Willingness to Pay and Compensation Demanded: Experimental Evidence of an Unexpected Disparity in Measures of Value." *Quarterly Journal of Economics* (forthcoming).

Krutilla, John V., "Conservation Reconsidered." *American Economic Review* 57(September 1967):777–786.

McConnell, Kenneth E., "Some Problems in Estimating the Demand for Outdoor Recreation." *American Journal of Agricultural Economics* 57(May 1975):330–334.

McConnell, Kenneth E. and I. Strand, "Measuring the Cost of Time in Recreation Demand Analysis: An Application to Sport Fishing." *American Journal of Agricultural Economics* 63(February 1981):153–156.

Meyer, Philip A., "Publicly Vested Values for Fish and Wildlife: Criteria in Economic Welfare and Interface with the Law." *Land Economics* 55(May 1979):223–235.

Randall, Alan and John R. Stoll, "Consumer's Surplus in Commodity Space." *American Economic Review* 70(June 1980):449–455.

Rowe, R., R. D'Arge and D. Brookshire, "An Experiment on the Economic Value of Visibility." *Journal of Environmental Economics and Management* 7(March 1980):1–19.

Smith, V. Kerry, "Travel Cost Demand Models for Wilderness Recreation: A Problem of Non-nested Hypothesis." *Land Economics* 51(May 1975):103–111.

Smith, V. Kerry and R. J. Kopp, "The Spatial Limits of the Travel Cost Recreation Demand Model." *Land Economics* 56(February 1980):64–72.

Sutherland, Ronald J., "Recreation and Preservation Valuation Estimates for Flathead River and Lake System." Kalispell: Flathead River Basin Commission, 1982.

Thayer, M., "Contingent Valuation Techniques for Assessing Environmental Impacts: Further Evidence." *Journal of Environmental Economics and Management* 8(March 1981):27–44.

Walsh, R. G., R. A. Gillman and J. B. Loomis, *Wilderness Resource Economics: Recreation Use and Preservation Values.* Denver: American Wilderness Alliance, 1982.

Willig, Robert D., "Consumer's Surplus without Apology." *American Economic Review* 66(September 1976):587–597.

Wilman, Elizabeth A., "The Value of Time in Recreation Benefit Studies." *Journal of Environmental Economics and Management* 7(September 1980):272–286.

AN APPLICATION OF THE HEDONIC TRAVEL COST FRAMEWORK FOR RECREATION MODELING TO THE VALUATION OF DEER

Robert Mendelsohn

I. INTRODUCTION

One of the critical problems facing outdoor recreation managers is the evaluation of site characteristics. Faced with scarce resources, should managers improve campgrounds, enhance wildlife stocks, maintain trails, preserve old growth, or devote their funds to some other activity? In order to address these pressing issues, managers need estimates of the benefits of changing the physical attributes of sites. Although a number of evaluation methodologies have been developed in the literature, most of the procedures focus upon valuing entire sites or the outputs of users. For example, the travel cost method (Clawson, 1959) and the travel cost de-

Advances in Applied Micro-Economics, Volume 3, pages 89–101.
Copyright © 1984 by JAI Press Inc.
All rights of reproduction in any form reserved.
ISBN: 0-89232-398-1

mand system (Burt and Brewer, 1971; Cichetti et al., 1972) approach focus on valuing single and systems of sites respectively.[1] The household production function approach (Charbonneau and Hay, 1978; Deyak and Smith, 1978; Bockstael and McConnell, 1981) values such outputs as activity days, size of kill, or number of sightings. Unfortunately, the value of household outputs and the value of specific sites do not readily lead to estimates of the benefits of changing site characteristics. A substantial fraction of outdoor recreational resource questions cannot be answered with the traditional travel cost and household production function approaches.

The only two approaches which directly evaluate site characterisics are the hedonic travel cost method (Brown and Mendelsohn, 1980; Mendelsohn and Roberts, 1983) and the own quality–own price travel cost model (Vaughn and Russell, 1982). As stated in the Mendelsohn and Brown (1983) review of revealed preference techniques, the own quality–own price technique suffers from the assumption that substitute sites do not matter. It is a strong assumption that a user would travel 60 miles to an average-quality site the same number of times regardless of whether there are a dozen high-quality sites closer to his residence or none.

The purpose of this paper is to describe the hedonic travel cost method and apply it to value deer density in Pennsylvania. The 1980 National Survey of Fishing, Hunting, and Wildlife-Associated Recreation was used to obtain information about hunter behavior in Pennsylvania. The price of deer density was calculated by observing how much further hunters were willing to travel to obtain higher deer density. In three of five residential areas, positive significant prices were estimated for deer density. The remaining two areas produced negative prices, but these areas were expected to yield low prices because of their proximity to good hunting sites. A demand function for deer density was estimated by comparing the average deer density purchased across hunters who faced different prices. The coefficient of price in the demand function was negative, significant, but small, suggesting that demand for deer density is price inelastic. Income was positive and significant, suggesting that deer density is a normal good.

The theory underlying the hedonic travel cost method is developed in detail in Brown and Mendelsohn (1980). Therefore, only a brief description is provided here in Section II. The data and its limitations are discussed in Section III, and the results are presented in Section IV.

II. THEORETICAL MODEL

The following model describes the outdoor recreational choices of a participant who takes one-day trips to hunt. For a more general model, which incorporates multiple-day trips, see Brown and Mendelsohn (1980). The individual has two sets of choices to make: he must decide how many trips he would like to take in a season and what average level of quality he would like to enjoy on these trips. A more complicated version of this model might also discuss the composition of trips the individual makes to arrive at his final choice of number of trips and average quality per season. At least in initial inquiries, however, this additional layer of micro description could not be supported by available data. Consumer's preferences for heterogeneity, however, deserves more attention in the economic literature.

Since the nearest site is the cheapest location to use, if all sites were alike everyone would travel only to their closest possible site. The fact that people are often willing to travel to more distant sites reflects the fact that these more distant sites must be superior to the closer sites. We assume, in this analysis, that the superiority of more distant sites is related to the objective characteristics of sites. That is, we assume the objective characteristics (Z_i) of sites enter the individual's utility function along with all other goods X and the number of trips T:

$$U(Z_1, \ldots, Z_n, T, X). \tag{1}$$

Adopting the assumptions of travel cost analysis, we further assume that the cost of purchasing a bundle of characteristics at a site is the travel cost associated with getting from the residence to that site. Technically any user fees associated with gaining access to the site should also be included. Since most sites have free access, we ignore user fees in this presentation. The budget constraint facing the individual is consequently

$$Y - SX + TV(Z), \tag{2}$$

where Y is income; S is a vector of prices of all other goods; T is the number of trips taken; and V(Z) is the travel cost associated with a site.

Maximizing utility (1) subject to the budget constraint (2) given the necessary second-order conditions yields the following first-order conditions:

$$U_{Z_i} - \lambda T V_{Z_i} = 0 \qquad (i = 1, \ldots, n);$$

$$U_T - \lambda V(Z) = 0; \tag{3}$$

$$U_X - \lambda S = 0.$$

The price of increasing the average level of each characteristic is the number of trips taken times the marginal transportation cost. The price of an additional trip is the transportation cost of getting to the site.

The budget constrained optimization of utility described by Eqs. (1),

(2), and (3) can be written in terms of two simultaneous demand functions:

$$Z_i = g(V_{Z_1}, V_{Z_2}, \ldots, V_{Z_n}, T, W) \qquad (i = 1, \ldots, n) \qquad (4)$$

and

$$T = h(V(Z), W), \tag{5}$$

where W is a vector of exogenous demand shift variables. Equations (4) and (5) describe the average level of each characteristic and the total number of trips the individual takes over a season.

In order to estimate the hedonic travel cost model, one must complete two distinct steps: (i) estimate the travel costs for each residential area, and (ii) estimate the demand functions (4) and (5). The travel cost function $V(Z)$ can be estimated by combining the insights of travel cost and hedonic analysis. In traditional hedonic analysis the cost of any component in a bundle of characteristics can be measured by regressing characteristics upon the total cost of the bundle. The travel cost approach essentially states that the total cost of the bundle is the expenditure on travel between the residence and the destination. By regressing travel cost on the characteristics of sites chosen by people from a particular residential area, the travel cost function $V(Z)$ can be estimated:

$$V(Z) = f(Z_1, Z_2, \ldots, Z_n).$$

Repeating this exercise for scattered residential areas reveals a set of prices or markets for the characteristics. Because the hunting sites are public goods and free, these nearby markets do not interfere with each other's prices. Marginal prices could also be estimated by simply measuring how far residents must travel to purchase various packages of characteristics and then regressing travel on characteristics. Care must be taken in using this latter approach, to eliminate inferior sites. The inclusion of dominated sites, locations which cost more but provide no additional characteristics, will tend to bias the prices of characteristics upward. Utilizing only sites that residents actually travel to eliminates this problem because inferior sites are not visited.

Note that travel costs include the total costs of traveling. In this analysis, we proxy these total costs with distance. Because some roads are faster than others, however, it would be preferable to have both distance and travel time. Separate characteristics prices could be estimated for both—a better-quality site being purchased by additional out-of-pocket travel costs and also longer travel time. These two prices could then be combined in an index depending upon both the dollar per mile cost as well as the dollar per travel hour cost. Unfortunately, this index is somewhat illusive—a serious problem with all the existing revealed preference techniques to value outdoor recreation.

Although the cost of travel time belongs in all travel cost models (including the hedonic travel cost), the cost of time at the site is not a travel expenditure. Although the length of time a user intends to stay at a given location may affect what he is willing to pay to go to that site, it does not affect what he must pay to get to the site. Thus, the length of time at the site might shift the demand for a characteristic but should not affect characteristic prices. McConnell (1975) and Wilman (1980) press for including time at the site in travel cost analyses because they mistakenly assume that the travel cost approach should be used to value the output of household production functions. As shown in Bockstael and McConnell (1981), however, only in unlikely circumstances can the travel cost method value household outputs.

The travel cost method focuses upon valuing the inputs (visits to the site), not the outputs (days of activities, catch, kill, etc.), of household production. To measure the demand for a site or site characteristics, one should not include the expenditures on other inputs such as time at the site as a cost of the characteristic. For example, to value an automobile, one would not normally include the 10-year cost of gasoline in addition to the purchase price. On the other hand, one could include the price of other inputs in the demand for the site. The wage rate of the individual could be included in the demand for site characteristics just as the price of gasoline might enter the demand for an automobile or the demand for automobile characteristics such as miles per gallon.

The prices for characteristics are simply the partial derivatives of the travel expenditure function with respect to each characteristic:

$$P_i \equiv \frac{\partial V}{\partial Z_i} (Z_1, \ldots, Z_n).$$

Note that in hedonic markets the prices for a particular characteristic may vary with the level of the characteristic. When the expenditure function is nonlinear, marginal prices are no longer exogenous to the individual because his choice of Z affects the marginal prices he faces. The price schedule $P(Z)$ is exogenous, but marginal prices are not. The specific marginal price at the optimum bundle is selected by the individual when he chooses a particular Z^*. When marginal prices are endogenous, the estimation of structural equations suffers from problems of identification and selectivity bias.[2] Because the advantages of better-fitting price equations often do not compensate for the complication of nonconstant prices, a linear hedonic price function is adopted in this paper.

Assuming that individuals in each of the residential areas are alike except for their observable differences (the vector of demand shift variables W), the prices estimated from the first-stage regressions can be used to compute demand curves. Regressing the level of characteristics purchased upon the price of characteristics, the number of trips, and the demand shift variables across residential areas, the demand for each characteristic can be revealed:

$$Z_i = f(P_i, P_j, T, W).$$

The demand for trips can be revealed by regressing the number of trips on the cost per trip and the demand shift variables:

$$T = g(V(Z), W).$$

Note that the average quality of trips and the number of trips an individual chooses is determined simultaneously. In practice, however, it appears that the actual number of trips and the actual average cost per trip can be entered as independent variables in the corresponding equations without affecting the results.

Although appropriate for valuing the characteristics of sites, the hedonic travel cost method is not particularly suited to value recreational sites themselves. Moreover, although the value of a site is only the sum of the values of its characteristics, the joint consumer surplus associated with the site being there or not is difficult to evaluate. A recreation site is a heterogeneous public, not private, good. A single private good is just one of many, and so it is worth the sum of its characteristics evaluated at existing prices. The public good, in contrast, will be the only combination of characteristics available to the user at a particular cost. A site cannot be evaluated at existing prices because, were it absent, the prices of characteristics would change. The evaluation of a single site through its characteristics consequently involves complex multiple price changes. Since more direct methods of site evaluation are available, the hedonic travel cost method is probably not the best method of valuing existing single sites.

III.   DATA

The information about user behavior in this study comes from the 1980 National Survey of Fishing, Hunting, and Wildlife-Associated Recreation. The focus of the study is upon deer, and the observations are limited to one state, Pennsylvania. Although additional states would be desirable, it is difficult to ascertain reliable site characteristic information. Because Pennsylvania keeps relatively superior deer information, it was chosen for this analysis. Over 300 persons in the survey hunted deer in Pennsylvania. Some of these persons visited more than one site and could be treated as a multiple observation of a recreation origin/destination, raising the initial number to 639 cases. For most of these cases the survey describes age, sex, income destination site, distance to site, number of trips and game hunted, as well as a number of other variables of less interest.

The destination site was one of seven groups of counties designated by Pennsylvania for the survey. For each of these game management regions, separate data were also collected from the Pennsylvania Game Commission detailing the estimated average deer populations. Four measures were computed for each region: aggregate deer population, deer population divided by aggregate square mile area, deer population divided by forested square mile area, and the percentage of males in the population. The deer density (population divided by forest area) for each regions is displayed in Figure 1.

When we confine the analysis to residents of Pennsylvania (since adjoining areas have insufficient numbers of observations), the sample size falls to 506. The sample is distributed across five of the seven regions in Pennsylvania, with especially heavy concentrations in the two urban areas Philadelphia and Pittsburgh. Of the 506 original observations, 466 contain all the desired socioeconomic and hunting behavior data.

The data appear to be representative of the hunting population. Hunters traveled to their favorite sites on average five times a year. The average site was 77 miles from home. The average age of the hunters was 35, average income was $21,000, and 97 percent of the sample was male.

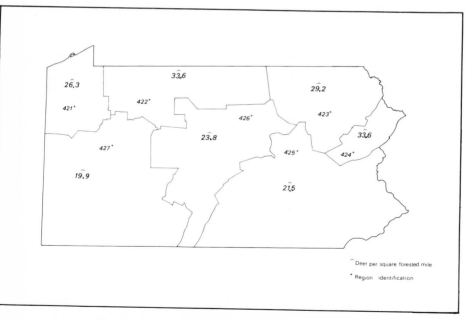

Figure 1.   Deer Densities in Pennsylvania.

IV. RESULTS

For each of the five regions with adequate data, distance was regressed upon site characteristics. Several functional forms were tried, but linear regressions performed the best—judging by the sign and significance of the coefficients. Relying upon linear price regressions also helps simplify the demand analysis. With nonlinear price gradients, the marginal prices are endogenous and must be replaced by an instrumental variable in the demand analysis (see Mendelsohn, 1983b). Several specifications were attempted, including different definitions of deer density and the percentage of males caught. Deer density, defined as estimated deer population per forested mile, performed best. Including the percentage of males distorted the price regressions, making deer density insignificant and producing highly significant coefficients on the male variable but widely varying signs. It appears that the male variable is acting as a proxy for special limited seasons. Because this regulatory effect is actually distorting the responses, it has been dropped from the regression.

The results of the best hedonic regressions are displayed in Table 1. Three of the five regressions displayed positive and significant deer density prices. People drove further to get higher-quality deer hunting. Residential areas 422 and 423, however, had negative coefficients. As one

Table 1.   Hedonic Price Regression[a]

Residential Site	Constant	Deer Density	R^2/F (No. observations)
421	− 107.	5.14	.189/9.16
	(2.26)	(3.02)	(36)
422	42.7	− 1.06	.103/12.45
	(4.91)	(3.53)	(99)
423	130.	− 3.65	.007/1.11
	(1.25)	(1.05)	(18)
425	− 152.	− 9.49	.302/83.54
	(5.75)	(9.14)	(191)
427	− 136.	8.46	.393/127.44
	(7.73)	(11.31)	(197)

Note:
[a] The regression was of the form:

$$distance = a_0 + a_1 \text{ deer density},$$

where deer density is defined as population of deer per forested area. The t-statistics are in parentheses. Distance is in miles.

can see from Figure 1, both of these areas had relatively high deer densities, so that low prices would be expected. The negative prices are unfortunately due to the aggregation of destinations. Anyone traveling to a nearby area in another region appears to be acting irrationally—driving further to get less. With more specific destination data and more site characteristics, even these observations would probably appear rational, with prices approaching zero or low positive numbers.

The size of the coefficients suggest that people living in the major metropolitan areas must travel an extra 9 miles each way to get one more deer per square mile. At prices of $0.20 per mile, this suggests that they pay $3.60 per deer per square forested mile given the current deer populations.[3] People who live outside of the Philadelphia and Pittsburgh regions face much lower prices, ranging from zero (negative) to $1.80 per deer per square forested mile.

Regressing deer density upon the prices estimated in Table 1 and age, sex, number of trips, and income reveals the demand function for deer density.[4] A second regression is estimated for number of trips. Unlike Table 1, where the observations are analyzed independently by residence, the structural equations are estimated across the entire sample. The results are displayed in Table 2.

With the demand for deer density, the price coefficients are negative, as expected, and highly significant. The deer density price coefficient states that huners select sites with 3.5 less deer per square mile for every mile per deer density that they must drive. Assuming travel costs of $0.20 per mile, if the price facing urban dwellers rose from $3.60 to $4.00 per deer density, they would on average purchase 3.5 less deer per square mile. Instead of purchasing their average deer density of about 24 at a total cost of $86 (24 * 3.6), the urban dwellers would choose about 20.5 at a total cost of $82 (20.5 * 4.0) per trip. Similarly, if the price dropped from $3.60 to $3.20, the urban dwellers would increase their deer density from 24 to 27.5 at a total of $88. At the high prices facing the urban dwellers, demand is elastic. At the low prices facing the rural dwellers, price is inelastic. The average price elasticity for the sample is .57. When constant elasticity demand curves are estimated, the price elasticity falls to .08.

Age had no detectable effect on the decision to purchase quality. Although males make up virtually the entire sample, females on average chose to go to higher quality sites. One must be slightly cautious interpreting sexual differences because some avid male hunters encourage female associates to participate in order to increase their legal harvest (by obtaining a second license). Higher-income individuals tended to purchase higher-quality sites. In general, one would expect that site quality is a normal good, but such results were not found in Brown and Men-

Table 2. The Demand Function[a]

	Deer Density	Number of Trips
Constant	33.8	4.28
	(79.94)	(2.46)
Age (years)	$-.19 \times 10^{-3}$	$.75 \times 10^{-2}$
	(.04)	(.37)
Sex (male)	$-.55$	1.55
	(1.51)	(1.03)
Income (thousands)	$.22 \times 10^{-3}$	$-.79 \times 10^{-3}$
	(3.34)	(2.90)
Constant price	$-.12$	$-.2 \times 10^{-2}$
	(26.80)	(.10)
Deer density price	-3.49	.20
	(37.36)	(.52)
Number of trips	.01	—
	(.90)	
R^2	.935	.05
F	1116.	5.97

Note:
[a] The t-statistic is in parenthesis. The total number of observations is 465. The prices are in terms of miles driven per deer per square mile.

delsohn's (1980) analysis of steelhead fishing. The number of trips was insignificant in the deer density equation, and the inclusion of trips had no effect on the other coefficient.

The demand for quality regression fits the data quite closely. Although this might seem surprising for cross-sectional data, one must remember that the individual observations have been aggregated by origin and destination. The aggregation of the dependent variable by eliminating much of the individual variation which is so hard to explain gives the misleading impression that the model is more reliable than it really is. Nonetheless, the overall results for the Pennsylvania study are quite encouraging.

The demand for number of trips was unresponsive to the prices of characteristics or even the level of characteristics purchased. At least with deer hunters in Pennsylvania, there appears to be no trade-off between the quality of hunting and the amount of hunting people do. The only significant explanatory variable for number of trips was income. Higher-income people tended to take fewer trips.

V. CONCLUSION

The hedonic travel cost method is aplied to measure the value hunters in Pennsylvania place on deer density. Using data collected in the 1980 National Survey of Fishing, Hunting, and Wildlife-Associated Recreation coupled with supply data for Pennsylvania, the prices and demand for deer density are calculated. Assuming total travel cost per mile is $0.20, the prices range from 0 to $3.60 per deer per square forested mile per trip. Deer density, like goods purchased in the market, has a downward sloping demand curve. For every dollar increase in the price of deer density, the typical hunter purchases 8.75 less deer per square mile. The price elasticity for deer density evaluated at the mean is .57. Thus, although hunters are willing to pay substantial sums to prevent significant deterioration of hunting sites, as the hunting quality of these sites improves dramatically the hunter's marginal willingness to pay for improvements falls dramatically.

Two areas of research concerning the hedonic travel cost deserve further attention. The first issue concerns improved measurements of travel cost. Although it is relatively easy to measure how many miles people travel to reach a site, it is difficult to know what value people would assign to each mile. Clearly they should be at least willing to pay the out-of-pocket costs of the trip. Would they also include depreciation of their car and the expected value of accidents? What value would they put on the travel time? Is driving as unpleasant as working, or do recreational trips provide substantial pleasure? Does the total cost per mile vary with the quality of the road or the scenery? Despite the reliance of virtually all the revealed preference outdoor recreation valuation techniques upon the answers to these questions, there has been virtually no research on these topics. The second area of research needing attention is a problem specific to the hedonic travel cost method. An important policy issue often facing resource managers is whether or not to improve some specific quality of a single site. If the improvement is marginal, the characteristic change can be evaluated by the price of that characteristic. Thus, if deer were to be increased from 24 to 25 deer per square mile, the approximate value of this change per trip is the price users currently pay for deer density. The total annual value of the change would be this price per trip multiplied by the number of trips per year. Nonmarginal changes at a single site are more difficult to assess. It is tempting to evaluate the change in terms of the consumer surplus in quantity space for the characteristic,[5] but in this case only one site out of the region has changed characteristics. In fact, this single-site change has altered the shape of the price gradient only in the neighborhood of the change. In order to evaluate what users are willing to pay for this nonlinear change in the price gradient, one would have to predict how users would respond to the change and then calculate how much they would pay to go from their original to their new consumption bundle. For example, one could adopt the procedure recommended by Hausman (1981). It remains to be seen whether simpler approaches might also be possible.

ACKNOWLEDGMENTS

Funding for this research comes from the U.S. Fish and Wildlife Service. I would like to thank Mike Hay and Kerry Smith for their helpful assistance.

NOTES

1. If the desired policy involves changing a site from its existing characteristics to the characteristics of other existing sites, the demand system approach is appropriate for measuring site quality changes. Among the types of sites included in the demand system would be the packages of characteristics before and after the change.

2. For a discussion of the identification problem, see Bockstael and McConnell (1981), Brown and Rosen (1982), and Mendelsohn (1983a). For a discussion of selectivity bias, see Hausman and Wise (1977), Heckman (1979), or Mendelsohn (1983b).

3. At costs of $0.30 per mile, the price of deer rise to $5.40 per deer per square forested mile. Because the figures are in terms of miles, not dollars, the reader can translate the results into dollars using whatever cost per mile is felt most appropriate.

4. The negative prices estimated in Table 1 were included in the demand regressions. Although one could argue the prices ought to be no less than zero, arbitrarily setting the prices to zero could bias the demand function.

5. See A. Randall and J. Stoll, "Consumer's Surplus in Commodity Space," *American Economic Review* 70:449–55 (1980).

REFERENCES

Bockstael, N. and K. McConnell, "Theory and Estimation of the Household Production Function in Wildlife Recreation." *JEEM* 8(1981):199–214.

Brown, G. and R. Mendelsohn, "The Hedonic Travel Cost Method." Institute for Economic Research, University of Washington, 1980.

Brown, J. and H. Rosen, "On the Estimation of Structural Hedonic Price Models." *Econometrica* 50(1982):765–68.

Burt, D. and D. Brewer, "Estimation of the Net Social Benefits from Outdoor Recreation." *Econometrica* 39(1971):813–29.

Charbonneau, J. and M. Hay, "Determinants and Economic Values of Hunting and Fishing." Presented at the 43rd North American Wildlife and Natural Resources Conference, Phoenix, Arizona, 1978.

Cichetti, C., A. Fisher and V. K. Smith, "An Economic and Econometric Model for the Valuation of Environmental Resources." Presented at Econometric Society Meetings, Toronto, 1972.

Clawson, M., "Methods of Measuring the Demand for the Value of Outdoor Recreation." Resources for the Future, Reprint No. 10, 1959.

Deyak, T. and V. K. Smith, "Congestion and Participation in Outdoor Recreation: A Household Production Function Approach." *JEEM* 5(1978):65–80.

Hausman, J., "Exact Consumer's Surplus and Deadweight Loss." *American Economic Review* 71(1981):662–76.

Hausman, J. and D. Wise, "Social Experimentation, Truncated Distributions, and Efficient Estimation." *Econometrica* 45(1977):919–38.

Heckman, T., "Sample Selection Bias as a Specification Error." *Econometrica* 47(1979):153–61.

McConnell, K., "Some Problems in Estimating the Demand for Outdoor Recreation." *American Journal of Agricultural Economists* (1975):330–34.

Mendelsohn, R., "Identying Structural Equations With Single Market Data." Mimeo, University of Washington, 1983a.

——, "Estimating the Structural Equations of Implicit Markets and Household Production Functions." Institute for Economic Research, University of Washington, 1983b.

Mendelsohn, R. and G. Brown, "Revealed Preference Approaches to Valuing Outdoor Recreation." *Natural Resources Journal* 23(1983):607–618.

Mendelsohn, R. and P. Roberts, "Estimating the Demand for the Characteristics of Hiking Trails: An Application of the Hedonic Travel Cost Method." Institute for Economic Research, University of Washington, 1983.

Vaughn, W. and C. Russell, "The National Recreational Fishing Benefits of Water Pollution Control." *JEEM* 9(1982):328–54.

Wilman, L., "The Value of Time in Recreation Benefit Studies." *JEEM* 7(1980):272–86.

University Library
GOVERNORS STATE UNIVERISTY

PART II

ECONOMIC IMPACT ANALYSIS AND CLIMATE CHANGE

INTRODUCTION TO PART II

V. Kerry Smith

Our recorded history provides extensive examples of mankind's ability to adapt to inhospitable environments. The human species displays a remarkable ability to adjust—to create conditions that are necessary to sustain and promote its continued existence. Since the Industrial Revolution, we have developed and come to recognize our ability to modify local environmental conditions. Such modifications were regarded as a natural component of economic development. Indeed, the modification of natural and environmental resources was widely regarded as improvements over their natural state.

It is difficult to state exactly when these views began to change among the general population. However, it is clear that during the late 1960s and 1970s, a change in attitude was widespread in the United States (and in most of the industrialized world).[1] Development was not necessarily synonymous with improvement. Local modification to the environment was not always judged to be desirable. Man's influence was not always regarded as a beneficial one. However, the problems these influences caused were generally regarded to be local environmental modifications. Transfrontier or transnational environmental externalities were consid-

Advances in Applied Micro-Economics, Volume 3, pages 105–108.
Copyright © 1984 by JAI Press Inc.
All rights of reproduction in any form reserved.
ISBN: 0-89232-398-1

ered to be more important for Western Europe, where the size and geography of the countries involved made local modifications into international problems.

The scope of mankind's potential influence was not fully appreciated. Over the past decade, there has been a growing awareness of the incomplete nature of this view of mankind's effects. There now appears to be sufficient evidence to conclude that man's activities can affect the global environment. One of the best examples of this phenomenon is the case of climate change. In the last generation, the concentration of carbon dioxide (CO_2) in the atmosphere increased by eight percent from 315 parts per million to over 340 parts per million by volume. The scientific community is generally agreed that increasing concentration of CO_2 in the atmosphere will lead to a change in the earth's climate conditions. Popularly referred to as the "Greenhouse Effect," increased atmospheric CO_2 affects the absorption of infrared radiation and, thereby, the earth's heat balance.

Recently, the Carbon Dioxide Assessment Committee of the National Academy of Sciences in their report *Changing Climate*, unambiguously confirmed the judgements of numerous past groups in suggesting that atmospheric CO_2 concentrations will continue to increase; and, as a consequence, we can expect that with a doubling in the atmospheric concentration, there would be a global warming of between 1.5°C to 4.5°C, with greater effects as one moves away from the equator. Such a change would be larger than any climatic modification in the last 10,000 years. The report was careful to point out the time span over which such a change would take place and the uncertainties present in our current information.

A doubling in atmospheric CO_2 is most likely to be realized by the third quarter of the next century. Thus, the change would be a slow one over the next 85 to 100 years.

Policy concern over the "CO_2 Problem" has run "hot and cold." It is difficult within our political system to develop the appropriate balance of research and policy initiative for problems with such a long time horizon. Nonetheless, the National Academy report suggests that the problem deserves sustained attention noting in its Executive Summary that:

> "Even very forceful policies adopted soon with regard to energy and land use are unlikely to prevent some modification of climate as a result of human activities. Thus, it is prudent to undertake applied research and development—and to consider some adjustments—in regard to activities, like irrigated agriculture, that are vulnerable to climate change." Carbon Dioxide Assessment Committee (1983), p. 3

This section of Volume III of *Advances in Applied Micro Economics* considers several of the most important research issues that must be addressed as part of any economic analyses of the impacts of climate change and of the design of policies under the uncertainty that characterizes our current knowledge of the problem.

The first essay by Kellogg provides an excellent overview of the problem, describing the nature of the carbon-cycle and climate models which suggest that increases in atmospheric CO_2 will raise global temperatures.[2] In the process, he discusses the sources of uncertainty in our models of the process. He concludes that:

> ". . .in its broadest sense the climate change issue can be seen as an unprecedented stimulus to long range planning and cooperation at all levels of society. . ."

How should economic analysis contribute to this planning process?

The remaining three papers in this section discuss various aspects of this problem. McFadden considers the influence of climatic uncertainty on the private actions of economic agents and how to modify conventional welfare analysis to evaluate the benefits or costs associated with a climate change. For the first of these tasks McFadden illustrates how recognized climatic uncertainty can be mitigated through the incorporation of flexibility in the technical design of production activities. While the analysis is undertaken for a firm, a comparable model could be developed for the household.

His second objective is to consider the application of conventional benefit cost analysis to the evaluation of changes in climate. His framework treats climate as a random variable and climate change as a change in one or more of the parameters of the distribution (i.e., the mean). Both of McFadden's models treat climate as exogenous to the decision process being modeled. For the firm's model, it is an exogenous random variable that influences production. For the welfare analysis it is a random variable that can influence both households' utility and firms' profit. By contrast, the second paper in this section, by Geoffrey Heal, focuses on the econ, omy-climate interactions. It recognizes that economic activities affect the character of the climatic uncertainty. Given the process is recognized but incompletely known, what are optimal economic policies? His analysis suggests that these policies can be defined for simple, stylized models. If, for example, the likelihood of a calamitous climate change was related to the rate of economic activity using the absorptive capacity of the environment, then society's attitude toward risk and discount rate would affect its willingness to undertake the activities that might lead to a climate change. Once the models become more complex, the optimal policy can become quite sensitive to the initial conditions of the model and therefore difficult to use for general conclusions.

The last paper concerns whether we can expect to learn the individual's valuation of desirable climatic regimes from conventional approaches to benefit measurement. Freeman's paper considers one of the most widely accepted of these methods—the hedonic price function. He concludes that while in principle it may be possible to use this method to measure the marginal valuation of climate attributes, there are likely to be significant problems. Among the most important of these is the prospect of quite different tastes for climate characteristics and the definition of the relevant markets for a hedonic price function with climatic variables.

These four papers provide both the background necessary to understand the climate change issue and an introduction to some of the issues that emerge from any attempt to consider the role of economic analysis in developing policies to respond to it.

ACKNOWLEDGMENTS

The research reported in this section was partially supported by the National Climate Program of NOAA. Special thanks are due Thomas Waltz for his interest in and encouragement to this research.

NOTES

1. Clearly, there have been numerous earlier concerns over the availability and conservation of natural resources. The Conservation Movement of the early 1900s is one such example. For an excellent overview of this movement, see Barnett and Morse (1963).

2. Kellogg's paper was written before the National Academy report *Changing Climate* was available. Nonetheless, it's primary conclusions and judgements closely parallel those in this report.

REFERENCES

Barnett, Harold J. and Chandler Morse, *Scarcity and Growth*. Baltimore: Johns Hopkins University, 1963.

Carbon Dioxide Assessment Committee, *Changing Climate*. Washington, DC: National Academy of Sciences, 1983.

MODELING THE PROSPECTS FOR CLIMATIC CHANGE:

CURRENT STATE OF THE ART AND

IMPLICATIONS

William W. Kellogg

I. INTRODUCTION

The *climate* of any locality is usually thought of as the weather that one has learned to expect from past experience. Thus, it can be defined for a given season of the year in terms of average temperature, rainfall and snowfall, hours of sunlight, wind, and so forth, together with the variances of these weather factors. Farmers and ranchers have to understand their climate, and they know that no two years are exactly the same but hope that over a period of several years the good and bad weather events will "average out." Thus, when times are bad they carry on with the conviction that sooner or later it will return to normal.

Advances in Applied Micro-Economics, Volume 3, pages 109–132.
Copyright © 1984 by JAI Press Inc.
All rights of reproduction in any form reserved.
ISBN: 0-89232-398-1

Lately a disturbing thought has been gaining in credence, and that is that the global climate could undergo a significant change in the next few decades. There have been articles about this in virtually every newspaper, and *Newsweek, Time,* and *L'Express* (of Paris) are among the weeklies that have covered it in some detail. These reports are not based on the pronouncements of a few publicity-seeking scientists, but rather on the findings of a succession of authoritative national and international scientific gatherings.

The suggestion that the carbon dioxide added to the atmosphere from all the worldwide burning of fossil fuel since the start of the Industrial Revolution could influence the global climate actually goes back to the turn of this century (Chamberlain, 1899; Arrhenius, 1903), but the Study of Man's Impact on Climate (SMIC, 1971), held near Stockholm in 1971, was one of the first to call world attention to this possibility. More recently there have been a number of responsible reviews of the carbon dioxide–climatic change question, at which the most recent results of research on the geochemistry of carbon dioxide and the way in which carbon dioxide affects the heat balance of the atmosphere and oceans were critically analyzed (NAS, 1977, 1979; SCOPE, 1979; IIASA, 1978; WMO, 1979a,b).[1]

All of these studies have converged on the same general opinion, namely, that if humankind continues on its present course of burning fossil fuel for its energy needs, plus (possibly) extensive cutting of its tropical forests, the average climate is likely to begin to be warmer. This is due to the absorption of more infrared radiation by the added carbon dioxide in the atmosphere, radiation that would otherwise escape to space and cool the surface and lower atmosphere. (This is the so-called greenhouse effect, though the analogy to a greenhouse is really not very satisfactory.)

It has also been pointed out that carbon dioxide is not the only actor in this drama, since we are adding other chemically stable and persistent trace gases that absorb infrared radiation as well, and these add further to the greenhouse warming. (Such trace gases are the chlorofluoromethanes used in refrigerators and spray cans, as well as methane, ozone, and nitrous oxide, which have increased or are likely to increase in concentration in the lower atmosphere, or *troposphere.*)

As will be shown in Section V, if our carbon-cycle and climate models are approximately correct, the average temperatures at the end of this century—in less than 20 years—will probably be warmer than at any time in the past 1000 years and will still be rising; and before the middle of the twenty-first century it may be warmer than at any time in the past million years. This assumes that we go on increasing our rate of burning of fossil fuels at about 4 percent per year, as has been the case for the past 100 years. (We will question this assumption below, however.)

Such an expectation creates an unprecedented situation in the history of civilization, a situation in which:

- We can foresee a climatic change decades ahead of time.
- We can now begin to visualize the disruptions and readjustments this may impose on us.
- We are already considering some possible actions that could be taken to mitigate the socioeconomic impacts of such changes.
- We are even contemplating the costs of averting the climatic change and weighing them against the risks of letting it happen.

Clearly these new considerations must involve an interdisciplinary effort involving geochemists, climatologists, oceanographers, agriculturalists, economists, political scientists, and others, all working toward a better definition of the alternative strategies that could be adopted to cope with future climatic changes and reduce societal vulnerability to such changes. The tools that such scientists are using most extensively are theoretical models, models that are designed to throw light on how complex systems respond to a given change of external conditions—and in some cases to predict the future state of that system.

The purpose of this report is to summarize the status of our ability to model the planetary system that determines the climate, sketched in Figure 1. If the geophysicists are successful they will be able to describe the

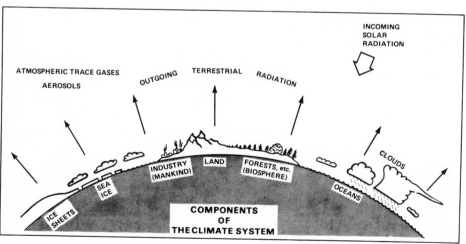

Figure 1. Schematic representation of the planetary system whose balance determines our climate. All the components are interconnected in one way or another, as will be shown in Figure 4 (in Section IV). (From Kellogg, 1979.)

future climate in some detail, given a certain pattern of human behavior. These descriptions of future climate we call *scenarios,* and they can serve as starting points for the climatic impact studies that social scientists (in the broadest sense) are just beginning to undertake.

II. THE CASCADE OF UNCERTAINTY

Before turning to the state of the art of modeling the climate system it would be useful, in the present context, to indicate where that effort properly fits in a climatic impact studies program. Raised as we are in an academic tradition that insists on disciplinary purity, we often find it uncomfortable to work at the fuzzy interface between disciplines. However, problems of the real world are rarely constrained to a single discipline, so now we are forced to think in interdisciplinary terms.

The components of a climatic impact study are all interconnected, as shown schematically in Figure 2. Since the circuit of cause and effect closes back on itself, there is strictly speaking no true beginning. Nevertheless, we would not be engaged in this activity if there were no climatic change at all, so it is probably fair to start with that as we trace the interactions.

Let us imagine for the moment that the geophysicists have been successful in their struggle to understand and predict the response of the climate system to a given increase of carbon dioxide and have presented the world with a set of climate scenarios describing the future changes of temperature, precipitation, soil moisture, and so forth on a region-by-region and season-by-season scale.

The changes anticipated can then, in principle, be interpreted in terms of their influence on a wide variety of specific human activities. We know how to do this for a few common crops (McQuigg, 1979; Katz, 1976); hydrologists are prepared to analyze the new stream flows and statistics of floods or empty reservoirs (Schaake and Kaczmarek, 1979); the effects on forests and rangelands can probably be estimated; and so forth. Moreover, many of these specific impacts can be interpreted in relative economic terms (d'Arge, 1979).

This first step in assessing climatic impacts is obviously not going to be very useful until the interactions between the various activities are taken into account: more rainfall may hurt some crops and encourage others; more snowfall raises the cost of snow removal but helps the ski resorts; higher temperature reduces heating energy requirements but increases those for air conditioning; and so forth. Thus, the economic system must be treated as an aggregate of all the sectors that are important to the economy (Hughes and Mesarovic, 1978). However, that ignores the fact that people and institutions were in place before the process

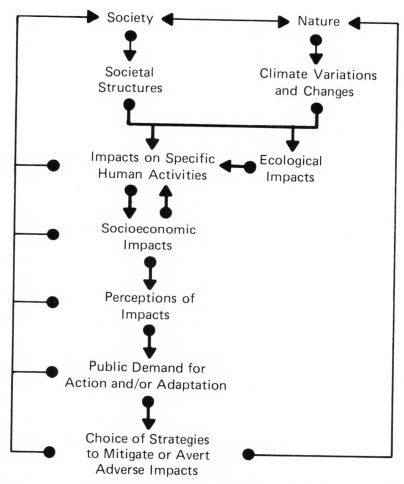

Figure 2. A flow diagram for a climatic impact study, including the feedback loops. (Adapted from R. W. Kates' proposal to SCOPE, 1979, by Aspen Institute.)

started, and their ability to respond and adjust to the changes may have an enormous effect on the socioeconomic impacts. It has been pointed out repeatedly that, notably in the poorer developing countries, such an event as a drought or flood will trigger instabilities in the socioeconomic system, and the resulting impact is therefore determined to a large extent by the preexisting structures of the society rather than the magnitude of the event itself (Garcia, 1978; Burton, 1979).

We will not carry this line of reasoning further here, but the message

Figure 3. The cascade of uncertainty for energy and food as they will be impacted by climatic change in the next 50 or so years. Time (or cause and effect) runs downward as the range of uncertainty increases. The response of governments as they adopt a variety of mitigating strategies will be especially hard to predict, and these strategies will, of course, have some influence on the climatic impact, as suggested in Figure 2. (From Kellogg and Schware, 1981).

is summarized in Figure 3. In that schematic diagram we have shown how, in the areas of food and energy, there are successions of cause and effect, and as one traces this cascade the uncertainties grow inexorably.

Somewhere, probably not too far from our starting point, it becomes fruitless to *predict* the impacts of a climatic change, no matter how well we are able to predict the character of the future climate itself. At present, as will be shown, *we cannot predict the carbon dioxide–induced climatic change in detail.* Thus, it becomes imperative to specify where our ability to predict the future is virtually nil. If we claim an ability that is beyond the state of our knowledge and our techniques, we may be justly accused of charlatanism—just as with the weather forecaster who claims that he can predict daily weather several months in advance.

The above leads to the question of how social scientists should think of the climate scenarios that are being generated by physical scientists. Some have feared that such climate scenarios might be viewed as real predictions of the future and might therefore be misused. This could happen, of course, even were the scenario accompanied by a set of caveats, including the statement that the scenario was based on a set of assumptions about the unpredictable future patterns of worldwide energy use.

A more proper way to present the output of our geochemical and climatic studies is in terms of a *set* of climate scanarios. Then no one scenario can be taken as an authoritative view of the future, but rather a range of possibilities would be given. It may even be possible to assign rough probabilities to this range for a given set of assumptions—a "best guess," for example, and reasonable upper and lower limits.

The social scientists who engage in studies of the future impacts of carbon dioxide–induced climatic change will have to learn to deal with such probabalistic sets of scenarios. They should not expect the geophysicists to do their homework any better than that—though, to be sure, the latter still have a long way to go to refine their sets of scenarios so that they will be more useful than they are now.

III. ACCESSIBLE LEVERS IN THE CLIMATE SYSTEM AND THE CARBON CYCLE

In Figure 1 we showed schematically the various interacting components of the global system whose balance determines the earth's climate. Although it may seem remarkable, we must now acknowledge that humankind's activities can actually influence these components: we can reach "levers" that alter that uneasy balance.

Since the atmosphere is in a real sense a gigantic heat engine that operates on the temperature difference between the equatorial region and the polar regions, anything that affects the planetary heat balance will

also affect the running of this engine. The motions generated by this process can be seen as the winds that transport heat and water vapor and as
the cyclonic eddies that carry with them storms and fair weather. It almost
goes without saying that these are complex processes, and we will discuss
them further in the next section.

Among the specific ways humankind has altered the heat balance of
the planet are the following:

- Changing patterns of land use that affect the solar radiation absorbed
  and the exchange of water vapor at the surface
- Direct release of large amounts of waste heat from the industrialized
  and urbanized regions of the world
- Addition of particles (aerosols) to the atmosphere that influence the
  radiation balance and that may also serve as condensation or freez-
  ing nuclei, thereby altering the growth of cloud droplets and precipitation
- Addition of trace gases to the atmosphere that remain for many
  decades or centuries and that can absorb infrared radiation, thereby
  changing the heat balance

While none of these can be neglected when we consider humankind's
total long-term influence on climate, it turns out that the last category,
the infrared-absorbing trace gases, is by far the most important (Budyko,
1977; Kellogg, 1977, 1978, 1979; Munn and Machta, 1979); and of the
trace gases that we are adding to the atmosphere, carbon dioxide will
almost certainly have the largest single effect on climate. Other infrared-
absorbing gases that we are adding to the lower atmosphere, notably
chlorofluoromethanes, methane, nitrous oxide, carbon monoxide, and
ozone, will simply add to the "greenhouse warming" of carbon dioxide
(Wang et al., 1976; Flohn, 1979a,b; Hameed et al., 1980). For that reason
we will concentrate here on the carbon dioxide situation—the carbon
cycle.

Ever since the beginning of the Industrial Revolution humankind has
been digging or pumping carbon stored in the earth as fossil fuels and
burning it, thereby creating carbon dioxide that spews out of smokestacks
and exhaust pipes throughout the world. This flow of new carbon dioxide
is now a staggering 20 gigatons per year [1 gigaton (Gt) equals 10^{15} grams],
corresponding to a little over 5 Gt of carbon; and furthermore the rate of
increase per year has been over 4 percent throughout most of this century.[2]

The result is an increase in the concentration of carbon dioxide from
290 ± 10 parts per million by volume (ppmv) in the last century to about
336 ppmv in 1979, a rise of about 16 percent. We have fairly good figures

on the mass of fossil fuel burned each year starting in 1860, and if we compare the cumulative amount of carbon dioxide released with that remaining in the atmosphere we find that 52 ± 4 percent is still airborne. This figure is based on the fairly accurate observational record of the past 20 years (Broecker et al., 1979).

This disappearance of roughly half the new carbon dioxide is not surprising, since the oceans have long been recognized as a potential sink for it. Furthermore, as carbon dioxide increases in the atmosphere plants grow faster (all other things being equal), and therefore living biota could potentially be another sink for the added carbon dioxide. This all seemed to balance out in an understandable way until the actual figures were looked at more closely, and now ecologists, oceanographers, and geochemists are locking horns in a battle to try to make the carbon cycle books balance (Björkström, 1979).

The situation is very complex, but the essence of the argument is that several leading oceanographers, relying on studies of the natural chemistry of the oceans and the way in which radioactive tracers from the nuclear tests of the period 1958–1962 were taken up by the oceans, believe that the oceans could only have taken up between 33 and 41 percent of the carbon dioxide added between 1958 (the start of continuous atmospheric concentration measurements) and the present (Stuiver, 1978; Broecker et al., 1979; Siegenthaler and Oeschger, 1978). This means that another 7–15 percent must have gone into another sink than the oceans.

While, as we have said, biota might have taken up this excess, "all things being equal," a study sponsored by the UN Food and Agriculture Organization (FAO) (Sommer, 1976) indicated that the mass of living things on the earth, the biomass, was probably shrinking instead of expanding. This was, the study claimed, due to the observation that a little over 1 percent of the tropical forests of the world were being cut down each year, and tropical forests constitute nearly two-thirds of the total terrestrial biomass (Bolin, 1977). When a tree is cut down and burned, its carbon goes into the atmosphere as carbon dioxide; if it is left to rot, the same thing happens over a longer time as it decays; and if it is used for timber, the process may take still longer but the end result is the same. Bolin (1977) and Woodwell et al. (1978) have considered the evidence, such as it is, and both conclude that the biosphere is most likely to be an additional source of carbon dioxide rather than a sink.

Where, then, is the "missing sink"? (The term is Björkström's.) It seems that the carbon-cycle books do not balance, and no one can think of a generally acceptable way to get rid of the unaccounted-for excess. Of course, either the oceanographers or the global ecologists could be wrong in their estimates by some 10 or 15 percent, and that could resolve the problem. If one were forced to guess which camp was most likely to be misled by poor data, it would seem to be the ecologists. For example, the FAO survey (Sommer, 1976) of the tropical forests that was quoted by Woodwell et al. (1978) bases its sweeping conclusion that 1 percent per year was falling to the axe on a sample of only 18 percent of the area of forests, and the area sampled was probably the most accessible part.

This difficulty will probably be resolved in the next few years as better data on the oceans and biosphere are obtained. Several current carbon-cycle models are conceptually quite complete, but some of the parameters remain uncertain and can only be determined empirically (SCOPE, 1979). Using these models it will eventually be possible to say with some assurance what the future atmospheric concentration of carbon dioxide will be for a given anthropogenic production of that trace gas.

It appears that the major uncertainty in the carbon-cycle picture in the future will be due not to a lack of knowledge of the geophysical quantities involved but rather to the unpredictability of humankind's use of fossil fuels, the recklessness of tropical deforestation, and the extent of efforts to replant trees—efforts being pursued already in parts of China, India, and Brazil.

IV. MODELING THE CLIMATE SYSTEM AND RECONSTRUCTING PAST CLIMATES

The components of the global system that determines our climate are sketched in Figure 1, and it is stated that they all interact with one another. That statement is perfectly true, of course, but when it comes to creating a theoretical model of the system it is practically impossible to include all the complex interactions. Figure 4 shows how these interactions occur, and even this enormously complicated network is probably an oversimplification.

Thus, the actual process of modeling the climate system has been an evolutionary one, in which each model in the hierarchy includes some additional factors that may be important. In the course of this process the climatologists are able to sort out those interactions or processes that are most important—and, of course, as in all creative efforts, intuition must play a part in the selection of the features that will be most significant.

In the earlier attempts to model the climate system and to assess its sensitivity to changes in external factors, or "boundary conditions," the atmosphere was taken as a single vertical column and the radiative transfer of solar and infrared radiation was calculated. The first successful estimate of the effects of a doubling of carbon dioxide was made with such a one-dimensional model by Manabe and Wetherald (1967), in which the other adjustments that would occur in water vapor and temperature

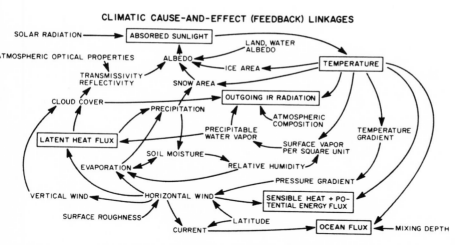

Figure 4. The interaction, linkages, and feedback loops in the climate system. As many of these as possible are included in the more sophisticated current climate models. Note that humankind has been left out, which makes the diagram incomplete. (From Kellogg and Schneider, 1974.)

distribution with height were all taken into account by certain assumptions about the lapse rate and relative humidity. This kind of model, called a "radiative–convective model," has been considerably refined and still serves a useful purpose for exploring specific factors in the radiative balance of the atmosphere (Ramanathan and Coakley, 1978).

The most advanced models are a far cry from the radiative–convective models. They include a three-dimensional and time-dependent model of the atmosphere, called a "general circulation model" (GCM). Such a model involves the "primitive equations" that govern the physical behavior of the atmosphere, most of them being time-dependent differential equations. These equations are combined and finite differences evaluated at each grid point on each height (or pressure) surface to calculate the change that would occur in a short time interval (the time step). Then the calculations are repeated for the next time step, and so on for as long as the modeler has money to pay for the computer time (or until something goes wrong with the model).

There is no ultimate limit to the detail that can be included in a GCM, as suggested in Figure 4, other than the practical limits of computer capacity and human ingenuity. For example, the more advanced GCMs calculate the formation of clouds and their effect on the radiation balance, rainfall, evaporation at the earth's surface, soil moisture, the effects of mountain ranges and land–sea contrasts, and so forth, in addition to the fundamental parameters of temperature, wind, and pressure. In the present context it is obviously essential that they calculate in some detail the radiative transfer in the atmosphere, taking into account the radiative effects of water vapor, carbon dioxide, ozone, and other trace constituents (Smagorinsky, 1974; Schneider and Dickinson, 1974).

A GCM by itself does not constitute a climate model, however, since the oceans are in some respects even more important in determining climate than is the atmosphere. They transfer as much heat from equator to pole at middle latitudes as does the atmosphere; they are the source of most of the atmospheric water vapor; they regulate the surface temperature of four-fifths of the globe; and so forth. Thus, a climate model must include the oceans in some way. Since oceans appear to be harder to model than the atmosphere, the climate models used so far in experiments to determine the response to increased carbon dioxide include oceans that are very highly simplified. One approach has been to let the simulated ocean be an infinite source of water vapor, but with no heat capacity and no circulation—indeed, very much like an enormous "swamp." Another approach has been to consider just the upper mixed layer of the ocean, the part some 70 meters deep that responds to seasonal changes of temperature, but again without any circulation or heat transport.

Recent experiments with atmosphere–ocean models to determine the response of the climate system have been carried out by the Geophysical Fluid Dynamics Laboratory (GFDL) of the National Oceanic and Atmospheric Administration (NOAA), the Goddard Instirue for Space Studies (GISS) of the National Aeronautics and Space Administration (NASA), Oregon State University (OSU), and the Lawrence Livermore Laboratory (LLL) (WMO, 1979b). The National Center for Atmospheric Research (NCAR) has used some simple models to study the effects of CO_2 and has just undertaken a CO_2 experiment with a more complete coupled atmosphere–ocean model in which a five-layer circulating ocean model is involved.

The way in which such models are used in these kinds of experiments deserves some comment. The procedure is first to run the model with current boundary conditions for a long enough period (model time) to establish "the climate" of the model, one which can then be compared with the real climate. This is the "control run." It is most important that the model, if it involves a primitive-equation GCM of the atmosphere and/ or ocean, be run long enough to obtain all the statistics necessary to characterize climate, including the *variability* or "noise" of the important parameters. If this is not done properly the results may be inconclusive.

The next step in the experiment is to run the model again with increased carbon dioxide concentration, usually double or quadruple the present value, all other factors and boundary conditions (with some exceptions) remaining the same as in the control run. The differences between the control run and the perturbed run are then presented and compared with the model noise, and if these differences ("signals") are larger than the model variability ("noise") the results of the experiment are considered as significant, in the statistical sense.

Results have been presented primarily in terms of temperature, both globally averaged and as a function of latitude (sometimes as a function of longitude as well). If the model includes a suitable hydrological cycle, results can also be presented in terms of precipitation, evaporation, and even soil moisture.

Several competent reviews have recently been conducted of the results of a number of such experiments with climate models (NAS, 1979; WMO, 1979b), and it turns out that seven more or less independently developed models have converged on the same result to within a factor of about 2 for the average surface temperature rise that would take place if the carbon dioxide concentration were doubled. The average temperature rise would be between 1.5° and 4°C (approximately 3° ± 1.5°C) according to these models, a condition that could occur in the first half of the next century, as will be shown in the next section.

It is necessary to emphasize that there is a certain amount of uncertainty in any such results due to the deficiencies of the models; specifically:

- The ocean part of the climate models has so far been rather rudimentary (either a "swamp" or a noncirculating mixed layer), though Warren Washington at NCAR has recently developed a coupled ocean model that has five layers and circulates.
- Even with an adequate coupled atmosphere–ocean model the present method of determining the equilibrium climate conditions for a doubling of carbon dioxide does not take account of the large heat capacity of the upper ocean and the resulting delay or lag in the response of the system. This lag could be as much as two decades (NAS, 1979), or almost half the time for the doubling to occur in the "upper limit" case to be discussed in Section V.
- The role of cloudiness is not adequately taken into account, though clouds play an important part in determining the radiation balance.
- The physical processes in the boundary layer and at the surface, including the effects of vegetation, soil moisture, and surface topography, are only included in an approximate fashion.
- The responses of the cryosphere (the snow and ice of the polar region) is taken into account rather crudely.

The climatologists involved in climate model development are in general the first to acknowledge the deficiencies of their models; nevertheless there does not seem to be any good reason for believing that they have neglected factors that would radically alter the conclusions of their experiments, as far as they go.

The greatest deficiency in the model experiments so far is the lack of detail, since it is of little value to a climatic impact study to be told that the global average temperature change will be thus and so, or even to be told the zonally averaged temperature change as a function of latitude. What is lacking still is a description of the *regional* and *seasonal* changes in temperature, precipitation, soil moisture, cloudiness, etc., and the *variances* as well as the *means*. The climate models have so far simply not provided this specific information, but they are developing rapidly and will undoubtedly begin to do so in the next few years.

In the meantime, and as an ultimate check on the veracity of the model results, we can turn to the past behavior of the real atmosphere for some hints as to what a warmer earth might be like, particularly with regard to precipitation patterns. There are several ways of going about this, not all of which have been pursued:

- Comparison of the warmest winters (or years) with the coldest, or with the average conditions, during the period of instrumental observations starting around 1900 for surface observations and 1948 for upper air observations (Wigley et al., 1980; Williams, 1980)
- An analysis of the period 1850–1950, during which average surface temperatures in the northern hemisphere rose by about 0.8°C.
- A reconstruction of the Altithermal (or Hypsithermal) period, 4500 to 8000 years ago, when the world was several degrees warmer than now (Kellogg, 1978, 1979; Flohn, 1979b).

The reconstruction of the Altithermal period is being pursued further by an international team, sponsored by the U.S. Department of Energy (DOE, 1980), which will reveal a great deal about the temperature and rainfall patterns by a careful analysis of evidence from lake bottoms, peat bogs, soil distributions, glacial moraines, etc., on a worldwide basis. An example of an earlier and somewhat cursory effort to do the same thing by the present author is shown in Figure 5.

It is natural that economists, social scientists, and government planners have already become impatient with the climatologists, who have not been able to provide the kind of detailed "climate scenarios" of the future that are called for. There is a concern on the part of the climatologists that, no matter how many cautionary statements are attached, these scenarios will be taken by the public as *predictions* of future climate, when in fact they are just examples of what could happen if certain trends continue. In spite of this valid concern, some climate scanarios ought to be prepared

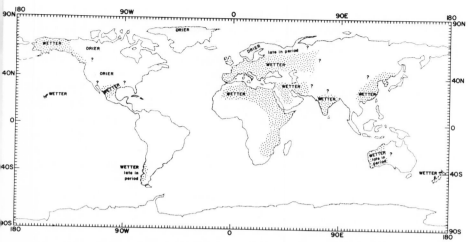

Figure 5. Regions of the world that were wetter or drier than the present (generally speaking, during the growing season) during the warm period some 4500 to 8000 years ago, known as the Altithermal (or Hypsithermal) period. The blank areas were not necessarily the same as now, there being large gaps in our reconstruction of the climate of that ancient time. (From Kellogg, 1977.)

in the near future that will allow others to test their economic tools to measure the impacts of a complex hypothetical climate change.

When climatologists do prepare one or more "surprise-free" scenarios of the future climate, they will most likely appear in the form of maps showing the patterns of average deviations of temperature, precipitation, soil moisture, etc. from the present mean conditions, patterns that might apply, for example, to a world with double the present carbon dioxide. Of even more importance to economists and planners, however, are the variances of these meteorological parameters—the probability of extreme events like floods and temporary droughts and early frosts. Such measures of variability of the weather are, as we have said in the introduction, a part of our climate record and of great practical importance, but unfortunately we cannot say for sure whether variability will grow or decrease as the earth grows warmer. Nevertheless, this element must be a part of a climate scenario to be useful.

V. SCENARIOS OF FUTURE CLIMATE

By now it should be clear that climatologists are not yet in a position to make a unique and credible prediction of the future carbon dioxide–governed climate change, partly because their knowledge of the factors that govern the carbon cycle and the climate is incomplete and partly because they do not know how much fossil fuel humankind will burn in the next few decades. Rather, they can provide a set of scenarios of future climate that are likely to encompass the possibilities.

As one attempt to bracket the range of possbilities, Figure 6 shows two cases of carbon dioxide production to the year 2050 A.D., the "upper limit" being a continued exponential growth of fossil fuel use at the same 4 percent per year as in the past century. We know that exponential growth cannot continue indefinitely, and the question is when will it begin to level out. This extreme scenario implies that fossil fuel will remain our main source of energy to at least 2050 A.D. and that the worldwide energy use will rise from the present 10 TW (terawatts; 1 TW equals 10^{12} watts) to a staggering 160 TW. The "lower limit" follows the compound interest law with a linearly decreasing growth rate, the governing equation being (Kellogg, 1979)

$$P(t) = P_0\left[1 + r_0\left(1 - \frac{t}{\tau}\right)\right]^t,$$

where P is rate of production of carbon dioxide; r_0 is the present rate of increase of 4 percent per year; and τ is the time it takes for the production rate to return to the present P_0 (after which the yearly addition of carbon dioxide to the atmosphere would be less than the present P_0 and diminishing). In this case τ is taken to be three doubling times at 4 percent per year, or 52.5 years, this being an optimistically short time for market penetration by nonfossil energy sources (Marchetti, 1979; Laurmann, 1979).

Another attempt to bracket the upper and lower limits of carbon dioxide production, carried out with a more detailed breakdown between various sources of energy as a function of time, is the study by the International Institute for Applied Systems Analysis, reported by Niehaus and Williams (1979). Their strategy leading to 50 TW of power by 2100 A.D., mostly powered by coal, leads to a doubling of carbon dioxide (600 ppmv) by 2030 A.D., close to our previous "upper limit;" and their 30-TW strategy ultimately powered by solar and nuclear sources barely reaches 400 ppmv around the middle of the next century, roughly corresponding to our "lower limit."

Combining Figure 6 with the "best guess" of 3°C for a doubling of carbon dioxide, and neglecting any delay in the warming due to thermal inertia of the oceans, we arrive at Figure 7, describing the increase of mean surface temperature with time for the two cases. Also shown are the estimates for the corresponding increases of temperature in the polar regions. Since the shaded area represents the natural variations of mean

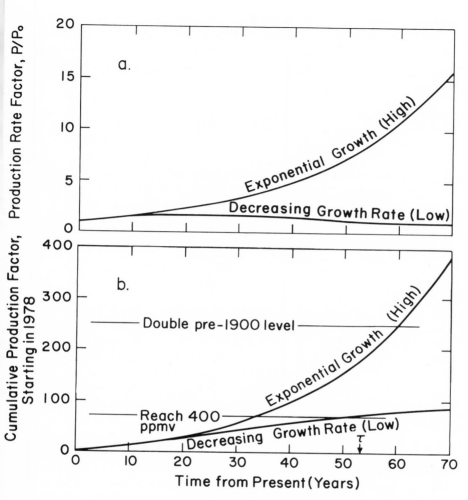

Figure 6. The rate of production of carbon dioxide from fossil fuel burning relative to the present (a), and the cumulative amount of new carbon dioxide remaining in the atmosphere, assuming that 50 percent of the added amount remains airborne (b). See the text for an explanation of the "high" and "low" limiting cases. (From Kellogg, 1979.)

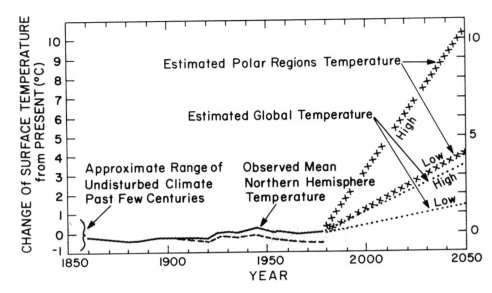

Figure 7. Estimated global mean and polar regions surface
temperature changes, past and future. The "high" and "low" cases
are the same as those shown in Figure 6. The shaded area represents
the approximate range of mean surface temperatures for the past 1000
years or more; and the dashed line is a theoretical estimate of the
course the temperature might have taken from 1900 to the present if
there had been no increase of carbon dioxide during that period. (From
Kellogg, 1979.)

temperatures during the past 1000 years or so, it can be seen that for the
"upper limit" case the mean temperatures will become warmer than at
any time since the early Middle Ages before the turn of the century,[3] and
even for the "lower limit" case this should occur before 2020 A.D. If the
mean temperature variations of the past can be treated as climatic
"noise," then those times may mark the emergence of the carbon dioxide
"signal" above the natural "noise" (or a signal-to-noise ratio of 1).

Recognizing that climatic impact studies cannot be carried very far
based on global mean temperature changes, the next step in the drawing
of scanarios must be to fill them in with indications of expected *regional*
and *seasonal* variations of temperature, precipitation, soil moisture, sun-
shine, and so forth. Our models are already capable of suggesting some
such changes rather crudely (Manabe and Stouffer, 1979; Manabe and
Wetherald, 1980), and further progress can be expected in the next year
or two. For example, we expect the warmer atmospheres and oceans to

cause more evaporation and more precipitation generally, and this increase will probably be most pronounced in the subtropics and equatorial zone. On the other hand, there may be less precipitation at midlatitudes in some locations.

As pointed out earlier, another approach to determining what a future warmer world would be like is to look at past warmer worlds. One such reconstruction is shown in Figure 5. It shows some of the regions that were wetter or drier during the Altithermal (or Hypsithermal) period some 4500 to 8000 years ago, determined mostly from analyses of the kinds of vegetation that grew at that time. Notice that, as predicted by the models, it does appear to have been wetter in the subtropics and drier at some midlatitude places—notably the central part of North America and northwestern Europe.

We cannot leave the subject of scenarios without discussing a feature of a warmer earth that has received considerable public attention lately— the possibility that sea level will rise. The great ice sheets of Greenland and the Antarctic contain over three-quarters of all the fresh water on the planet (corresponding to about 65-meters depth of ocean water), and the large fluctuations of sea level in the past have almost certainly been due to growth and decay of continental ice sheets. There has been considerable speculation that this could happen again if the polar regions are warmed, and attention has focused recently on the West Antarctic ice sheet. This ice sheet is sitting on bedrock below sea level, and it has been seriously suggested that the warmer ocean water working its way underneath could induce it to shift more rapidly and even break up (Hughes, 1973; Mercer, 1978; Thomas et al., 1979). If all of this mass of ice were to slide into the surrounding ocean it could raise sea level by about 5–7 meters.

At the present time glaciologists are rather sharply divided about the likelihood of this West Antarctic ice sheet disintegration, and they are divided even more as to the timetable for the process. The most recent evidence seems to indicate that this ice sheet is not likely to surge or break up in the next century or two, even in the face of a pronounced warming, but the question is still open (Radok, 1978). The possibility of a rise of sea level of this magnitude, even spread over a century or more, certainly raises the specter of enormous economic and societal readjustments in all countries with coastlines—which includes most of them.

VI. SOME GENERAL CONCLUSIONS AND VALUE JUDGMENTS

The subject of this paper is the impact of a carbon dioxide–induced climatic change. While this promises to have very great consequences throughout the world, it must be seen in perspective, since there are other human activities that are likely to have equally great (or greater) consequences in the years and decades ahead. To mention a few:

- Loss of fertile soil and erosion
- Desertification
- Depletion of natural resource reserves
- Spread of toxic or environmentally damaging substances

It is likely that over the short period, before climatic change becomes a real and present issue, these problems will be perceived as more deserving of attention by the community of nations and especially by developing nations.

On a longer time scale, however, climatic change probably looms as a dominant factor during the difficult period of transition from the *exploitative* fossil-fuel-powered society (ours) to a society that has learned to rely on renewable or longer-lasting resources—a *sustainable* phase, sometimes referred to as "the Postindustrial Society" (Kahn et al., 1976). It may be more feasible to describe this future sustainable phase than the many impacts (including climatic impacts) during the transition period. It would undoubtedly be useful to do so, since then the long-term directions to be taken would become clearer; and, indeed, it is long-range planning with which we are concerned here.

The patterns of climatic change and climatic variation that we will experience in the transitional decades ahead will be complex, and there are bound to be some countries that will be "winners," others that will be "losers." It is hard to imagine an international superauthority with the ability and the power to decide whether the climatic change is "good" or "bad" for the world as a whole—necessarily a value judgment, of course—and which would then be able to direct the reduction of fossil fuel use on a worldwide basis, thereby averting further climatic change. Perhaps a way will be found to ellicit voluntary cooperation in the matter, though such cooperation would be something new.

Rather, the most likely course to be followed will involve many decisions and the adoption of national and regional strategies to mitigate the impact of the changes. The strategies that will make the most sense are those which make "good sense" generally, not solely as regards coping with climatic change. Examples of measures that will contribute to a mitigation of the climatic change problem and that should probably be pursued anyway, for other fairly obvious reasons, are the following:

- Limitation of deforestation and encouragement of reforestation, especially in the tropics

- Conservation of fossil fuel resources, which will be needed by future generations for a variety of nonenergy purposes
- Management of water resources to increase resilience to fluctuations of rainfall and snowfall
- Transfer of technology from advanced to developing countries to increase the latter's ability to adapt to the effects of climatic variability on food production, an ability that might indeed allow them to adapt better to the effects of a gradual climatic change as well
- A similar transfer of non-fossil-fuel energy technology, taking advantage of renewable resources
- Land use and urban renewal programs that take into account the possibility of a slow rise of sea level and give priority to measures that alleviate flooding from any cause

Thus, in its broadest sense the climatic change issue can be seen as an unprecedented stimulus to long-range planning and cooperation at all levels of society, from the local to the national to the international (Kellogg and Schneider, 1974; Kellogg and Mead, 1977; Brown et al., 1977). It is an issue that involves the entire world, both in its inevitable impacts and in the sense of responsibility for the cause, and it can therefore hardly fail to be a unifying influence. Such unifying influences will be badly needed during the future period of transition to a world that we hope will be more stable than the present one.

ACKNOWLEDGMENTS

The National Center for Atmospheric Research (NCAR) is sponsored by the National Science Foundation. The study of impacts of carbon dioxide-induced climatic change at the Aspen Institute was sponsored by the U.S. Department of Energy.

NOTES

1. Since this paper was prepared several authoritative reviews of the CO_2/climate issues have been developed. These reviews are cited in the References section.
2. Since 1973 it has dropped to a little under 2 percent per year.
3. It turns out that the year 1981 witnessed the warmest average surface temperature for the entire northern hemisphere since the invention of the thermometer—a real record breaker! We have probably *already* passed the point of a signal-to-noise ratio equal to 1 (WMO, 1982).

REFERENCES

Arrhenius, S., *Lehrbuch der Kosmischen Physik 2.* Leipzig: Hirzel, 1903.
Aspen Institute, *Consequences of a Hypothetical World Climate Change Produced by In-*

creasing Atmospheric Carbon Dioxide (background report sponsored by Department of Energy). Boulder, Colo.: Aspen Institute, 1980.

Bach, W., J. Pankrath, and J. Williams (eds.), *Interactions of Energy and Climate*. Dordrecht, Holland: D. Reidel Publishing Co., 1980.

Bach, W., A. Crane, A. Berger, and A. Longhetto (eds.), *Carbon Dioxide: A Text on Current Views and Developments in Energy/Climate Research* (second course of International School of Climatology, Erice, Sicily, July 1982). Dordrecht, Holland: D. Reidel Publishing Co., 1983.

Berger, A. (ed.), *Climate Variations and Variability: Facts and Theories* (first course of International School of Climatology, Erice, Sicily, March 1980). Dordrecht, Holland: D. Reidel Publishing Co., 1980.

Bjorkstrom, A., "Man's Global Redistribution of Carbon." *Ambio* 8(1979):254–259,

Bolin, B., "Changes of Land Biota and their Importance for the Carbon Cycle." *Science* 196(1977):613–619.

Broecker, W. S., T. Takahashi, H. J. Simpson, and T.-H. Peng, "Fate of Fossil Fuel Carbon Dioxide and the Global Carbon Budget." *Science* 206(1979):409–418.

Brown, S., N. W. Cornell, L. L. Fabian, and E. B. Weiss, *Regimes for the Ocean, Outer Space, and Weather*. Washington, D.C.: Brookings Institution, 1977.

Budyko, M. I., "On Present-Day Climate Changes." *Tellus* 29(1977):193–204.

Burton, I., "Social and Behavioral Responses to Climate Change and Variability: The Role of Perception and Information." Paper presented at AAAS/DOE Workshop, Annapolis, Maryland, April 1979.

Chamberlain, T. C., "An Attempt to Frame A Working Hypothesis of the Cause of Glacial Epochs on an Atmospheric Basis." *J. Geology* 7(1899):575, 667, 751.

d'Arge, R. C., "Climate and Economic Activity." Chapter in *Proc. World Climate Conference*, WMO No. 537. Geneva: World Meteorological Organization, 1979, pp. 652–681.

DOE, "Carbon Dioxide Effects Research and Assessment Programs," *Annual Research Report*. Washington, D.C.: Department of Energy, 1980.

DOE, *Proceedings: Carbon Dioxide Research Conference: Carbon Dioxide, Science and Consensus*. (Berkeley Springs, W. Va., September 1982), CONF-820970. Washington, D.C.: Department of Energy, 1983.

Flohn, H., "A Scenario of Possible Future Climates—Natural and Manmade." Chapter in *Proc. World Climate Conference*, WMO No. 537. Geneva: World Meteorological Organization, 1979a, pp. 243–266.

———, "Possible Climatic Consequences of a Manmade Global Warming," IIASA WP-79-86. Laxenburg, Austria: International Institute for Applied Systems Analysis, 1979b.

Garcia, R., "Climate Impacts and Socio-Economic Conditions." Chapter in *International Perspectives on the Study of Climate and Society*. Washington, D.C.: National Academy of Sciences, 1978, pp. 43–47.

Hameed, S., R. D. Cess, and J. S. Hogan, "Response of the Global Climate to Changes in Atmospheric Chemical Composition due to Fossil Fuel Burning." *J. Geophys. Res.* 85(1980):7537–7545.

Hughes, B. B., and M. D. Mesarvoic, "Population, Wealth and Resources Up to the Year 2000." Futures (August 1978):267–282. [See also M. Mesarovic and E. Pestel, *Mankind at the Turning Point* (the Second Report to the Club of Rome), New York: E. P. Dutton, 1974 (210 pp.).]

Hughes, T., "Is the West Antarctic Ice Sheet Disintegrating?" *J. Geophys. Res.* 78(1973):7884–7910.

IIASA, "Carbon Dioxide, Climate, and Society." In J. Williams (ed.), *Proc. International Institure for Applied Systems Analysis Workshop*, Laxenburg, Austria. Oxford: Pergamon Press, 1978.

Kahn, H., W. Brown, and L. Martel, *The Next 200 Years: A Scenario for America and the World*. New York: William Morrow and Co., 1976.

Katz, R. W., "Assessing the Impact of Climatic Change on Food Production." *Climatic Change* 1(1976):85–96.

Kellogg, W. W., *Effects of Human Activities on Global Climate*. World Meteorological Organization, Tech. Note No. 156 (WMO No. 486). Geneva: World Meteorological Organization, 1977.

———, "Global Influences of Mankind on the Climate." Chapter 13 in J. Griblin (ed.), *Climatic Change*. Cambridge: Cambridge University Press, 1978, pp. 205–227.

———, "Influences of Mankind on Climate." *Ann. Rev. Earth Planet. Sci.* 7(1979):63–92.

Kellogg, W. W., and S. H. Schneider, "Climate Stabilization: For Better or For Worse?" *Science* 186(1974):1163–1172.

Kellogg, W. W., and M. Mead (eds.), *The Atmosphere: Endangered and Endangering*. Fogarty International Center Proc. No. 39 (DHEW Publ. No. NIH-77-1065). Washington, D.C.: National Institute of Health, 1977.

Kellogg, W. W., and R. Schware, *Climate Change and Society: Consequences of Increasing Atmospheric Carbon Dioxide*. Boulder, Colo.: Westview Press, 1981.

———, "Society, Science and Climate Change." *Foreign Affairs* 60(1982):1076–1109.

Laurmann, J. A., "Market Penetration Characteristics for Energy Production and Atmospheric Carbon Dioxide Growth." *Science* 205(1979):896–898.

Manabe, S., and R. J. Stouffer, "A CO_2-Climate Sensitivity Study with a Mathematical Model of the Global Climate." *Nature* 282(1979):491–493.

Manabe, S., and R. T. Wetherald, "Thermal Equilibrium of the Atmosphere with a Given Distribution of Relative Humidity." *J. Atmos. Sci.* 24(1967):241–259.

———, "On the Distribution of Climate Change Resulting from an Increase in CO_2 Content of the Atmosphere." *J. Atmos. Sci.* 37(1980):99–118.

Marchetti, C., "Multicompetition and the Diffusion of New Technology in the Energy System." *Chem. Econ. Engineering Rev.* 11(1979):7–13.

McQuigg, J. D., "Climatic Variability and Agriculture in the Temperate Regions." Chapter in *Proc. World Climate Conference*, WMO No. 537. Geneva: World Meteorological Organization, 1979, pp. 406–425.

Mercer, J. H., "West Antarctic Ice Sheet and CO_2 Greenhouse Effect: A Threat of Disaster." *Nature* 271(1978):321–325.

Munn, R. E., and L. Machta, "Human Activities that Effect Climate." Chapter in *Proc. World Climate Conference*, WMO No. 537. Geneva: World Meteorological Organizatin, 1979, pp. 170–209.

NAS, *Energy and Climate*. Washington, D.C.: Geophysical Research Board, National Academy of Sciences, 1977.

———, *Carbon Dioxide and Climate: A Scientific Assessment*. Report of ad hoc Study Group on Carbon Dioxide and Climate, Woods Hole, Mass., July 1979. Washington, D.C.: Climate Research Board, National Academy of Sciences, 1979.

———, *Carbon Dioxide and Climate: A Second Assessment*. Washington, D.C.: Climate Board/Committee on Atmospheric Sciences, U.S. National Research Council, 1982.

Niehaus, F., and J. Williams, "Studies of Different Energy Strategies in Terms of their Effects on the Atmospheric CO_2 Concentration." *J. Geophys. Res.* 84(1979):3123–3129.

Radok, U., *Climate Roles of Ice*. Tech. Doc. in Hydrology, International Hydrology Program. Paris: UNESCO, 1978.

Ramanathan, V., and J. A. Coakley, Jr., "Climate Modeling through Radiative-Convective Models." *Rev. Geophys. Space Phys.* 16(1978):465–489.

Schaake, J. C., Jr., and Z. Kaczmarek, "Climate Variability and the Design and Operation of Water Resource Systems." Chapter in *Proc. World Climate Conference*, WMO No. 537. Geneva: World Meteorological Organization, 1979, pp. 290–312.

Schneider, S. H., and R. E. Dickinson, "Climate Modeling." *Rev. Geophys. Space Phys.* 12(1974):447–493.

SCOPE, *The Global Carbon Cycle,* edited by B. Bolin, E. T. Degens, S. Kempe, and P. Ketner, Scientific Committee on the Problems of the Environment (SCOPE) of I.C.S.U., Report No. 13. Chichester, New York, Brisbane and Toronto: John Wiley and Sons, 1979.

Siegenthaler, U., and H. Oeschger, "Predicting Future Atmospheric Carbon Dioxide Levels." *Science* 199(1978):388–395.

Smagorinsky, J., "Global Atmospheric Modeling and Numerical Simulation of Climate." Chapter 18 in W. N. Hess (ed.), *Weather and Climate Modification.* New York: John Wiley and Sons, 1974, pp. 633–686.

SMIC Report, *Inadvertent Climate Modification: Report of the Study of Man's Impact on Climate.* Cambridge, Mass.: M.I.T. Press, 1971.

Smith, V. K., "Economic Impact Analysis and Climate Change: A Conceptual Introduction." *Climatic Change* 4(1982):5–22.

Sommer, A., "Attempt at an Assessment of the World's Tropical Moist Forests." *Unasylva* (FAO) 28(1976):5–25.

Stuiver, M., "Atmospheric Carbon Dioxide and Carbon Reservoir Changes." *Science* 199(1978):253–258.

Thomas, R. H., T. J. O. Sanderson, and K. E. Rose, "Effect of Climatic Warming on the West Antarctic Ice Sheet." *Nature* 277(1979):355–358.

Wang, W. C., Y. L. Yung, A. A. Lacis, T. Mo, and J. E. Hansen, "Greenhouse Effects Due to Manmade Perturbations of Trace Gases." *Science* 194(1976):685–690.

Wigley, T. M. L., P. D. Jones, and P. M. Kelly, "Scenario for a Warm, High-CO_2 World." *Nature* 283(1980):17–20.

Williams, J., "Anomalies in Temperature and Rainfall during Warm Arctic Seasons as A Guide to the Formulation of Climate Scenarios." *Climatic Change* 2(1980):249–266.

WMO, *World Climate Conference Proceedings* (including Declaration and Supporting Documents), WMO No. 537. Geneva: World Meteorological Organization, 1979a.

———, *Climatic Effects of Increased Carbon Dioxide,* Report of ad hoc Study Group of Carbon Dioxide Working Group of WMO Commission for Atmospheric Science. Geneva: World Meteorological Organization, 1979b.

———, Report of the JSC/CAS Meeting of Experts on *Detection of Possible Climate Change* (Moscow, October 1982), Rapporteur: W. W. Kellogg, World Climate Programme Report No. 29. Geneva: World Meteorological Organization, 1982.

Woodwell, G. M., R. H. Whittaker, W. A. Reiners, G. E. Likens, C. C. Delwiche, and D. B. Botkin, "The Biota and the World Carbon Budget." *Science* 199(1978):141–146.

WELFARE ANALYSIS OF INCOMPLETE ADJUSTMENT TO CLIMATIC CHANGE

Daniel McFadden

"The devil you know is better than the devil you don't."

I. INTRODUCTION

A "catastrophe" is variously defined as an "abrupt or sudden change" or a "disaster." Since the long-run consequences of a change may be desirable rather than undesirable, the habit of equating catastrophes and disasters presumably reflects the costs of accommodating an unanticipated change, as well as aversion to uncertainty about long-run outcomes. Consider, for example, a catastrophic change in global temperatures induced by increased atmospheric CO_2 due to burning fossil fuels. With accompanying changes in rainfall patterns, there may be major shifts of arability of land areas. The long-run impact of such shifts will not necessarily be to reduce the carrying capacity of the land. However, the transitional costs of large-scale migration and reorientation of activity are likely to be sufficiently large to be labeled a disaster. In addition, uncertainty about the long-run outcome, particularly when there is a possibility

Advances in Applied Micro-Economics, Volume 3, pages 133–149.
Copyright © 1984 by JAI Press Inc.
All rights of reproduction in any form reserved.
ISBN: 0-89232-398-1

that carrying capacity may fall, will be accorded a cost in the welfare calculations of a risk-averse society.

The primary economic impacts of climatic change are on technology, and the primary economic response will be modifications in the level and channels of capital accumulation and in technological design. Since uncertainty about climate is an important feature of the problem, the appropriate tools for economic analysis will be drawn from the theory of economic behavior under uncertainty. A systematic sampling of this theory can be found in Diamond and Rothschild (1978).

I believe that the least difficult path to a dynamic model of climate and economics will start from a synthesis of the following three relevant literatures:

First, the dynamics of investment and savings behavior is likely to be similar to that found in optimal growth models with uncertainty. Most of these models deal with the problem of optimal rules for capital accumulation by a risk-averse society facing uncertain technological possibilities; the uncertainty is readily interpreted as due to climate, although no technological feedback from economic activity to this source of uncertainty is usually considered. The particular specialization and elaboration of this subject to treat uncertain exhaustible resources provides a number of models and insights which can be adapted to the analysis of irreversible climate changes, as Heal (1980) has done. A comprehensive survey of optimal growth theory can be found in Mirrlees and Stern (1973).

The second relevant literature is that dealing with precautionary, flexible strategies as a response to an uncertain environment. Fuss and McFadden (1978) have analyzed the economic choice of flexible technologies in the presence of price uncertainty. This treatment allows a full dynamic structure and specifies a framework for econometric analysis, but it does not emphasize the type of uncertainty most likely to be associated with climate: technological uncertainty causing social risk which affects general equilibrium. More useful may be the studies of explicit technological uncertainty in a market context; see particularly Rothenberg and Smith (1971), Carleton (1977), and Sheshinski and Dreze (1976).

These studies can be viewed as addressing the question of the extent to which technological uncertainty is spread or shared by the market system, as well as the extent to which individual agents can accommodate uncertainty by technological flexibility and can hedge against uncertainty by market transactions. The methodological contribution of these studies is to clarify the distinct effects of technological uncertainties and pecuniary uncertainties—the latter being generally advantageous to a flexible, risk-neutral firm, although possibly unattractive to risk-averse owners. In policy analysis, these models are potentially useful for quantifying the extent to which precautionary flexibility should be built into long-lived investment projects such as irrigation systems.

On the consumer side of the market, the extensive literature on savings under uncertainty and portfolio choice provides some guidance; see Leland (1968), Laffont (1976), and Nelson and Winter (1964). These studies develop in more detail than do optimal growth models the implications for level and type of investment of individual consumer attitudes toward uncertainty, particularly in the presence of incomplete or costly information. An important feature of these models is the role of markets in signaling information about states of nature and permitting pooling of risk. The portfolio problem also emphasizes the role of transactions costs and technological flexibility in determining liquidity (i.e., the ability to accommodate fluctuations in income or needs). A particularly good synthesis of the portfolio problem and the literature on technological flexibility is that of Goldman (1975).

The third relevant literature is concerned with the statistical problem of learning about the state and response characteristics of a system subject to control, where payoff depends on current and future values of controls and the system state. Using a Bayesian approach, Zellner (1966) and Taylor (1978) have established optimal protocols for control of simple systems. The focus of these analyses is on deliberate perturbations of the system in the short run in order to tune controls in the future. While control manipulation for statistical purposes is unlikely in the climate problem, the statistical methods in this literature may be useful.

A stylized model of the production of a commodity for which the demand varies with climate is outlined in Section II. An analysis of this model determines the degree to which it is desirable to build precautionary flexibility into a technology as a hedge against possible climatic changes. It should be possible to adapt the methods used in this example to quantify the optimal level of flexibility in realistic models of climate and technology.

The criterion for optimality in Section II is simply maximum expected present value of profit for risk-neutral firms. In reality, firm owners are likely to be averse to the social risks associated with climate changes which cannot be fully hedged in the market. Then an explicit welfare calculation is required. Section III reviews the basic problems of carrying out benefit–cost calculations for policies involving a phenomenon like climate which has nonmarket as well as market impacts.

II. A STYLIZED MODEL OF PARTIAL ADJUSTMENT TO CLIMATE VARIATION

A full development of a technological model incorporating all the interactions of technology and climate, as well as the full trade-off of flexibility and efficiency, will require a great deal of work to synthesize existing data on climate and technology in different regions at different times. I

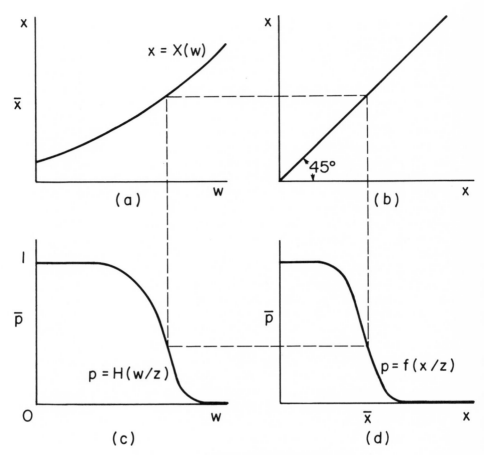

Figure 1.   Distribution of Demand.

shall develop here a very specialized and stylized model of the production of a commodity such as fuel for space heating or water for irrigation for which the demand varies with climate. This will help to fix ideas and may suggest the type of data required to quantify impacts in realistic models.

Let w be a single climate variable, e.g., average temperature during the growing season of an agricultural product. Let $x = X(w)$ be demand for a commodity as a function of w. We assume X is strictly increasing in w. The case in which x is the demand for irrigation water has this feature. Figure 1(a) illustrates such a demand function.

Let $H(w \mid z)$ be the probability that the weather variable exceeds the level w. This probability distribution summarizes expectations about climate formed on the basis of history and models of climate. This distribution may depend on a vector of parameters z, some of which may be influenced by economic activity. For example, the expected distribution of average temperatures during the growing season may be influenced by CO_2 levels, which are in turn affected by fossil fuel consumption and by long-term variations in the earth's orbit. These are then components of z. Figure 1(c) illustrates the H distribution for a specified level of the z vector.

For the example, we shall interpret H as the expected distribution of the climate variable in a future steady state. The spread in this distribution reflects uncertainty as to what the future holds. The better historical information and climate models are in narrowing the range of uncertainty, the less will be the spread in this distribution. In elaborations of this example, the model can be made explicitly dynamic by considering w as a multivariate vector over time. Then H will incorporate expectations on predictable cycles and trends in climate as well as summarizing uncertainty.

Using the demand function $x = X(w)$ and the climate distribution $H(w \mid z)$, we can derive the probability distribution of the levels of demand for the commodity. The probability that demand is at least x is

$$f(x \mid z) = H(X^{-1}(x) \mid z), \tag{1}$$

where $w = X^{-1}(x)$ is the inverse demand function. This distribution is illustrated in Figure 1(d). The derivation of f is illustrated in Figure 1 for the quantity $\bar{x}$. From Figures 1(a) and 1(c), this quantity or more is demanded for levels of w which occur with probability $\bar{p}$. Reflecting x through Figure 1(b) yields a point $(\bar{x}, \bar{p})$ in Figure 1(d) on the f distribution.

Suppose there are three alternative designs for producing the commodity, ranging from one extreme which has high capital cost and low operating cost and is efficient for producing a fixed output requirement, to the other extreme which has zero capital cost and high operating costs and is most suitable for "emergency" output requirements. The following notation is employed for these three activities:

	Activity 1	Activity 2	Activity 3
Capital cost per unit of capacity	k_1	k_2	0
Present value of full capacity operating cost	c_1	c_2	c_3

Assume that the activities have $k_1 > k_2 > 0$ and are ranked $k_1 + c_1 < k_2 + c_2 < c_3$ in the cost of producing continuous capacity output. Assume constant returns in construction and operation.

For the example of irrigation water, these activities may correspond to different methods of transportation: gravity aquaduct (1), pumping (2), and trucking (3). In this model, the technological coefficients k_i and c_i do *not* vary with climate. I shall comment later on how the analysis is modified in the (likely) case that climate influences technology directly in addition to influencing demand.

In optimal operation, demand is met first by activity 1, second by activity 2, and finally by activity 3. Suppose a capacity α is constructed in activity 1, and $(\beta - \alpha)$ in activity 2. Then the expected present value of total cost equals

$$
C = \alpha k_1 + (\beta - \alpha)k_2 + c_1 \int_0^\alpha f(x \mid z)\, dx
$$
$$
+ c_2 \int_\alpha^\beta f(x \mid z)\, dx + c_3 \int_\beta^\infty f(x \mid z)\, dx. \tag{2}
$$

The first two terms in this expression are capital costs for the amount of capacity installed. The third term gives the expected present value of operating costs associated with activity 1. To derive this term, note that activity 1 will always be used up to capacity before any other activities are used. If demand is x, then $\min(x, \alpha)$ will be produced using activity 1. The probability density of demand x is $-\partial f(x \mid z)/\partial x$. Under the assumption of constant returns, the expected cost of operating activity 1 is

$$
c_1 \int_0^\infty \min(x, \alpha)(-\partial f(x \mid z)/\partial x)\, dx
$$
$$
= c_1 \int_0^\alpha x(-\partial f(x \mid z)/\partial x)\, dx + c_1 \int_\alpha^\infty \alpha(-\partial f(x \mid z)/\partial x)\, dz
$$
$$
= c_1 \left[(-xf(x \mid z))\Big|_0^\alpha + \int_0^\alpha f(x \mid z)\, dx - \alpha(f(x \mid z))\Big|_\alpha^\infty \right] \tag{3}
$$
$$
= c_1 \left[-\alpha f(\alpha \mid z) + \int_0^\alpha f(x \mid z)\, dx + \alpha f(\alpha \mid z) \right]
$$
$$
= c_1 \int_0^\alpha f(x \mid z)\, dx.
$$

The steps in this derivation are first to break the integral into two ranges, next to use integration by parts on the first integral and integrate the second, and third to collect terms. Analogous arguments yield the last two integrals in the expression for the expected present value of total cost, corresponding to the operating costs of the last two activities. Define $\rho = (k_1 - k_2)/(c_2 - c_1)$ and $\sigma = k_2/(c_3 - c_2)$. Then ρ is the level of capacity utilization at which activities 1 and 2 yield the same total cost, and σ is the level at which activities 2 and 3 yield the same total cost. Assume $\sigma > \rho$, so there is a range of levels of capacity utilization where activity 2 has the least cost.

Consider the problem faced by the firm in choosing the capacity levels α and β. Assume that demand must be met and that the firm is risk neutral and seeks to minimize the expected present value of cost. Differentiating C yields

$$\frac{\partial C}{\partial \alpha} = (c_2 - c_1)(\rho - f(\alpha \mid z))$$

and

$$\frac{\partial C}{\partial \beta} = (c_3 - c_2)(\sigma - f(\beta \mid z)).$$

(4)

Hence the ex ante minimum cost design satisfies $f(\alpha \mid z) = \rho$ and $f(\beta \mid z) = \sigma$.

Figure 2 illustrates the determination of optimal α and β. Figure 2(a) reproduces the distribution of demand levels from Figure 1(d). Figure 2(b) graphs the present value of total cost for each activity when it is installed at unit capacity and operated at a fixed level of output. Consider for example the line from k_1, the cost of installing a unit of capacity of activity 1 and not operating it, to $k_1 + c_1$, the cost of installing a unit of capacity and operating it at full capacity. By constant returns, the line between these points gives the present value of total cost of operating activity 1 at any specified utilization level. The line from k_2 to $k_2 + c_2$ gives the corresponding cost for activity 2, and from 0 to c_3 the cost for activity 3. Activity 1 is most economical for high levels of utilization, and activity 3 is most economical for low levels. At utilization level ρ, activities 1 and 2 give equal cost, $k_1 + c_1\rho = k_2 + c_2\rho$. Similarly, at utilization level σ, activities 2 and 3 give equal cost, $k_2 + c_2\sigma = c_3\sigma$. The optimal level of capacity in activity 1, satisfying $f(\alpha \mid z) = \rho$, is determined graphically by reflecting the output level ρ from the 45° line in Figure 2(a) and determining the output level α at which $f(\alpha \mid z) = \rho$.

From Figure 2, we see that an increase in k_1 or c_1 will increase ρ and decrease α. The less the uncertainty about future climate, the steeper the ogive in Figure 2(a) and the closer to mean demand the level of capacity in activity 1. In the extreme case of no uncertainty about climate, with demand fixed at a level μ, production will be by activity 1 only at capacity μ and total cost $\mu(k_1 + c_1)$. When uncertainty is present, the optimal configuration of production provides capacity in activities 2 and 3 as a hedge, achieving flexibility at lower expected cost than would be incurred if only activity 1 were used.

As a simple example, assume

$$f(x) = \begin{cases} 1 & x < \mu - \theta \\ (\mu - x + \theta)/2\theta & \mu - \theta < x < \mu + \theta \\ 0 & x > \mu + \theta. \end{cases}$$

(5)

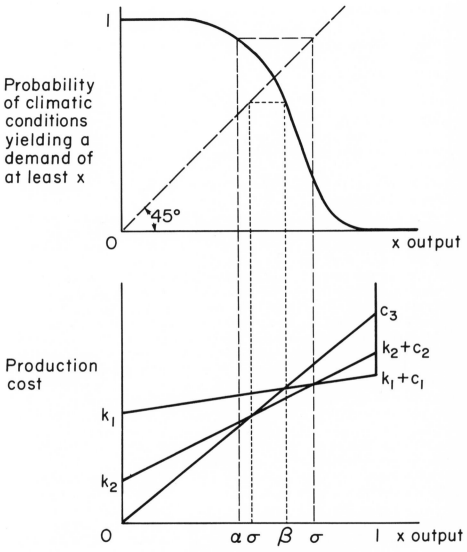

Figure 2. Optimal Technological Flexibility.

Then x has mean μ and variance $\theta^2/3$. The optimal design satisfies

$$\alpha = \mu + \theta(1 - 2\rho) \tag{6}$$
$$\beta = \mu + \theta(1 - 2\sigma),$$

and the associated cost is

$$C = (k_1 + c_1)\mu + \theta\gamma, \tag{7}$$

with $\gamma = k_1 + c_1 - (k_1 - k_2)^2/(c_2 - c_1) - k_2^2/(c_3 - c_2)$ satisfying $c_1 < \gamma < c_1 + k_1$. Thus, increased uncertainty increases cost, but by less than the cost of meeting all demands using activity 1 alone. Note that the less the uncertainty, the closer α and β to mean demand μ. The amount of capacity in activity 1 may either increase or decrease when uncertainty falls, depending on the magnitude of ρ, which is determined by relative costs.

The preceding stylized model of optimal technological design as a hedge against climatic uncertainty can be extended in several directions. First, the technology itself may be directly affected by climate. This can be modeled by assuming the operating costs c_i to be functions of climate and therefore (via the demand function) of level of output. The expression for expected present value of total cost does not reduce to the compact form in the previous case; however, the first-order conditions for optimal designs are the same as before, with operating cost terms now interpreted as conditional expectations of operating costs which depend on the capacity levels. More generally, it is often possible to model the direct impacts of climate in terms of changing input requirements or prices and invariant technological parameters. Then most of the analytical simplifications in the stylized model can be retained (see Fuss and McFadden, 1978).

A second extension is to make the model dynamic by explicitly considering investment over time in capacity in the alternative activities. In this framework one could incorporate a feedback from activity levels to the distribution of climate.

III. WELFARE ANALYSIS OF CLIMATIC IMPACTS

The objective of this section is to clarify the issues involved in applying traditional benefit–cost methods to long-term uncertain global changes of the sort that may be associated with major climatic shifts.

I shall follow Smith's (1980) general approach to describing climate. Meteorological conditions at a location at time t are described by a vector w_t. The w_t follow a stochastic process centered on a vector of state variables z_t which define the climate at time t and which can be estimated by time averages of the w_t. The z_t may evolve over time as a result of natural forces (e.g., precession of the earth's axis) or man's activities.

I begin by considering a simple static economy influenced by weather; later this will be reinterpreted as a representation of the steady state. Suppose the economy has goods n = 1, . . . , N and a technology set T(q, w) containing the feasible net supply vectors to consumers, including resource endowments. This set depends on a vector of design parameters q and on the weather vector w. (We define w to include seasonal variables such as heating and cooling degree days for the year, seasonal precipitation, etc., so that it is unnecessary to write T as a function of an explicit weather history.) The design parameters q contain information on technological features which determine the flexibility of production in accommodating changes in weather; examples could be inventory rules for storing grain in case of crop failure, or the development of crops which are insensitive to extremes in precipitation.

An example is a two-good economy in which the commodities are food (F) and leisure (L), consumer endowment consists of one unit of leisure, and there is a production function $F = A(q, w)(1 - L)^\theta$ for food from labor with $0 < \theta < 1$ and $A(q, w)$ a positive function with $\partial A/\partial w > 0$, $\partial A/\partial q < 0$, and $\partial^2 A/\partial w \partial q < 0$. Then increasing the design parameter q yields a more conservative technology which is less productive on average, but also less sensitive to weather. The technology set for this example is $T(q, w) = \{(F, L) \mid F \leq A(q, w)(1 - L)^\theta \text{ for } 0 \leq L \leq 1\}$.

With the simplifying assumption of competitive markets, there is associated with the technology a profit function

$$\pi = \Pi(p, q, w) = \max\{p \cdot x \mid x \in T(q, w)\}, \tag{8}$$

which specifies the maximum profit attainable given a price vector p, a design q, and weather w. For the example,

$$\pi = \max\{p_F F + p_L L \mid F = A(q, w)(1 - L)^\theta\}$$
$$= P_L + (1 - \theta)\theta^{\theta/(1-\theta)}A(q, w)^{1/(1-\theta)}p_F^{1/(1-\theta)}p_L^{-\theta/(1-\theta)} \tag{9}$$

attained at $F = \theta^{\theta/(1-\theta)}A(q, w)^{1/(1-\theta)}(p_F/p_L)^{\theta/(1-\theta)}$ and $L = 1 - [\theta A(q, w)p_F/p_L]^{1/(1-\theta)}$. A consequence of the envelope theorem of maximization is that the profit-maximizing net supply vector satisfies

$$x = \Pi_p(p, q, w) \tag{10}$$

where $\Pi_p = \partial\Pi/\partial p$ denotes the vector of partial derivatives of Π with respect to p. One can verify this condition for the example, where $F = \partial\Pi/\partial p_F$ and $L = \partial\Pi/\partial p_L$.

Suppose the aggregate demand of consumers can be treated *as if* it were generated by a single utility-maximizing consumer with indirect Von Neumann–Morgenstern utility function u = V(y, p, w), where y is income and weather w may influence utility directly. This function gives the maximum utility attainable within the budget constraint $y \geqq p \cdot x$, where the consumption vector x is chosen *after* the weather vector w is observed. From consumer theory, Roy's identity implies that demand satisfies

$$x = - \frac{V_p(y, p, w)}{V_y(y, p, w)}, \tag{11}$$

where $V_p = \partial V/\partial p$ and $V_y = \partial V/\partial y$.

Continuing the example of the two-commodity economy, one possible indirect utility function is

$$V(y, p, w) = \frac{y}{p_L} - \frac{B(w)(p_F/p_L)^{1-\lambda}}{1 - \lambda}, \tag{12}$$

where $\lambda > 0$. This yields demand functions $F = B(w)(p_L/p_F)^\lambda$ and $L = y/p_L - B(w)(p_L/p_F)^{\lambda-1}$. Since all consumer endowments are included in the technology set, consumer income equals firm profit, $y = \Pi(p, q, w)$. Market equilibrium requires that demand equal supply, or

$$\Pi_p(p, q, w) = - \frac{V_p(\Pi(p, q, w), p, w)}{V_y(\Pi(p, q, w), p, w)}, \tag{13}$$

where income has been set equal to profit. This condition determines the price vector p up to a normalization; say, taking the first commodity as numéraire and fixing its price at 1. I shall assume this equilibrium is unique for each (q, w) vector and denote it by $p = P(q, w)$.

For the example of the two-commodity economy with $p_L = 1$, the equilibrium price satisfies

$$p_F = \left[\frac{B(w)}{\theta^\theta A(q, w)} \right]^{1/[\theta + \lambda(1 - \theta)]}. \tag{14}$$

Assume weather to have a probability distribution F(w − z), with F symmetric about zero so that climate z is the mean of w. Expected utility then satisfies

$$U(q, z) = \int_{w=-\infty}^{+\infty} V(\Pi(P(q, w), q, w), P(q, w), w) \, dF(w - z)$$

$$= \int_{w=-\infty}^{+\infty} V(\Pi(P(q, w + z), q, w + z), P(q, w + z), w + z) \, dF(w),$$

$$\tag{15}$$

with the second integral obtained by changing variables. Evaluation of this integral provides a direct measure of the consequences of different climates z and the impacts of designs q to ameliorate the effects of climate.

The welfare calculation can also be expressed in "willingness to pay," as pointed out by Smith. From a base $(q°, z°)$, define a compensating variation $\delta(q, z)$ to satisfy

$$U(q°, z°) \equiv \int V(\Pi(P(q, w + z), q, w + z)$$
$$- \delta(q, z), P(q, w + z), w + z) \, dF(w). \quad (16)$$

Then, $\delta(q°, z°) = 0$, and $\delta(q, z)$ is the net willingness to pay to be in state (q, z) rather than $(q°, z°)$.

The impact on utility of a small change in climate satisfies

$$\frac{\partial U(q, z)}{\partial z} = \int_{w = -\infty}^{+\infty} [V_w(y, p, w + z)$$
$$+ V_y(y, p, w + z)\Pi_w(p, q, w + z)] \, dF(w) \quad (17)$$
$$+ \int_{w = -\infty}^{\infty} [V_y(y, p, w + z)\Pi_p(p, q, w + z)$$
$$+ V_p(y, p, w + z)]P_w(q, w) \, dF(w),$$

where $y = \Pi(p, q, w)$ and $p = P(q, w)$. But the bracketed term in the second integral is zero from the condition for market equilibrium. Hence, the impact of climate change on utility is an average of the direct marginal impact of weather on consumer satisfaction, V_w, and the marginal impact of weather on profit, Π_w, weighted by the marginal utility of income V_y. Pecuniary effects net out of the utility calculations, giving

$$\frac{\partial U(q, z)}{\partial z} = \int_{w = -\infty}^{+\infty} [V_w + V_y\Pi_w] \, dF(w). \quad (18)$$

Similarly, starting from the compensating variation condition (16) and differentiating with respect to z yields

$$0 = \int V_y \, dF(w) \left[-\frac{\partial\delta}{\partial z} \right] + \int [V_w + V_y\Pi_w] \, dF(w) \quad (19)$$
$$+ \int [V_y\Pi_p + V_p]P_w \, dF(w)$$

or

$$\frac{\partial\delta}{\partial z} = \int [V_w + V_y\Pi_w] \, dF(w) \Big/ \int V_y \, dF(w)$$
$$= \left[\frac{\partial U(q, z)}{\partial z} \right] \Big/ \int V_y \, dF(w), \quad (20)$$

so that the change in compensating variation equals the change in utility divided by the expected marginal utility of income.

For the example of the two-commodity economy, the compensating variation can be shown after some manipulation to satisfy

$$\frac{\partial \delta}{\partial z} = \int \left[\frac{A_w}{A} - \frac{1}{1 - \lambda} \frac{B_w}{B} \right] [\theta^{\theta\lambda} A^\lambda B^{\theta/(1 - \theta)}]^{1/[\theta + \lambda(1 - \theta)]} \, dF(w). \quad (21)$$

The impact on utility of a small change in the design of technology satisfies

$$\frac{\partial U(q, z)}{\partial q} = \int_{w = -\infty}^{+\infty} V_y \Pi_q \, dF(w), \quad (22)$$

since again the pecuniary effects of q on P(q, z) cancel out. Similarly,

$$\frac{\partial \delta(q, z)}{\partial q} = \int_{-\infty}^{+\infty} V_y \Pi_q \, dF \bigg/ \int_{-\infty}^{+\infty} V_y \, dF. \quad (23)$$

Under what conditions can traditional consumer surplus measures be used to calculate the compensating variation δ(q, z) associated with a nonmarket shift such as a climate change? The answer is that special structures of technology and preferences are required. To illustrate, consider the two-commodity economy given above as an example. The demand for food has income elasticity zero, so that Marshallian and Hicksian consumer surplus measures agree. Figure 3 illustrates a traditional calculation of the willingness to pay for a climatic change. Here, solid curves give expected (average) demand and supply before the change; dashed curves give expected demand and supply after the change. Consumer surplus is measured by the area of the triangle formed by the demand and supply curves. The traditional measure of net willingness to pay for the climate change is the difference in consumer surpluses, or area A minus area B. For this example, V(y, p_F, w) = y + g(p_F, w) with g having the concrete functional form given in (12). Then the compensating variation (16), an exact measure of willingness to pay, is

$$\delta(q°, z) = \int_{w = -\infty}^{+\infty} [\Pi(P_F(q°, w + z), q°, w + z)$$

$$+ g(P_F(q°, w + z), w + z)] \, dF(w) \quad (24)$$

$$- \int_{w = -\infty}^{+\infty} [\Pi(P_F(q°, w + z°, q°, w + z°)$$

$$+ g(P_F(q°, w + z°), w + z°)] \, dF(w).$$

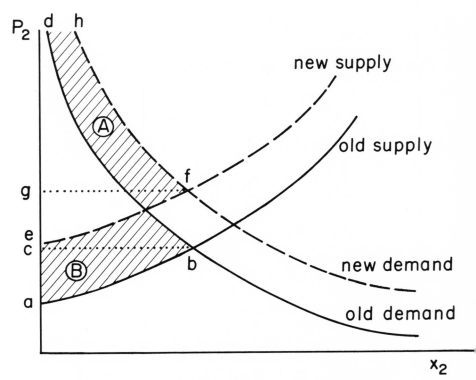

Figure 3. Willingness to Pay for a Climatic Change.

Rearranging terms,

$$\delta(q^\circ, z) = \int_{w=-\infty}^{+\infty} [\Pi(P_F(q^\circ, w + z), q^\circ, w + z)$$

$$- \Pi(P_F(q^\circ, w + z^\circ), q^\circ, w + z^\circ)] \, dF(w) \qquad (25)$$

$$+ \int_{w=-\infty}^{+\infty} [g(P_F(q^\circ, w + z), w + z)$$

$$- g(P_F(q^\circ, w + z^\circ), w + z^\circ)] \, dF(w).$$

The first integral in (25) can be rewritten as

$$\int_{w=-\infty}^{+\infty} \left[\int_0^{P_F(q^\circ, w+z)} \Pi_p(p, q^\circ, w + z) \, dp \right.$$

$$\left. - \int_0^{P_F(q^\circ, w+z^\circ)} \Pi_p(p, q^\circ, w + z^\circ) \, dp \right] dF(w) \qquad (26)$$

$$= \int_{w=-\infty}^{+\infty} [\text{area(efg)} - \text{area (abc)}] \, dF(w),$$

where the areas are indicated in Figure 3. This relationship uses the envelope condition (10) to identify the price derivative of the profit function with the supply curve. Note that in the definition of these areas, Figure 3 is interpreted as holding for a particular value of w. Then the areas are averaged over w.

Similarly, the second integral in (25) can be rewritten as

$$\int_{w=-\infty}^{+\infty} \left[\int_{P_F(q^\circ, w+z)}^{\infty} g_p(p, w + z) \, dp \right.$$

$$\left. - \int_{P_F(q^\circ, w+z^\circ)}^{\infty} g_p(p, w + z^\circ) \, dp \right] dF(w) \qquad (27)$$

$$= \int_{w=-\infty}^{+\infty} [\text{area(gfh)} - \text{area(cbd)}] \, dF(w)$$

provided these area in Figure 3 are defined and finite for each w. This result uses Roy's identity (11).

When (27) exists, the exact compensating variation measure (25) equals area A less area B in Figure 3, where these are computed for each w and then averaged over w. Now compare this calculation with the traditional consumer surplus calculation of area A minus area B for the expected demand and supply curves. Two conditions are required for the traditional and exact measures to coincide. First, the area (gfh) must be finite for each w. This condition is met if the demand for the affected commodity is sufficiently price elastic. For the functional form (12) in the example, the condition is met for $\lambda > 1$ but fails for $0 < \lambda < 1$. Second, the averaged values of the areas must equal the areas subtended by the average value of demand and supply. This condition is met in the unlikely case that equilibrium price is independent of weather, since then in (26) and (27) the average with respect to w can be interchanged with the integral over price, and the areas can be interpreted as those subtended by the average demand and supply curves. For the functional forms in the example, this condition requires that $b(w)/A(q, w)$ be independent of w. More generally, it is likely that equilibrium price will be dependent on weather and that the traditional consumer surplus measure will give an incorrect measure of willingness to pay. Since the evaluation of the exact willingness to pay formula (25) is not fundamentally more difficult than the measurement of average demand and calculation of consumer surplus, it seems best to abandon the traditional geometric approach to assessing welfare impacts for the climate problem.

The technical issue of evaluating willingness to pay is one aspect of a broader question of developing a methodology for assessing policies which affect climate. One approach which has confronted many of the conceptual problems which arise in climate policy is that utilizing transportation benefit–cost analysis and priority programming methods. Much of this literature has been concerned with the development of practical management-oriented programmatic methods for project evaluation; references include American Association of State Highway Officials (1977), Barrell and Hills (1972), Cambridge Systematics (1977), Crumlish (1966), Gulbrandsen (1967), Hibbard and Miller (1974), Hoch (1961), and Positer and Larson (1976). A reexamination of the theoretical foundation of these methods, particularly with regard to the evaluation of nonmarket changes and the treatment of uncertainty, can be found in Hau (1980) and Turvey (1971).

IV. QUESTIONS FOR FUTURE RESEARCH

The modeling approaches suggested in this note should be adaptable to problems of determining optimal economic response to uncertainty about climate. A static or comparative steady-state analysis, utilizing the theoretical description of the design of flexibility in technology as a response to climatic uncertainty outlined in this paper, should be quite feasible. Econometric parameterizations of this approach have been worked out (Fuss and McFadden, 1978). The primary missing element in such an analysis is a systematic mapping of the demand and technological conditions which will prevail for a range of climates. Modeling dynamic economic behavior, feedbacks from economic activity to climate, and optimal dynamic policy pose some unsolved but largely familiar problems for the economist, and such issues will certainly require attention in any comprehensive research program. However, the first priority for research on climate and economics is systematic study of the "preeconomic" relationship between climate and technological opportunities.

REFERENCES

American Association of State Highway and Transportation Officials, *A Manual on User Benefit Analysis of Highway and Bus Transit Improvements*. Washington, D.C., 1977.

Barrell, David W. F. and Peter J. Hills, "The Application of Cost–Benefit Analysis to Transport Investment Projects in Britain," *Transportation* 1(May 1972):29–54.

Cambridge Systematics, *Recommendations for an Improved Statewide Programming Methodology*. Prepared for the Wisconsin State Department of Transportation, Madison, Wisconsin Department of Transportation, February 1977.

Carleton, D., "Uncertainty, Product Lags, and Pricing." *American Economic Review Proceedings* 67(1977):244–49.

Crumlish, Joseph D., *Notes on the State-of-the-Art of Benefit–Cost Analysis as Related to Transportation*, Technical Note No. 294. Washington, D.C.: U.S. National Bureau of Standards, 1966.

Diamond, P. and M. Rothschild, *Uncertainty in Economics*. New York: Academic Press, 1978.

Fuss, M. and D. McFadden, "Flexibility vs. Efficiency in the Economic Analysis of Production." In M. Fuss and D. McFadden, *Production Economics,* Volume 1. Amsterdam: North Holland, 1978.

Goldman, S., "Portfolio Choice and Flexibility: the Precautionary Motive." University of California, Berkeley, Economic Theory and Econometrics Working Paper, 1975.

Gruver, James E., et al., "Highway Investment Analysis Package." *Transportation Programming, Economic Analysis, and Evaluation of Energy Constraints,* Transportation Research Record 599. Washington, D.C.: Transportation Research Board, 1976, pp. 13–18.

Gulbrandsen, Odd, "Optimal Priority Rating of Resources—Allocation by Dynamic Programming." *Transportation Science* 1(November 1967):251–260.

Hau, T., *Cost Benefit Analysis of Urban Highway Investment: An Expenditure Function Approach.* Ph.D. thesis, University of California-Berkeley, 1980.

Heal, G., "Interactions between Economy and Climate: A Framework for Policy Design under Uncertainty." University of Sussex working paper, 1980.

Hibbard, Thomas H. and Fred Miller, "Applications of Benefit–Cost Analysis: The Selection of 'Non-Construction Projects.'" *Cost–Benefit and Other Economic Analyses of Transportation,* Transportation Research Record 490. Washington, D.C.: Transportation Research Board, 1974, pp. 31–39.

Hoch, Irving, "Benefit–Cost Methods for Evaluating Expressway Construction." *Traffic Quarterly* 15(April 1961):208–225.

Laffont, J., "Risk, Stochastic Preference, and the Value of Information." *Journal of Economic Theory* 12(1976):483–487.

Leland, H., "Savings and Uncertainty: The Precautionary Demand for Savings." *Quarterly Journal of Economics* 82(1968):465–473.

Lin, Feng-Bor and Lester A. Hoel, "Structure of Utility-Based Evaluation Approaches." *Transportation Engineering Journal of the ASCE* 103, No. TE 2(March 1977):307–320.

Mirrlees, J. and N. Stern (eds.), *Models of Economic Growth.* London: MacMillan, 1973.

Nash, Christopher, et al., "Criteria for Evaluating Project Evaluation Techniques." *American Institute of Planners Journal* 41(March 1975):83–89.

Nelson, R. and S. Winter, "A Case Study in the Economics of Information and Coordination: The Weather Forecasting System." *Quarterly Journal of Economics* 78(1964):420–441.

Positer, Theodore H. and Thomas D. Larson, "Administering State Mass Transit Programs in Pennsylvania." *Management of Transportation and Environmental Review Functions,* Transportation Research Record 603. Washington, D.C.: Transportation Research Board, 1976, pp. 1–7.

Rothenberg, T. and K. Smith, "The Effect of Uncertainty on Resource Allocation." *Quarterly Journal of Economics* 85(1971):440–53.

Sheshinski, E. and J. Dreze, "Demand Fluctuations, Capacity Utilization, and Costs." *American Economic Review* 66(1976):731–42.

Smith, V. Kerry, "Economic Impact Analysis and Climate Change." University of North Carolina Working paper, 1980.

Taylor, J., "Estimation and Control of Macroeconomic Model with Rational Expectations." Discussion Paper 77-7821, Columbia University Economics Workshops, 1978.

Turvey, R., *Economic Analysis and Public Enterprise.* London: Allen and Unwin, 1971.

Zellner, A., "On Controlling and Learning about a Normal Regression Model." University of Chicago Working Paper, 1966.

INTERACTIONS BETWEEN ECONOMY AND CLIMATE:
A FRAMEWORK FOR POLICY
DESIGN UNDER UNCERTAINTY

Geoffrey Heal

I. INTRODUCTION

It is now widely recognized that economic activities affect the world's climate, and that there is at least some possibility that these effects may be sufficiently substantial to be a cause of serious concern. Many mechanisms have been suggested as carriers of the impact of economic activities on the climate. Prominent among these are the emission of carbon dioxide (CO_2) as a result of the combustion of fossil fuels, the emission of waste heat, particularly from power generation, the contamination of the atmosphere with aerosols and particulates, and changes in the ecological balance as a result of agricultural activities.[1]

Advances in Applied Micro-Economics, Volume 3, pages 151–168.
Copyright © 1984 by JAI Press Inc.
All rights of reproduction in any form reserved.
ISBN: 0-89232-398-1

The generation of CO_2 and of aerosols and particulates is thought to change the reflective and absorbtive characteristics of the atmosphere for electromagnetic radiation, thus possibly changing the rates at which the earth heats and cools. The emission of waste heat may, like intensive agricultural activities, change the local climate, and if this is done on a sufficiently large scale in geographic terms there is a possibility of such effects becoming global.

Although there is general agreement that all of these effects *may* provide mechanisms whereby economic activities affect the climate, there is unfortunately substantial uncertainty about the magnitudes and characteristics of these effects. To be precise, there is uncertainty on several counts.

1. The *time scale* on which climate might respond to economic activity is not clear. There is general agreement that none of the effects concerned is likely to be immediate, but beyond this there is little common ground. Some commentators see a chance of significant responses in this century, whereas others see them at least half a century distant.

2. There is also a wide range of opinions about the possible magnitudes and directions of economic impacts on the climate. It is not clear whether we should expect increases or decreases in global mean temperatures, variance of temperatures, precipitation, etc.

3. Finally, there is little information about the effects of possible climate changes on human activity in general, and on economic activity in particular. It is not clear whether any particular change is likely to be harmful or beneficial to agricultural activities, or to enforce major and costly changes in patterns of settlement or energy use.

It might be helpful to illustrate briefly the types of uncertainty involved. Clearly one of the most important mechanisms for interactions between economy and climate is the emission of CO_2 into the atmosphere, with its possible effects on the transmission and absorption of electromagnetic radiation. The main source of such emission is the combustion of fossil fuels: CO_2 is released into the atmosphere by combustion and removed from it by photosynthesis and by solution into the oceans. In order to make a forecast as to the effects of CO_2 release, it is clearly necessary to predict:

1. The use of fossil fuels
2. The rate of removal of CO_2 from the atmosphere
3. The effect of changes in CO_2 concentration on climate
4. The economic effects of climate changes

A little reflection reveals that every one of these tasks is clearly very difficult. The first—the prediction of fossil fuel consumption—is perhaps the simplest, yet most energy economists would attach little confidence to any prediction of energy consumption more than 10 or 15 years hence. One has to predict gross national product (GNP), the relationship between GNP and energy consumption, and the shares of different fuel types in supplying this consumption. Most existing long-run predictions of energy consumption are based essentially on an extrapolation of existing energy–GNP relationships and so of course lead to the prediction that as the currently less-developed countries industrialize, energy consumption, and hence fossil fuel consumption and so the release of CO_2, will rise greatly on a worldwide basis. However, recent studies of energy consumption in the Third World[2] have suggested that official statistics for many poor countries greatly understate the true levels of energy consumption because of the extensive reliance on energy sources such as firewood, dung, and animal power, none of which is recorded in official energy statistics. This omission will of course bias *upward* the apparent relationship between energy consumption per head and GNP per head because of the underreporting of energy consumption at low income levels and will also bias *downward* estimates of current emission of CO_2 into the atmosphere. Such climatic effects as are observed will thus be attributed to less CO_2 than is actually released, overestimating the impact of CO_2. It thus emerges that a simple shortcoming in official statistics—a shortcoming of a kind that is very common—may give a misleading appearance to the problem.

I have so far discussed only the first of the four links in the chain of reasoning needed to predict the effect of CO_2 release on economic activities via its effect on the climate. It is clear that even this, almost surely the simplest link, involves great uncertainties. This is quite sufficient for the present purpose, which is merely to emphasize that our knowledge of the structure of the problem with which we are concerned is extremely partial and imperfect. It is therefore of great importance that any decision making in the field of economy–climate interactions should be carried out in the light of an explicit recognition of the immense uncertainties involved.

The remaining sections of this paper attempt to raise some of the issues involved in giving due recognition to these uncertainties. I present two very simplified models of stochastic economy–climate interaction and derive optimal decision rules for both of them. Neither can claim to be more than extremely partial; nevertheless they appear to demonstrate that the relevant issues can be formalized quite tractably.

Both models are dynamic and have as a central feature the fact that the *timing* of any response of climate to economic activity is very uncertain but that this timing is at least partially controllable via the level of economic activity. Thus we do not know when a given sustained rate of release of CO_2 into the atmosphere will lead to major changes, but we do know that, at least in expected value terms, lower rates of fossil fuel burns will delay the changes.

The first of the two models, discussed in Section II, is very simple and hence admits a complete analytical solution. The second, given in Section III, has analytical solutions only for very special cases. The model of Section II is based on the idea that the atmosphere has a limited capacity to absorb emissions such as CO_2 and particulates before undergoing a major change. However, this capacity is unknown; we only discover it when we reach the limit and notice the changes. The only information we have a priori is a probability distribution over possible values of this absorbtive capacity. The model then addresses the question: given this probability distribution, how should we control our emission-producing activities?[3]

The second model, discussed in Section III, is considerably more complex. It is supposed that the climatic environment may be in one of two states, either *favorable* or *unfavorable* to economic activity. It is initially in the favorable state, and it may move stochastically to the unfavorable state with probabilities that depend on the history of economic activities persued to date. Given that the dependence of these probabilities on economic activities is a known function, the question naturally arises: how should the economic activities be controlled over time?

In both cases, then, there is an uncertain dependence of irreversible climatic changes on cumulative economic activities. The uncertainty is described by a probability distribution on a stochastic process, and the issue is how the relevant economic activities should be controlled over time.

Before beginning the formal analysis, it is perhaps appropriate to comment on the role and value of the highly simplified models that are about to be discussed. Clearly they tackle the issues involved only at a very high level of abstraction and simplification. I think it can be argued that this is an essential characteristic of a first step in this area: one has to pick out the basic issues, see how to formalize them, and determine whether they are tractable. The issue, in this case, is not so much whether the model is too simple as whether the simplications are the right ones. If they are, then the models analyzed below can be used as "building blocks" in the construction and analysis of more complete and integrated pictures of the overall problem. They can also be used to highlight the key relationships and parameters, so that we know where it is most important to improve our knowledge.

II. UNCERTAIN ABSORBTIVE CAPACITY

It is supposed that the atmosphere has a total capacity A to absorb emissions. As far as the decision makers are concerned, A is an unknown random variable with a marginal density function f(A):

$$f(A) \geq 0, \qquad \int_0^\infty f(A) \, dA = 1.$$

Here A is not, of course, truly a stochastic variable: in principle its value can be known, so the uncertainty facing decision makers stems from a lack of information rather than from the random nature of the environment. Once the total absorbtive capacity A has been utilized, then there is a major irreversible and harmful change in the climate—a true catastrophe. The analysis does not require a precise specification of this change, so that the reader may be left to exercise a vivid imagination on this issue.

It is supposed that the rate of emission at time t is E_t, a nonnegative real number, and that there are benefits of value $V(E_t)$ associated with a rate of emission of E_t. The value of the catastrophe when it occurs, measured in the same units as benefits, is C. The overall decision-making problem thus has as an objective:

$$\text{maximize expectation} \left\{ \int_0^T V(E_t)e^{-\delta t} \, dt + Ce^{-\delta T} \right\}, \qquad (1)$$

where $\delta \geq 0$ is a discount rate to be applied to future benefits; T is the date at which the total absorbtive capacity A is exhausted and at which the catastrophe occurs, and the expectation is over all possible values of T; $V(E_t)$ is of course a continuous real-valued increasing function and will usually be assumed to be strictly concave. On occasions it will however be of interest to investigate the impact of certain threshold effects which can be represented by a nonconcavity in V(E).

The structure of the problem can now be set out more formally. The choice variable is E, the emission rate, as a function of time, E_t. Any particular emission policy, say $\hat{E}_t$, taken in conjunction with the density function f(A) describing possible values of A, induces a probability distribution over possible values of T, the date at which absorbtive capacity is exhausted and the climatic catastrophe occurs. This distribution is given by

$$\text{proby}(T = T') = f\left(\int_0^{T'} \hat{E}_t \, dt \right). \qquad (2)$$

For convenience we let

$$Z_t = \int_0^t E_\tau \, d\tau, \qquad \frac{dz}{dt} = \dot{Z}_t = E_t, \tag{3}$$

so that (2) becomes

$$\text{proby}(T = T') = f(Z_t).$$

The problem (1) can now be restated as

$$\max \int_0^\infty f(Z_t) \left\{ \int_0^T V(E_t)e^{-\delta t} + Ce^{-\delta T} \right\} dZ_t \tag{4}$$

subject to $\dot{Z}_t = E_t$ [i.e., Eq. (3)].

The maximization of (4) subject to (3) is now a well-defined dynamic optimization problem,[4] which may be solved as follows. Rewrite the maximand as

$$\int_0^\infty f(Z_t) \frac{dz}{dt} \left\{ \int_0^T V(E_t)e^{-\delta t} + Ce^{-\delta T} \right\} dt$$

$$= \int_0^\infty f(Z_t)E_t \left\{ \int_0^T V(E_t)e^{-\delta t} + Ce^{-\delta T} \right\} dt.$$

We now simplify the problem by choosing the origin of the payoff function so that

$$C = 0.$$

This is clearly an acceptable normalization. Defining

$$\int_T^\infty f(Z_t)E_t \, dt \equiv \int_{Z_T}^\infty f(Z_t) \, dZ = F(Z_t)$$

and integrating by parts, the maximand becomes

$$\int_0^\infty V(E_t)e^{-\delta t} \left\{ \int_T^\infty f(Z_t)E_t \, dt \right\} dt$$

$$= \int_0^\infty V(E_t) \, F(Z_t)e^{-\delta t} \, dt. \tag{5}$$

The relevant optimization problem is now that of maximizing (5) subject to the differential Eq. (3). This may readily be solved by, for example, Pontryagin's maximum principle. Letting p_t be the shadow price or co-state variable associated with the constraint, the Hamiltonian is

$$H = V(E) \, F(Z)e^{-\delta t} + pEe^{-\delta t}$$

and the conditions necessary for a solution are, assuming an interior solution,

$$V'(E) F(Z) = -p, \tag{6}$$

where $V'(E) = dV/dE$ and

$$\dot{p} - \delta p = -V(E) F'(Z). \tag{7}$$

Notice from (6) that as $V(E)$ is an increasing function, $p \le 0$. Intuitively the state variable Z is a "bad" rather than a "good" variable and so has a negative shadow price.

$$F'(Z_t) = \frac{d}{dZ_t} \int_{Z_T}^{\infty} f(Z_t) \, dZ = -f(Z_t).$$

Differentiation of (6) leads to

$$\frac{V''E}{V'} \frac{\dot{E}}{E} - \frac{fE}{F} = \frac{\dot{p}}{P},$$

which in combination with (7) gives

$$\frac{V''E}{V'} \frac{\dot{E}}{E} - \frac{fE}{F} = \delta + \frac{V}{V'} \frac{F'}{F}. \tag{8}$$

Defining

$$y(E) = \frac{V''E}{V'}$$

and

$$q(Z) = \frac{f(Z)}{F(Z)}$$

so that $q(Z)$ is the conditional probability of the change occurring at cumulative emission level Z, given that it has not occurred previously, (8) may be simplified to

$$\frac{\dot{E}}{E} = \frac{\delta}{y(E)} + \frac{q(Z)}{y(E)} \left\{ E - \frac{V(E)}{V'(E)} \right\}.$$

This, in turn, can conveniently be rewritten in final form as

$$\frac{\dot{E}}{E} = \frac{\delta}{y(E)} + \frac{q(Z)}{y(E)} \frac{.E.}{V'} \left\{ V'(E) - \frac{V(E)}{E} \right\}. \tag{9}$$

This is a differential equation governing the optimal rate of change of emissions over time. For any strictly concave function, we have

$$y(E) < 0$$

and

$$V'(E) < \frac{V(E)}{E},$$

as for any such function the marginal payoff $V'(E)$ is strictly less than the average $V(E)/E$. Hence for a strictly concave function the first term in the expression for $\dot{E}/E$ is negative and the second positive. This second term tends to zero as $q(Z)$, the conditional probability of the catastrophe, tend to zero.

It is clear from (9) that $E = 0$ if and only if

$$E\left\{\frac{\delta}{y} - \frac{qV}{yV'} + \frac{q}{y}E\right\} = 0.$$

Thus $E = 0$ is a locally stable stationary solution, with a second stationary solution given by

$$E = \frac{V}{V'} - \frac{\delta}{q}.$$

As V, V', and q are not in general constants, $E = 0$ is in general the only stationary solution.[5] Hence a solution to the overall optimization problem will consist of picking a time path for E which converges to zero according to (9). It is clear from this that the rate of decline of E is greater, the greater is the discount rate δ applied to future benefits and the nearer is the payoff function to linear.

A ready intuitive interpretation can be provided for these results. The atmosphere has a limited (though uncertain) absorptive capacity, and an increase in the discount rate represents a change in preferences toward using up that absorptive capacity now rather than later: it hence tends to produce an emission path which starts higher but falls faster than would be the case with a lower discount rate. It is worth noting that, in the context of an uncertain problem, the elasticity of the marginal payoff function, $y(E)$, has a natural interpretation as an index of risk aversion. Hence we can say from (9) that an increase in society's risk aversion vis-à-vis the uncertainties of climatic change will lead to a decline in the rate at which emissions should fall over time. This decline in the steepness of the profile will be accompanied by a decrease in the initial emission level, producing a flatter profile with less variation in emission levels and a smaller cumulative emission through to any given date. It is clear, then,

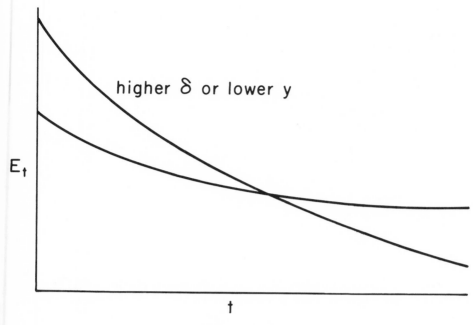

higher δ or lower y

E_t

t

Figure 1

that changes in the discount rate and the index of risk aversion have very much the effects that might be expected. Figure 1 illustrates these points.

The role of the difference between average and marginal payoffs, {V' − V/E}, is less immediate but nevertheless quite comprehensible. To understand this, recall that the choice of any particular emission profile E amounts to a choice of a probability distribution over dates at which absorptive capacity will be exhausted. Corresponding to a particular profile, say $\hat{E}_t$, is an expected exhaustion date, say $\hat{T}$. Suppose that the level of emission just prior to $\hat{T}$ is reduced by one unit: then the loss of payoff is $V'e^{-\delta\hat{T}}$. The unit of absorptive capacity thus saved could be used to prolong the period in which this capacity remained effective; and if emission were held constant at its terminal rate, then the extra time thus gained would be $1/E_{\hat{T}}$, with the associated increase in payoff of $e^{-\delta\hat{T}}V/E$. Thus the net decrease in payoff from a marginal reduction in emissions just prior to exhaustion is

$$e^{-\delta T}\left\{V' - \frac{V}{E}\right\},$$

which explains the form of the second term in (9). For a concave function,

$(V' - V/E)$ is always negative, and the more negative it is, the greater is the decrease in payoff from a postponement of emissions. In such a situation, $(V' - V/E)$ contributes, through division by $y < 0$, a positive term to $\dot{E}/E$.

In the context of the role of the term $(V' - V/E)$, it is interesting to consider briefly the results of replacing a strictly concave $V(E)$ by a function such as that shown in Figure 2. Here $V(E) = 0$ for $E \leq \underline{E}$: for $E \geq \underline{E}$, $V(E)$ is a strictly concave function. Hence there is a threshold level $\underline{E}$ of emissions: levels of emission below this contribute nothing to the payoff. Such a function has the property that

$$V' \gtreqless \frac{V}{E}, \qquad E \lesseqgtr E^*,$$

and

$$V' = \frac{V}{E}, \qquad E = E^*.$$

Hence for a payoff function of this sort, the second term in Eq. (9) will change sign, being positive as before for $E > E^*$, but being negative for $E < E^*$. Thus the threshold effect in the payoff function reinforces the tendency for the optimal E_t to decline with time.

It is now time to summarize the conclusions of this section. Clearly the model is too simple to be anything other than a guide to thinking on this issue, but in this role it seems useful. It suggests that one essential element

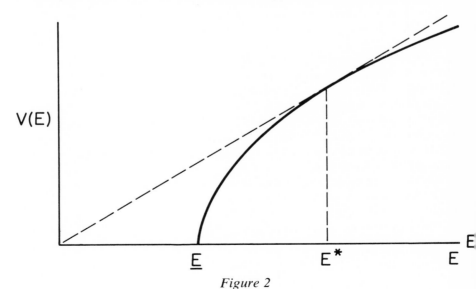

Figure 2

of our problem is that we are in danger of exhausting the unknown absorptive capacity of the atmospheric environment. How optimally to deplete an unknown absorbtive capacity is the problem that can be posed in a convenient form and that proves amenable to relatively standard analytical techniques. It can therefore be used as an element of any more general formulation of the problem of decision making in the context of economy–climate interactions.

III. A MODEL OF RESOURCE DEPLETION AND EMISSIONS

This section addresses a slightly different formulation of the problem. It is supposed that the atmospheric environment is a common property resource which enters as an input into the production function. This environment may be in one of two states—either favorable or unfavorable to economic activity. These are denoted by $\overline{A}$ and $\underline{A}$, respectively. The environment is initially in the favorable state $\overline{A}$ but may transit stochastically into the unfavorable state $\underline{A}$: $\underline{A}$ is absorbing in the sense that once the environment is in state $\underline{A}$ it will remain there for ever. The probability of a transition from $\overline{A}$ to $\underline{A}$ is endogenous and in particular depends on cumulative emissions into the atmosphere. The source of these emissions is the use of an exhaustible resource in production: the rate of use of this at time t is R_t; and in addition to R_t and A, the remaining input to production is the capital stock, K_t. Thus production is described by

$Y = Q(K, R, A)$, where Y is total output, $A = \overline{A}$ or $\underline{A}$, and $Q(K, R, \overline{A}) > Q(K, R, \underline{A})$ for all K and R.

We thus have a production process that depends on inputs of capital and resources, and a cooperating climatic or environmental factor. The state of the atmospheric environment depends on cumulative emissions, which in turn depends on cumulative resource use. Obviously the motivation for this model is the emission of CO_2 by the combustion of fossil fuels: this is a clear case of an emission which might change the state of the climatic environment and whose magnitude depends on cumulative use of the resource fossil fuel.

The rest of the model can be formalized as follows. The rate of emission at date t is E_t and is directly proportional to the rate of resource use R_t at time t. The constant of proportionality can be set equal to unity, and we can therefore identify E_t and R_t, and from now on will refer just to R_t. Cumulative resource depletion up to date t is denoted by Z_t:

$$Z_t = \int_0^t R_\tau \, d\tau, \qquad \dot{Z}_t = R_t.$$

The evolution of the climatic environment A is as follows:

There exists $T > 0$ such that $A = \overline{A}$, $0 \leqslant t \leqslant T$; $A = \underline{A}$, $T < t \leqslant \infty$. Here T is a random variable whose marginal density function f has as its argument cumulative emission and depletion Z_t, thus $f = f(Z_t)$.

It follows from this formulation that the probability that the date of the change T lies in any interval (t_1, t_2) is

$$\text{Prob}(T \in (t_1, t_2)) = \int_{Z_{t_1}}^{Z_{t_2}} f(Z_t)\, dt$$

Hence, if $Z_{t_1} = Z_{t_2}$ and there is no depletion or emission in the interval (t_1, t_2), then the probability of a climatic change in that interval is zero. It is also the case that, when there is emission in the interval (t_1, t_2), the probability of a change depends not only on the level of emission in (t_1, t_2) but also on cumulative emissions prior to t_1. Although there is little formal discussion of these issues in the literature on climatic change, these seem very desirable properties.[6]

Total output Y_t may be divided between investment $\dot{K} = dK/dt$ and consumption C_t. Consumption yields value or utility at a rate given by $U(C_t)$, where $U(C_t)$ is a strictly concave function and the objective is to maximize the expected present discounted value of utility of consumption.

In addition to the production constraint, there is a constraint on total resource use steming from the fact that only a finite amount S_0 is available:

$$\int_0^\infty R_t\, dt \leqslant S_0$$

The overall problem is thus:

$$\max E \int_0^\infty U(C_t) e^{-\delta t}\, dt$$

$$\text{subject to } \int_0^\infty R_t\, dt \leqslant S_0$$

$$\dot{K} + C = Q(K, R, A).$$

The expectation operator here is over the realizations of the stochastic process governing T, the date of transition from $\overline{A}$ to $\underline{A}$.

We define

$$S_t = S_0 - \int_0^t R_\tau\, d\tau, \qquad \dot{S}_t = -R_t,$$

and also

$$W(K_T, S_T) = \max \int_T^\infty U(C_t) e^{-\delta(t-T)}\, dt,$$

where the maximization is subject to the technological conditions operative after T and the initial conditions K_T and S_T at T: $W(K_T, S_T)$ is thus a state valuation function for the state variables of the system at the transition date T. Hence we may write the maximand as

$$E \left\{ \int_0^T U(C_t)e^{-\delta t} \, dt + W(K_T, S_T)e^{-\delta T} \right\}$$

$$= \int_{Z_0}^{Z_\infty} f(Z) \left\{ \int_0^T U(C_t)e^{-\delta t} \, dt + W(K_T, S_T)e^{-\delta T} \right\} dZ$$

$$= \int_0^\infty f(Z)R \left\{ \int_0^T U(C_t)e^{-\delta t} \, dt + W(K_T, S_T)e^{-\delta T} \right\} dT.$$

Define

$$F(Z_t) = \int_T^\infty f(Z_t)R_t \, dt$$

and recall that

$$Z_t = S_0 - S_t.$$

Then the maximization can finally be written as:

$$\max \int_0^\infty U(C_t) F(S_0 - S_t)e^{-\delta t} \, dt + \int_0^\infty W(K_t, S_t) f(S_0 - S_t)R_t e^{-\delta t} \, dt$$

subject to $C_t + \dot{K}_t = Q(K_t, R_t, \overline{A})$,

$\dot{S}_t = -R_t$,

$\lim_{t \to \infty} S_t \geq 0$.

Once again the problem has been converted into a relatively tractable dynamic optimization problem which can be solved by the maximum principle. The problem is essentially an optimal resource depletion problem, with the added complication that resource depletion generates emissions whose cumulative impact may be to trigger a climatic change which affects the production possibilities of the economic system.[7] In fact it is clear that, as everything after capital T is summarized in a state valuation function, one could equally well suppose that the climatic change alters the nature of the payoff or utility function, for example, by making the climate less (or more) pleasant.

Letting λ_t and μ_t be costate variables, the Hamiltonian is

$$H = U(C)F(S_0 - S_t)e^{-\delta t} + W(K_t, S_t)f(S_0 - S_t)R_t e^{-\delta t}$$
$$+ \lambda(Q(K, R, \overline{A}) - C)e^{-\delta t} - \mu R_t e^{-\delta t}$$

and the conditions necessary for a maximum, assuming an interior solution, are

$$U'(C) F(S_0 - S_t) - \lambda = 0, \qquad (10)$$

$$W(K_t, S_t) f(S_0 - S_t) + \lambda Q_R - \mu = 0, \qquad (11)$$

(where $Q_R = \partial Q/\partial R$), and

$$\dot{\lambda} - \delta\lambda = -\lambda Q_k, \qquad (12)$$

$$\dot{\mu} - \delta\mu = UF' + W_s fR + W f'R. \qquad (13)$$

In the case of a "pure" optimal resource depletion problem, the equivalent of (13) would be $\dot{\mu} = \delta\mu$, with the shadow price of the resource constraint rising at the rate δ. Clearly matters are a great deal more complex in the present case: note that $F' < 0$ and f' may be positive or negative, so that in turn $\dot{\mu}$ may have either sign. The possibility that the shadow price on the resource constraint may fall and even become negative is quite in accordance with intuition. The resource is of course a scarce input and for this reason should have a positive and growing shadow price. But it is also a source of emissions which clearly have a negative economic value, and this creates a tendency in the opposite direction.

Once again defining

$$q(z) = \frac{f(z)}{F(Z)}, \qquad y(c) = \frac{U''C}{U'},$$

(10) and (12) yield

$$\frac{\dot{C}}{C} = \frac{\delta}{y} + q\frac{R}{y} - \frac{Q_k}{y}. \qquad (14)$$

For a pure resource depletion problem where resource use has no environmental side effects, one would derive an equation identical to (14) except that the term qR/y would be missing (precisely as when the conditional probability q is zero or the rate of emission R is zero). We can therefore regard (14) as the result for the pure resource depletion model with the discount rate augmented by an amount of qR, which depends both on the conditional probability of a climatic change and on the rate of emission.

From (11) and (13), together with the simplifying assumption that $W_s = 0$, it is possible to derive

$$\frac{1}{Q_R} \frac{d}{dt} (Q_R) = Q_k + \frac{1}{FU'Q_R} (\delta Wf + UF'). \qquad (15)$$

Equation (15) is again identical to a result that emerges from the pure resource depletion model except for the presence of the second term on the right-hand side. Without this second term, it is simply a statement of the obvious efficiency condition that the rate of return to the resource R (which equals the rate of change of its price, which in turn under competitive conditions equals its marginal product Q_R) should equal that to the capital good, which is given by its marginal productivity Q_K.

In the present context, however, there are two components to the return to the resource—one connected with its productive use, and the other associated with its impact on the climate. Recalling that $F' < 0$, and noting that if $\underline{A}$ is very much worse than $\overline{A}$, it is clear that the second term on the right-hand side in (15) is likely to be negative. Hence in this case the rate of return to the productive use of the resource is to be equated to a lower value than in the pure depletion case, so that its private (as opposed to social) marginal product will rise more slowly. This in turn indicates, as one would expect, that the solution path will have a lower rate of depletion of the resource than in the case of no climatic side effects.

IV. CONCLUSIONS

The object of this paper has been to discuss decision rules in the field of economy–climate interactions, with particular emphasis on the appropriate reaction to uncertainty. The most natural reaction to a highly uncertain problem is to attempt to simplify it by invoking certainty equivalence results and replacing it by an equivalent certain problem. The properties of such an approach have been studied extensively (see, for example, Theil, 1961; Malinvaud, 1972; Henry, 1974), and it is known to be optimal in the linear-quadratic-Gaussian (LQG.) case. However, certainty equivalence results which depend on the system to be studied being LQG. are almost certainly of little use in the present area because of the very complex nonlinearities that may be present in environmental systems and because there is no evidence that a normal distribution is the most appropriate formulation of the stochastic element of the problem. My approach has therefore been to model directly the nonlinear, nonnormal aspects of the system. There are occasions when certainty equivalence results are available for dynamic nonlinear nonnormal systems, as shown in Dasgupta and Heal (1974); some such results are apparent in Section III, but they are of limited generality.

The particular phenomenon that I have been concerned to model is one of a discrete and calamitous change in environmental conditions induced by cumulative economic activity. The melting of the polar icecaps would perhaps be the stereotype of such an event. It is an open question whether

such discrete and calamitous changes are the ones most likely to occur—
though, by definition, they are the ones most likely to be important if
they do occur. Possibly therefore their expected impact, in the statistical
sense, is greatest. This is an issue that must be resolved by further work
in the physical sciences. However, it is I think important to emphasize
that the methods and models used here are by no means limited to the
analysis of discrete and unpleasant events, although these provide a striking and simple framework for displaying their potential. The essence of
the models and techniques developed here is that there is a date, random
but endogenous, at which cumulative economic activity induces climate
changes. One could adapt the model to the analysis of a sequence of
relatively minor events or to the analysis of a gradual shift of climatic
regime, the beginning date of which was uncertain. This latter case would
be modeled by having the stochastic process in the model describe the
date of initiation of a process of alteration of the production possibilities
in the model. It seems that the only important possibility to which this
framework could not be adapted is a series of very local but significant
climate changes induced by global economic activities: this would seem
to require a more disaggregated approach. Analysis of this type of phenomenon would also seem to require disaggregation of the global climate
models now in use, in order to supply data about possible patterns of
microclimate change.

There is relatively little literature to which the analysis of this paper
can be related. As indicated in the previous sections, there are papers
with similar analytical structures, but they are usually focused on rather
different issues. Those most closely related are Cropper (1976) and Heal
(1979). The former specifically considers the regulation of activities having random and possibly catastrophic environmental effects. Cropper's
paper in fact contains two distinct models—one encompassing the regulation of activities having potentially catastrophic environmental effects,
and the other encompassing the optimal depletion of an unknown resource
stock. The second model is similar to that of Section II of this paper but
gives a rather less detailed analysis of the solution paths. The first of
Cropper's models is a more complex version of that in Section II above,
allowing both for natural regeneration of the environment and for a nonlinear relationship between the level of economic activity and additions
to the stock of emissions. This case appears to admit the possibility of
stationary optimal solutions other than those on which $E = 0$, but conditions for the existence of such stationary solutions are not given. In the
model of Section II above, conditions for the existence of nonzero stationary values of E would involve quite unreasonable assumptions about
the functions and parameters, and this would be true even if the model

were extended to include natural regeneration of the atmospheric environment or nonlinear stock-flow interactions.

Another related analysis is that of Heal (1982), which is based on the earlier work by Heal and Ryder (1973). This also analyzes the optimal control of pollution-emitting activities which have a cumulative impact, but in this case within a deterministic framework. The environment is not seen as having a fixed absorptive capacity in that model but as undergoing gradual deterioration as the pollutant stock increases. Such a model is quite different from the ones already discussed, focusing on a rather different set of issues. It is therefore of interest that its behavior is in some respects similar to that of Cropper's model, with the possibility of a multiplicity of nonzero stationary values of the pollution variable. This model also suggests that the optimal pollution policy is very sensitive to the initial conditions of the model, being quite different for different initial regimes.

It is perhaps appropriate to end this paper by indicating an important aspect of the problem that has not been discussed here. As mentioned above, the models analyzed are very aggregative and treat the system as a uniform whole. In fact there is some indication that long before major global changes in the environment occur, significant local changes could occur in some regions. Recent trends in the sub-Saharan belt provide an example of a purely regional but nonetheless very significant climatic change. In some cases these changes could be beneficial and in others harmful. This suggests that when these micro-level effects are considered there could be a considerable international divergence of interests, with some nations or regions standing to gain and others to lose from the continuation of climate-affecting activities. In all cases, of course, both the timing and the magnitude of the gains and losses would be very uncertain. Obviously considerations of this type raise questions about the scope for international agreements in this field, and it could perhaps be important to analyze this issue within a game-theoretic or bargaining context.

ACKNOWLEDGMENTS

I am grateful to Graciela Chichilnisky, Kerry Smith, and others for helpful suggestions.

NOTES

1. These issues are surveyed in detail in other papers in this section of the volume. See also International Workshop on Climate Issues (1978), Frisken (1973), and Larmuth (1979). The impact of agricultural activities on the climate is given little prominence in most reviews,

but Larmuth quotes the startling fact that in 1872 some 14 percent of potential usable land was desert whereas by 1977 this figure had risen to 55 percent. He also attributes most of the change to overintensive agricultural use.

2.   Private communication, Science Policy Research Unit, University of Sussex.

3.   In an earlier paper, Cropper (1976) has analyzed environmental problems in a very similar framework.

4.   This formulation of the problem draws heavily on Heal (1979), which discusses inter alia the optimal depletion policy for an exhaustible resource whose initial stock is unknown. The analogy with the present problem will be immediately clear. This problem was studied earlier by Cropper (1976, Sec. III), Kemp (1976), Gilbert (1976), and Loury (1978).

5.   Cropper (1976), in a related but more complex model, investigates possible stationary solutions: she can characterize them, but not guarantee their existence.

6.   An analogous stochastic optimization problem is discussed in Dasgupta et al. (1976, 1980). There the same assumptions about the probabilities have a very clear grounding in the structure of the problem.

7.   The problem discussed in Dasgupta and Heal (1974) could be regarded as the "pure depletion" version of the present problem. There resource depletion has no impact on the stochastic process to which the economy is subject.

REFERENCES

Cropper, M. L., "Regulating Activities with Catastrophic Environmental Effects." *Journal of Environmental Economics and Management* (1976).

Dasgupta, P. S. and G. M. Heal, "The Optimal Depletion of Exhaustible Resources." *Review of Economic Studies*, Symposium, 1974.

Dasgupta, P. S., G. M. Heal and M. K. Majumdar, "Resource Depletion and Research and Development." In M. D. Intriligator (ed.), *Frontiers of Quantitative Economics*, Vol. III.B. Amsterdam: North Holland, 1976.

Dasgupta, P. S., G. M. Heal and A. K. Pant, "Optimising R and D Expenditure in the Development of Resource Substitutes." *Applied Mathematical Modelling* (1980).

Frisken, W. R., *The Atmospheric Environment*. Baltimore: Johns Hopkins Press for Resources for the Future Inc.

Gilbert, R. J., "Optimal Depletion of an Uncertain Stock." I.M.S.S.S. Stanford Discussion Paper No. 207, 1976.

Heal, G. M., "Uncertainty and the Optimal Supply Policy for an Exhaustible Resource." In R. Pindyck (ed.), *Advances in the Economics of Energy and Resources*, Vol. 2. Greenwich, Conn.: JAI Press, 1979.

Heal, G. M., "The Use of Common Property Resources." In V. Kerry Smith and John V. Krutilla (eds.), *Explorations in Natural Resource Economics*. Baltimore: Johns Hopkins Press for Resources for the Future, 1982.

Henry, C., "Option Values in the Economics of Irreplacable Assets." *Review of Economic Studies*, Symposium, 1974.

International Workshop on Climate Issues, *International Perspectives on the Study of Climate and Society*. Washington, D.C.: National Academy of Sciences, 1978.

Kemp, M. C., "How to Eat a Cake of Unknown Size." Chapter 23 in M. Kemp, *Three Topics in the Theory of International Trade*. Amsterdam: North Holland, 1976.

Larmuth, J., "Desert and Man." In *Third World Quarterly*, 1979.

Loury, G. C., "The Optimal Exploitation of an Unknown Reserve." *Review of Economic Studies* (October 1978).

Malinvaud, Edmund, *Lectures in Microeconomic Theory*. Amsterdam: North Holland, 1972.

Theil, Henri, *Economic Forecasts and Policy*. Amsterdam: North Holland, 1961.

THE HEDONIC PRICE TECHNIQUE
AND THE VALUE OF CLIMATE AS A
RESOURCE

A. Myrick Freeman, III

I.   INTRODUCTION

Human activity could lead to changes in climate at a global, regional, or local level. Such climatic changes could affect human welfare through a variety of channels. For example, changes in rainfall or temperature could affect agricultural productivity. The availability and cost of raw materials could be affected. Populations could respond to changes in climate by migration and the relocation of the economic activity. And there might be direct effects on utility or welfare due to changes in the amenity attributes of climate.

There are difficult conceptual and empirical problems in predicting, quantifying, and valuing these potential effects of climate change. For example, it seems likely that any economic assessment would have to

Advances in Applied Micro-Economics, Volume 3, pages 169–186.
Copyright © 1984 by JAI Press Inc.
All rights of reproduction in any form reserved.
ISBN: 0-89232-398-1

deal with the fact that many prices would be affected simultaneously, thus requiring a general equilibrium framework. Also, interregional transfers of economic activity and welfare may be significant, thus calling for an explicit analysis of redistribution effects. Finally, the time span over which climate changes are likely to occur may make the typical neoclassical assumptions of fixed technology and unchanging tastes and preferences implausible.

For these reasons, the conventional tools and methods of welfare economics and benefit estimation may not be very useful in dealing with the special features of climate change. There must be a search for new tools and methods. The purpose of this paper is to consider one such tool which has been applied with some success to the problem of using housing price data to measure the demand for the aesthetic and amenity aspects of cleaner air—the hedonic price technique. I will examine to what extent the hedonic price technique can be used to analyze the economic effects of differences in climate variables across regions, and whether information from the hedonic price technique can be used to shed some light on the shadow prices or values of climate attributes. The hedonic price approach is a technique for measuring the implicit prices of goods or characteristics that are not themselves explicitly traded in markets but which are characteristics of marketed goods. Section II of this paper reviews the hedonic price technique. Section III describes how information on implicit prices of characteristics might be used to estimate the inverse demand functions or marginal willingness to pay functions for these characteristics. I then turn to a discussion of the possible use of variations in property values and wage rates across regions as a means of inferring values of those climatic attributes that vary across regions.

II.   A REVIEW OF THE HEDONIC PRICE THEORY

The hedonic technique is a method for estimating the implicit prices of the characteristics which differentiate closely related products in a product class. The hedonic price technique was developed by Griliches (1971) and others initially for the purpose of estimating the value of quality change in consumer goods. Rosen (1974) has used the hedonic price concept to analyze the supply and demand of the characteristics which differentiate products in competitive markets. Anderson and Crocker (1972), Bishop and Cicchetti (1975), and Freeman (1974, 1979a) have also discussed the application of the hedonic price technique to the measurement of the demand for environmental quality characteristics such as clean air.

In principle, if there are enough finely differentiated models of a good within a product class, each with different combinations of characteristics, it is possible to estimate an implicit price relationship which gives the

price of any model as a function of the quantities of its various characteristics. The derivatives of this function with respect to the characteristics give the implicit prices. For example, the difference in price between
two automobile models which have engines of different horsepower but
which are identical in all other respects can be interpreted as the implicit
price of horsepower.

It is necessary to assume that all of the relevant models are sold in a
single market in which all potential buyers have full information on the
range of alternatives and their prices. It is also necessary to assume that
the market is in equilibrium and that these prices just clear the market.[1]

More formally, let X represent the product or commodity class. Any
unit of X, say x_i, can be completely described by a vector of its characteristics, Z_j. The price of x_i is a function of the levels of these characteristics:

$$P_{xi} = P_x(Z_{i1}, \ldots, Z_{ij}, \ldots, Z_{im}). \tag{1}$$

The function P_x is the hedonic or implicit price function for X. If P_x can
be estimated from the observations of the prices and characteristics of
different models, the price of any possible model could be calculated from
knowledge of its characteristics. The marginal implicit price of a characteristic can be found by differentiating the implicit price function with
respect to that characteristic. Thus,

$$\frac{\partial P_x}{\partial Z_j} = P_{zj}(Z_j) \tag{2}$$

gives the increase in expenditure on X that is required to obtain a model
with one more unit of Z_j, other things equal.

If Eq. (1) is linear in the characteristics, then the implicit prices are
constants for households. But if Eq. (1) is nonlinear, then the implicit
price of an additional unit of a characteristic depends on the quantity of
the characteristic being purchased and, depending upon the functional
form of (1), perhaps on the quantities of other characteristics as well.
Equation (1) need not be linear. Linearity will occur only if consumers
can "arbitrage" characteristics by untying and repackaging bundles of
attributes (Rosen, 1974, pp. 37–38). For example, if individuals are indifferent as to the choice between owning two 6-foot long cars and one
12-foot car, other things equal, they can create equivalents of 12-foot cars
by repackaging smaller units. If both sizes exist on the market, the larger
size must sell at twice the price of the smaller one and the implicit price
function will be linear in length. The example suggests that nonlinearity
will not be uncommon.

Assume that Eq. (1) has been estimated for housing in an urban area.
If the household is assumed to be a price taker in the market for this good,

it can be viewed as facing an array of implicit marginal price schedules for various characteristics. A household maximizes its utility by simultaneously moving along a marginal price schedule for each characteristic until it reaches a point where its marginal willingness to pay for an additional unit of a characteristic just equals the marginal implicit price of that characteristic. If a household is in equilibrium, the marginal implicit prices associated with the model chosen must be equal to the corresponding marginal willingnesses to pay for these characteristics.

Figure 1(a) shows the partial relationship between the price of a good and one of its characteristics, Z_j, as estimated from Eq. (1) holding all other characteristics constant. Figure 1(b) shows $P_{Z_j}(Z_j)$, the marginal implicit price of Z_j. It also shows the demand functions for Z_j for two households, A and B, and the equilibrium positions of these households. Each household chooses a model such that its marginal willingness to pay for Z_j is equated with the marginal implicit price of Z_j. Thus the implicit price function is a locus of household equilibrium marginal willingnesses to pay.

The marginal implicit price paid by a household for a characteristic can be interpreted as the shadow price or value of that characteristic. The benefit of a marginal change in the level of the characteristic available to all households can be found by summing the marginal implicit prices for all households. But it is not possible to compute benefits for nonmarginal changes in the characteristic without knowledge of the demand or inverse demand functions for the characteristic.[2] Estimation of demand functions is discussed in the next section. It also should be noted that the technique yields a unique shadow price for the characteristic only when the hedonic

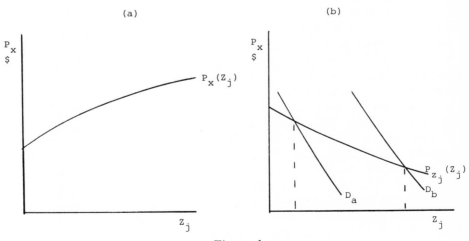

Figure 1

equation is linear. Otherwise the shadow price is itself a function of the level of the characteristic taken by each household.

III. ESTIMATING DEMAND FUNCTIONS AND BENEFITS

The analysis described in the preceding section provides a measure of the implicit price of the characteristic; but it does not directly reveal or identify the demand function for the characteristic. Here I shall take up two questions: First, under what circumstances it is possible to identify the underlying demand or inverse demand function on the basis of the data on marginal implicit prices and quantities given by Eq. (1)? The second question concerns the specification of the inverse demand function, especially what variables need to be included.

Taking up the latter specification question first, demand estimation requires the assumption of identical utility functions or underlying structures of preferences for all households. Whenever observations of households' prices and quantities are pooled to estimate demand functions, it is necessary to assume that all households in the pool have structures of demand which are the same except for those variables which are controlled for in the regression equation. The control variables normally include income, but they also could be extended to include other socio-economic characteristics postulated to affect demand. Examples might include age, family size, or education.

Some type of restriction on the assumed form of the underlying utility function may be useful in simplifying the demand or inverse demand function to be estimated. Separability is perhaps the most helpful form of restriction in that it makes the demand for a good a function only of the prices of those goods in the same utility branch. Other prices and quantities can be omitted from the demand function being estimated without biasing the price coefficients. The simplest case is if the utility function is separable in the climate characteristic. Then the inverse demand function makes marginal willingness to pay a function only of the characteristic, income, and other taste parameters.

If the utility function is not in fact separable, then the omission of other price or quantity variables will bias the estimate of the effect of the climate characteristic on marginal willingness to pay. A less restrictive assumption would be that the utility function is separable in the attributes of the differentiated good. Even this form of separability may be too restrictive in principle. There could be other goods or services which are either complements to or substitutes for various attributes of this good. However, even where no separability conditions can be reasonably invoked, one can still reasonably argue that many cross-price effects are close enough to zero to be ignored. Also, individuals in a single unified market

face identical prices for most undifferentiated goods and services. Therefore, the prices of those goods that are the same across all individuals
can be omitted from the demand function specification. Finally, there may
be cases where one would expect the marginal willingness to pay for a
characteristic to depend upon the quantity of some other good or service.
An example might be the ownership of musical instruments and the marginal willingness to pay to avoid noise. Then variables reflecting these
consumption patterns should be included in the marginal willingness to
pay function. But the justification is that they are proxies for differences
in the underlying preference structure. Whether some form of separability
assumption should be invoked seems not to be an important question in
itself. What is important is the list of variables to be included in the model
specification. And here judgment and experience with the data will probably turn out to be the best guide.

Turning now to the question of identification, there are two special
cases. First, if the hedonic price function is linear in the characteristic,
estimation of the demand function is not possible. This is because the
marginal implicit price is constant for all households. With no variation
in implicit prices across the data set, nothing is revealed about the relationship between implicit price and quantity of the characteristic. However, even in this case the income elasticity of demand could be estimated.
The second special case arises when all households have identical incomes
and utility functions. In this case, the marginal implicit price function,
Eq. (2), is itself the demand function. Recall that the marginal implicit
price curve is a locus of points on households' demand curves. With
identical incomes and utility functions, these points all fall on the same
marginal willingness to pay curve.

Where neither special case applies, Sherwin Rosen (1974) and I (Freeman, 1979a) had argued that the identification problem would be solved
with the appropriate analysis of the supply side of the market. We argued
that estimates of marginal implicit prices from a single market could be
used to estimate the demand function for the individuals in that market
if those individuals had identical utility functions and provided that the
standard identification problem could be solved. It has now become apparent that our analysis was incorrect. James N. Brown and Harvey S.
Rosen (1982) have shown that these conditions are not sufficient. The
problem is that the data from a single market reveal only the outcome of
a single market experiment. As Brown and Rosen (1982, p. 176) put it:

> Contrary to [Sherwin] Rosen's original statement, we claim that marginal attribute
> prices constructed as above will not necessarily play the same role in estimation that
> direct observations on prices would play if they were available. Because such con-
> structed prices are created only from observed sample quantities, any new information
> that they may provide (i.e., any information beyond that already provided directly

by observed sample quantities) can only come from *a priori* restrictions placed on the functional form of the price function [$P_X(Z)$]. In the absence of such additional restrictions, second-stage "structural" estimation of the sort suggested by Rosen may only reproduce the information already provided by the first-stage estimation of the [$P_X(Z)$] function. [Notation in brackets changed by the present author.]

Although the Freeman–Rosen technique for identifying demand functions is invalid, there are at least two ways in which estimates of demand functions can be obtained from hedonic analysis. The first is to increase the quantity of information contained in marginal implicit prices by estimating hedonic price functions for several separate markets and then pooling the cross-sectional data on the assumption that the underlying structure of supply and demand is the same in all markets (Freeman, 1974; Brown and Rosen, 1982). The second approach is to impose additional structure on the problem by invoking a priori assumptions about the form of the underlying utility function. For example, Quigley (1982) has shown how estimates of marginal implicit prices from a single market can be used to estimate the parameters of the previously specified generalized constant elasticity of substitution utility function. If the utility function correctly describes preferences, then, once its parameters are known, estimating the benefits of changes in attributes is straightforward.

In summary, in the last two sections we have outlined the hedonic theory of implicit price estimation and shown that implicit prices of non-marketed attributes can be derived from the hedonic price function. Furthermore, with reasonable assumptions, it is possible to use implicit price and quantity information to identify demand functions for characteristics. Once the household marginal willingness to pay function has been identified, it is possible to provide ex ante estimates of the benefits of postulated changes in the levels of characteristics or in their marginal implicit prices. This is done by integrating the relevant demand or inverse demand function over the relevant range. These estimates have the advantage of being derived directly from the demand functions as manifestations of the underlying utility functions. They do not have some of the problems of interpretation which plague ex post observations of responses to actual climate changes: Is adjustment complete? Did other variables change violating ceteris paribus assumptions? And so forth.

IV.   APPLYING THE TECHNIQUE TO CLIMATE

In this section, I shall take up several issues concerning the application of the hedonic price technique to climate as a characteristic which differentiates housing, agricultural land, and jobs across regions. In broad terms, the questions to be addressed are the following: Is estimation of hedonic price functions feasible? How are they to be interpreted? And can they be used to provide information on the structure of demand for climatic characteristics? These questions are addressed in the context of the specification of climate and its influence on utility, and the possible application of the hedonic technique to prices of housing, agricultural land, and labor.

How Does Climate Enter Utility Functions?

One problem, of course, is that climate is not a one-dimensional variable. A reasonably complete description of the climate at a particular point in space would include data on both the mean and the variation of parameters such as temperature, precipitation, wind, humidity, and perhaps other dimensions of climate. The question of which variables and which moments of their probability distributions are most important to people and hence should be included in hedonic price functions can only be settled by further empirical research.

A more fundamental problem arises because it does not appear to be possible on a priori grounds to specify the sign with which some climate variables enter utility functions—and therefore the expected sign of these variables in hedonic price functions. An implicit assumption in the literature on the hedonic price technique is that characteristics are unambiguously either good or bad. But both casual observation and some more formal evidence suggest that preferences for climate variables are heterogeneous. For example, some people seem to prefer the more rigorous climate of New England, with its lower average temperature and greater extremes, whereas others prefer the warmth and greater uniformity of southern California. More formal evidence comes from a survey conducted by Bradley and Larson (1975). They surveyed people who had recently moved to Riverside, California, to determine their preferences with regard to number of rain days, number of hot days (temperature greater than 90°F), and number of cold days (temperature less than 30°F). The results showed that the sample divided nearly evenly with respect to preferences for rainy days, that is, with some preferring more and others preferring fewer rainy days. There was a slight preference for more hot days. But still, over one-third of the sample preferred fewer hot days. Two-thirds of the sample preferred fewer cold days, but almost 20 percent of the sample preferred more cold days.

Consider the characteristic Z_j, which by assumption can take values ranging from zero to $\bar{Z}_j$. Figure 2 shows demand functions for Z_j for four groups of households. The demand function (D_a) for Group "a" shows that, for all positive values of the characteristic, Z affects utility negatively. Households in this group would have to receive increasing compensation to induce them to accept larger quantities of Z_j. Households in Group "d"

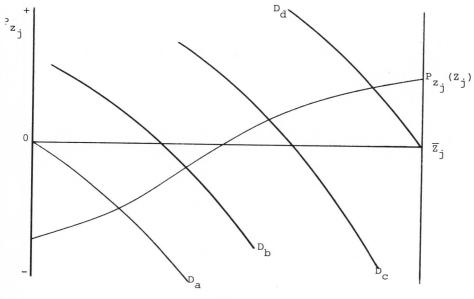

Figure 2

have a positive preference or willingness to pay for Z_j at all levels. Households in Groups "b" and "c" have optimal levels of the characteristic and are willing to pay positive amounts to increase the amount of Z_j up to their optimum, but require compensation to accept further Z_j beyond their optimum.

The numbers of households in each group interact with the available supplies of models with different levels of Z_j to determine an equilibrium hedonic price function which just clears the market. The hedonic price function could take a variety of shapes. For example, it could be U-shaped, in which case it would yield a marginal implicit price function that was upward sloping with both negative and positive segments, as is that shown in Figure 2. But other shapes and forms are equally plausible, depending upon the interaction of demand and supply of the characteristic.

One implication of this analysis is that it is not possible to specify a priori the functional form of the hedonic price function to be estimated. It is necessary to experiment with a variety of functional forms, including those which would allow for a change of sign in the marginal implicit price function as the magnitude of the characteristic changes. To my knowledge, no hedonic price studies of climate variables have attempted to do this.

If the marginal implicit price function has been correctly estimated, is it then possible to estimate the demand functions for the characteristics? Whenever observations of households' prices and quantities are pooled to estimate demand functions, it is necessary to assume that all households in the pool have structures of demand which are the same except for those variables which are controlled for in the regression equation. The control variables normally include income but could also be extended to include other socioeconomic characteristics postulated to effect demand. The demand functions of Figure 2 could be estimated from the implicit price data only if it were possible to parameterize the taste differences across the different groups of households and to include that parameter as a control variable on the assumption that otherwise preferences were identical across all groups of households. It may be possible to do this if one can identify observable characteristics of households which can be taken as proxies for the structural differences in utility. For example, number of preschool and school-aged children might be a proxy for strong demand for quality of schools in the analysis of housing prices.

Finally, where preferences for the characteristic are heterogeneous, a marginal increase in the level of the characteristic in all models purchased by households could have little or no net effect on welfare. For example, in Figure 2, a marginal increase in Z_j for all units of the good would impose marginal losses on households in Groups "a" and "b" and marginal gains in households in Groups "c" and "d". Net benefits could be positive, negative, or zero. And it is possible that the only significant impact on welfare would arise through the redistribution of benefits across households.

Residential Property Values

Since measures of climate vary across space, these measures can be considered as characteristics of locations. There is a substantial body of research on the influence of locational characteristics such as proximity to the central city or air quality on housing values in urban areas.[3] This suggests the possibility of using housing values to estimate the marginal implicit prices and, perhaps, demand functions for climate variables.

One approach is simply to add some measures of climate as explanatory variables in the analysis of housing values in an urban housing market. The main question is whether there is sufficient variation in the climate variables within the urban area to lead to statistically significant results. Crocker et al. (1975) introduced three measures of climate into an earlier analysis of the determinants of housing values in the Washington, D.C., SMSA (standard metropolitan statistical area). The measures were average annual minimum temperature, average annual precipitation, and spring–winter temperature difference. Each variable was entered singly in a separate regression equation. The equations were linear in the logs. None of the climate measures was significant. These results are inconclusive, however, for two reasons. The first is the small range of variation of the climate variables within the single urban area. The second is that the authors acknowledge some uncertainty as to the expected sign of two of the climate measures. But, as I argued above, it is possible that households in the urban area had heterogeneous tastes regarding these variables. If this were the case, then the log linear functional form could be a misspecification and the estimated regression coefficients could be biased toward zero.

A second approach is to take advantage of the substantial variation in climate across some urban areas by pooling data from several cities in a single regression equation.[4] However, this requires the assumption that all housing units in the sample are part of a single unified housing market. If this is not the case, then the market can be said to be segmented or stratified. Straszheim (1974) was the first to raise the question of market segmentation in the context of estimating hedonic price functions for housing. He argued that even in a single urban area, the housing market really consisted of a series of separate, compartmentalized submarkets with different hedonic price functions in each segment. As evidence in support of the segmentation hypothesis, Straszheim showed that estimating separate hedonic price functions for different geographic areas around San Francisco Bay reduced the sum of squared errors for the sample as a whole.[5]

For different hedonic price functions to exist in a market, two conditions must be met. First, purchasers in one market stratum must not participate significantly in other market strata. In other words, there must be some barrier to the ability of buyers to move among market strata. These barriers could be due to geography, discrimination, or lack of information. The second condition is that either the structure of demand, the structure of supply, or both must be different across strata. Either buyers in separate submarkets must have different structures of demands or the structure of characteristics of the housing stocks must be different. Even with buyer immobility, if demand and supply structures are the same in all strata, they will produce similar structures of hedonic prices. And perfect mobility and information on the part of buyers will eliminate differences in the implicit prices for any characteristic across market strata.

It should be noted that the existence of market segmentation does not render the hedonic price technique invalid; rather, it makes its application more difficult. If the appropriate basis for segmentation can be identified, it is conceptually possible to estimate separate implicit price functions for each submarket. Although these functions would be different across markets, they each would accurately reflect the outcome of market processes in each submarket. Thus they could be used to estimate equilibrium marginal willingnesses to pay.

Applying this analysis to the case of using housing price data from several cities, it seems likely that lack of mobility and information costs would lead to segmentation and differences in price structures across cities. But if separate equations are estimated for each segment, that is, each city, then climate variation within the segment may not be sufficient to yield statistically significant results.

A third alternative is to estimate separate hedonic equations for several urban areas, omitting climate variables, and then to investigate the influence of climate on the marginal implicit price functions for certain attributes. To the extent that a climate variable such as heating degree days was related to a housing attribute such as quantity of insulation, marginal implicit price functions could be affected by climate in such a way as to permit some inferences about the value of climate change.

To be more specific, let Z_{jk} represent the jth attribute of housing in the kth city, and C_k represent climate in the kth city. After estimating implicit price functions for housing of the form of Eq. (1) for each city, it is possible to compute the marginal implicit price function for an attribute Z_j for each city. Assume that there is some a priori basis for hypothesizing that the demand for this attribute is a function of climate, among other things. For expositional purposes, assume that the implicit price functions are linear in the logs.[6] Then the marginal implicit price function for Z_j in city k is

$$P_{Zjk} = b_{jk} \frac{P_{Xk}}{Z_{jk}},\qquad(3)$$

where b_{jk} is the estimated coefficient on Z_j in city k. If the demand for Z_j is related to climate, then climate differences across cities should have an impact on the marginal implicit price functions. A reasonable formulation would be

$$b_{jk} = d + eC_k,\qquad(4)$$

which can be estimated from the data across cities.[7] The economic implications of this can be seen by substituting (4) into (3):

$$P_{Zjk} = d \frac{P_{Xk}}{Z_{jk}} + eC_k \frac{P_{Xk}}{Z_{jk}}.\qquad(5)$$

This shows that the effect of Z_j on housing prices can be partitioned into two components, a stable bivariate relationship depending on Z_j alone and identical across cities and a component reflecting an interaction between Z_j and climate.

It should be possible to use this information to carry out the second stage of hedonic analysis and estimate inverse demand functions. This would be done by computing $P_{Z_{jk}}$ for each household in each city, assuming that it is equal to marginal willingness to pay for Z_j, and using an estimating technique appropriate to this specification of the supply side. The inverse demand for Z_j would be a function of Z_j, income, climate, and perhaps other variables.

Finally, it might in some cases be possible to use this relationship to compute benefits for changes in climate by assuming weak complementarity between C and Z_j.[8] A climate change would shift the demand curve for Z_j. The benefit would be the relevant area between the two demand curves.

Although this approach may have theoretical appeal, it is an open question whether it will turn out to be of practical importance. There are three points to be made. First, the approach assumes a particular structure for the way that climate affects the demands for attributes, and whether this is valid can only be determined by empirical research. Second, climate might affect housing demand and prices through several channels or attributes. Any benefit estimate would be incomplete unless it identified and examined all of the relationships between climate and the relevant attributes prices. Finally, and perhaps of most importance, this approach can only capture those aspects of climate change which work themselves out through some complementary or substitute relationship with other housing attributes. If the utility function is separable in climate, then climate differences will have no effect on the marginal implicit prices of other attributes; and this analysis could not shed any light on the way climate differences affect housing prices or utility.

Agricultural Land Prices

Agricultural land is an asset used in the production of marketed goods. Although the hedonic price technique was developed to deal with characteristics entering directly into household utility functions, the technique can be applied to producers' goods as well. Assume that all farmers have made their optimizing or profit-maximizing adjustment to climate conditions, soil conditions, demand, technological opportunities, and so forth. Further, assume that there are no speculative or developmental premia built into the structure of land prices. Given these assumptions, land prices can be taken as measures of the present values of the stream of agricultural rents. A regression of land prices on the attributes of land including location and climate would give a hedonic price function explaining land prices as a function of the productive characteristics of land. The marginal implicit price of a characteristic could be interpreted as the value of marginal product of that characteristic.

It should be noted that even in the case of agricultural land, it may not be possible to specify a priori the signs with which some climate variables enter the hedonic price function. For some fertility variables such as pH and some climate variables such as rainfall, there may be optimum values with the marginal implicit prices decreasing for changes away from the optimum level on either direction.

It would be necessary to utilize price data for land over a substantial geographic area to assure sufficient variation in the climate measures. Because of this, one could question whether the condition of a single market would be met. On the one hand, farmers participate in a national market for their outputs and major inputs (equipment, seed, fertilizer). But on the other hand, information costs, barriers to mobility, local markets for farm labor, and so forth may combine to prevent differences in price structures from being eliminated over time. Any empirical study of agricultural land prices should include tests for the presence of market segmentation.

If the hedonic price functions and marginal implicit prices can be estimated, it should be possible to use this data to estimate demand functions for the attributes of agricultural land. The specification of the attribute demand functions can be derived from the underlying agricultural production function. Then the benefits or costs of climate change can be estimated by integrating under the appropriate attribute demand functions.

Wages

There have been several studies of the determinants of wage rates which have been based implicitly or explicitly on hedonic price theory. For example, Lucas (1977) examined the relationship between wage rates and certain job characteristics such as work environment, repetitious nature of the work, and supervisory responsibility. Others have looked at the relationship between wage rates and risk of accident, ill health, and mortality (Thaler and Rosen, 1976; Smith, 1976; Viscusi, 1976). Some studies have focused not on job characteristics but on the characteristics of the urban areas in which the jobs are located, for example, population density and urbanization (Nordhaus and Tobin, 1972; Meyer and Leone, 1977), and climate (Hoch and Drake, 1974; Meyer and Leone, 1977).

When the hedonic price technique is applied to the study of wage rates, the theory must be modified to take account of an important feature of labor market. In the typical application of the theory, the producer is viewed as selling a good embodying a package of characteristics and as being indifferent to the characteristics of the purchaser of the good. In wage studies, the employer is viewed as selling a package of job characteristics (including environmental characteristics associated with the job location); but at the same time the employer is purchasing work effort and cannot be indifferent to the productive characteristics of employees. Lucas (1977) has shown that in these circumstances the hedonic wage equation can be interpreted as a reduced-form equation reflecting the interaction of workers' demands for job characteristics and employers' demand for worker characteristics. Both worker and job characteristics should be included as arguments in the estimated wage equation. However, neither of the hedonic wage rates studies utilizing climate variables (Hoch and Drake, 1974; Meyer and Leone, 1977) used worker characteristics in their regression analyses.

The problem of market segmentation referred to above in the discussion of property value studies can also arise in the hedonic analysis of wage rates. It is necessary that all of the jobs and/or workers for which wage data are analyzed be part of a single unified market. In actuality, labor markets can be segmented on the basis of geography with moving costs and lack of information on job alternatives imposing barriers between labor markets in different parts of the country with different climate characteristics. Markets can also be segmented on the basis of education and skill requirements, for example, as between blue collar and professional/managerial workers. Geographic segmentation can lead to different marginal implicit price schedules in different regions. Segmentation on the basis of occupation or educational level can lead to different marginal implicit price functions across occupational categories. If it can be assumed that the underlying demand functions are the same across market segments, then the inverse demand function can be estimated directly.

One approach to the problem of geographic segmentation is to estimate the hedonic wage function only for occupational groups which are believed on a priori grounds to be part of a national labor market. For example, Meyer and Leone (1977) estimated separate hedonic wage functions for skilled workers and for computer analysts on the assumption that workers in these categories would be more aware of job opportunities in other cities. In general, the extent of market segmentation and its significance for empirical estimation of hedonic wage functions is not known. This is one of the first issues which must be settled if substantial efforts are to be made to estimate the values of climate variables from hedonic analysis of wage data.

V. CONCLUSIONS

Climate can be considered to be a characteristic differentiating classes of goods such as houses, agricultural land, and jobs. Thus in principle it may be possible to utilize the hedonic price technique to estimate the marginal implicit prices of climate characteristics and, perhaps, to estimate the relevant demand or inverse demand functions for these characteristics. However, this brief review of the hedonic price technique and its application to climate has uncovered two potentially significant problems:

The first is heterogeneous tastes for climate characteristics and the possibility that a given climate variable might at the same time be both a good and a bad for different subgroups of the relevant population. This does not preclude the possibility of hedonic price estimation. But it makes the estimation more difficult because the model specification and the estimation technique should allow for the possibility that the hedonic price function may have both positively and negatively sloped segments. This also makes estimation of demand functions more difficult since it is necessary to control for those characteristics of individuals which account for the heterogeneity of preferences.

The second problem is the possibility of market segmentation. Study areas must be large enough to provide substantial variation in climate characteristics. But communication costs, moving costs, and other barriers to mobility may prevent such large areas from developing into single unified markets with a single structure of implicit prices throughout the area.

Neither of these problems makes it impossible in principle to utilize the hedonic price technique in the analysis of climate data. However, if the use of the hedonic price technique is to be extended beyond its traditional areas of application (for example, to urban property value differences and air quality), then these problems must be confronted head on.

ACKNOWLEDGMENT

I am grateful to V. Kerry Smith for a number of helpful comments on an earlier draft.

NOTES

1. For a further discussion of these assumptions, particularly the equilibrium assumption, and an assessment of some criticisms of the application of the hedonic technique to the analysis of housing values, see Freeman (1979b).

2. For a discussion of some approaches to approximating the benefits of nonmarginal changes, see Freeman (1979a, pp. 143–147).

3. See Freeman (1979a,b) for discussions of conceptual and empirical issues in this body of research and surveys of recent results.

4. See, for example, Smith (1976).

5. For further discussion of evidence on segmentation in urban housing markets, see Freeman (1979b).

6. For discussion of the importance of proper specification and some of the features of alternative functional forms, see Freeman (1979a, pp. 139–142).

7. For further discussion of this approach and the econometric issues involved, see Saxonhouse (1977).

8. See Mäler (1974, pp. 183–189) and Freeman (1979a, pp. 72–79).

REFERENCES

Anderson, Robert J., and Thomas Crocker, "Air Pollution and Property Values: A Reply." *Review of Economics and Statistics*, 54 (November 1972):470–473.

Bishop, John, and Charles Cicchetti, "Some Institutional and Conceptual Thoughts on the Measurement of Indirect and Intangible Benefits and Costs." In Henry M. Peskin and Eugene P. Seskin (eds.), *Cost Benefit Analysis and Water Pollution Policy*. Washington, D.C.: The Urban Institute, 1975.

Bradley, Richard, and Robert Larson, "Conceptualization of Aesthetic Damages Induced by Climatic Change." In U.S. Department of Transportation, *Economic and Social Measures of Biologic and Climatic Change*, Climatic Impact Assessment Program, monograph 6. Washington, D.C.: U.S. Department of Transportation, 1975.

Brown, James N., and Harvey S. Rosen, "On the Estimation of Structural Hedonic Price Models." *Econometrica* 50(May 1982):765–768.

Crocker, Thomas, Larry Eubanks, and Robert Horst, Jr. "Estimation of Climatic Impact Through Property Value Analysis." In U.S. Department of Transportation, *Economic and Social Measures of Biologic and Climatic Change*, Climatic Impact Assessment Program, monograph 6. Washington, D.C.: U.S. Department of Transportation, 1975.

Freeman, A. Myrick, III, "On Estimating Air Pollution Control Benefits from Land Value Studies." *Journal of Environmental Economics and Management* 1(May 1974):74–83.

———, *The Benefits of Environmental Improvement: Theory and Practice*. Washington, D.C.: The Johns Hopkins University Press, 1979a.

———, "Hedonic Prices, Property Values and Measuring Environmental Benefits: A Survey of the Issues." *Scandinavian Journal of Economics* 81(1979b):154–173.

Griliches, Zvi (ed.), *Price Indexes and Quality Change*. Cambridge, Mass.: Harvard University Press, 1971.

Hoch, Irving with Judith Drake, "Wages, Climate and The Quality of Life." *Journal of Environmental Economics and Management* 1(1974):268–295.

Lucas, Robert E. B., "Hedonic Wage Equations and Psychic Wages in the Returns to Schooling." *American Economic Review* 67(September 1977):549–558.

Mäler, Karl-Göran, *Environmental Economics: A Theoretical Inquiry*. Baltimore: Johns Hopkins University Press, 1974.

Meyer, John R., and Robert A. Leone, "The Urban Disamenity Revisited." In Lowdon Wingo and Alan Evans (eds.), *Public Economics and the Quality of Life*. Baltimore: Johns Hopkins University Press, 1977.

Nordhaus, William D., and James Tobin, "Is Growth Obsolete?" In National Bureau of Economic Research, 50th Anniversary Colloquium, Volume 5, *Economic Growth*. New York, National Bureau of Economic Research, 1972.

Quigley, John M., "Nonlinear Budget Constraints and Consumer Demand: An Application to Public Programs for Residential Housing." *Journal of Urban Economics* 12(September 1982):177–201.

Rosen, Sherwin, "Hedonic Prices and Implicit Markets: Product Differentiation in Pure Competition." *Journal of Political Economy* 82(January/February 1974):34–55.

Saxonhouse, Gary R., "Regressions from Samples Having Different Characteristics." *Review of Economics and Statistics* 59(May 1977):234–237.

Smith, Robert S., *The Occupational Safety and Health Act: Its Goals and Achievements.* Washington, D.C.: American Enterprise Institute for Public Policy Research, 1976.

Smith, V. Kerry, *The Economic Consequences of Air Pollution.* Cambridge, Mass.: Ballinger, 1976.

Straszheim, Mahlon, "Hedonic Estimation of Housing Market Prices: A Further Comment." *Review of Economics and Statistics* 56(August 1974):404–406.

Thaler, Richard H., and Sherwin Rosen, "The Value of Saving A Life: Evidence From the Labor Market." In N. E. Terleckyj (ed.), *Household Production and Consumption.* New York: Columbia University Press, 1976.

Viscusi, W. Kip, "Labor Market Valuations of Life and Limb: Empirical Evidence and Policy Implications." *Public Policy* 26(Summer 1976):359–386.

PART III

ISSUES IN MODELING PUBLIC PROVISION OF EDUCATION AND CRIME PROTECTION

INTRODUCTION TO PART III

Ann Dryden Witte

The three papers in Part III are quite different from those in Parts I and II. They are concerned with the effect of public agency actions on desired social outcomes (e.g., student achievement levels, crime rates). This is an extremely important issue and one that provides a wealth of challenges to the applied researcher. To understand how agency actions affect social outcomes, the researcher must understand the way in which the agency provides its goods or services and the way in which the public goods and services provided affect the desired social outcome. Further, the researcher desiring to provide policy guidance must take great care in data collection and analysis. One of the major conclusions that can be drawn for the papers in Part III is that no single study can provide definitive policy prescriptions. We would do better to encourage a series of studies and to use only those results which emerge consistently as guides to policymaking. Other insights and research suggestions emerge from a more detailed consideration of the three papers in this part.

Professor Summers and Wolfe conduct a process analysis of the provision of junior high school education. Elsewhere (Summers and Wolfe, 1977; Witte, 1980) they have argued that the traditional economic ap-

Advances in Applied Micro-Economics, Volume 3, pages 189–197.
Copyright © 1984 by JAI Press Inc.
All rights of reproduction in any form reserved.
ISBN: 0-89232-398-1

proach to analyzing the nature of productive activity (i.e., the estimation of profit functions, production functions, cost functions, and factor demand equations) which was developed for the private sector is not appropriate for an analysis of the provision of educational services. They feel that differences in goals, the heterogeneity of both inputs and outputs, and pervasive economic inefficiency make the traditional economic approaches inappropriate. Researchers studying the provision of other public goods and services have reached conflicting conclusions regarding the usefulness of the economic approach.[1] Those studying public agencies which produce physical outputs (e.g., water, electricity, refuse collection) with well-defined inputs and known technological processes find economic constructs such as production and cost functions most useful in understanding the way in which goods are provided. Traditional economic constructs, when adjusted for differences in input and output quality and external constraints imposed on the public manager (e.g., legal due process, approved medical procedures) have proven useful in studying intermediate types of publically provided goods and services (e.g., hospitals, libraries, prisons). Traditional economic constructs appear to be least useful for analyzing the provision of public services that require extensive interaction between public employees and the individuals receiving services (e.g., education, probation and parole, and other social services) or where projection of demand is difficult (e.g., police and fire departments). For social services individual skills are extremely important, and the exact way in which services are provided may vary substantially from employee to employee. When analyzing these kinds of services, a type of process analysis which uses client (e.g., pupil) specific data may be most helpful in providing insights concerning the nature of the productive process.

What are the major factors which determine whether or not traditional economic constructs will prove useful when analyzing a public organization? One observation seems obvious: traditional economic constructs will prove most useful when analyzing goods which are both publically and privately provided (e.g., water, refuse collection). Other distinctions are more difficult to draw. Niskanen (1971) has suggested that public organizations are most likely to cost minimize (a traditional economic goal) when the nature of the productive process is relatively well known, when output can be relatively easily projected, and when public interest in and desire for the service is not excessive. Panelists at a session on the "Economics of Public Delivery Systems"[2] felt that additional factors were the following: the extent and effectiveness of pressures for cost minimization; the degree of unionization; the degree to which the operation of the organization had been politicized (e.g., politically appointed versus professional management); the availability and quality of cost-related data; and the degree to which output could be easily and accurately measured and related to the operation of the public organization.

The first analysis conducted by Summers and Wolfe uses pupil-specific data to conduct a process analysis of the provision of junior high school education. Their work provides results which are quite different from the work which uses data which has been aggregated to a higher level (e.g., the school or school district). Most importantly Summers and Wolfe find that increases in certain types of resources can improve student achievement.

In addition to conducting a process analysis of education production using unusually rich and pupil-specific data, Summers and Wolfe explore the robustness of their results by estimating similar models of educational process using other data for the same school district (i.e., the Philadelphia school district) and time period. They find some of their conclusions to be quite robust and to be confirmed in all of their analyses. For example, they find that large numbers of unexcused absences provide a useful "trouble signal" for schools, that differential pay for teachers with education beyond the Bachelor of Arts degree is not warranted, and that higher pay for more experienced math and English teachers is warranted. Some other conclusions could not be replicated. For example, their original work indicated that school size had no significant effect on achievement, but their later work suggested that smaller schools might improve student achievement. Comparison of the results they obtain in their various analyses is fascinating and provides a useful warning to researchers who are willing to make policy suggestions based on the results of a single study. Replications of the type carried out by Summers and Wolfe or a survey of all available studies related to the policy issue at hand are likely to provide a far more reliable basis for decision making.[3]

The Summers and Wolfe paper also provides an interesting approach to the missing data problem. This problem has been considered quite extensively in time series settings and methods have been developed to obtain BLUE estimates of missing data.[4] Indeed, the method used by Summers and Wolfe is a cross-section analogy of the time series work. However, we know nothing about the statistical properties of the estimates used by Summers and Wolfe.[5]

The papers by Votey and Phillips are quite different from the Summers and Wolfe paper, both in subject matter and in approach. Votey and Phillips are interested in modeling crime rates. Crime rates, like student achievement, are affected by both public agency actions and other factors (e.g., the level of private protection, the age structure of the population, the legitimate opportunities available). Thus, in modeling crime rates or student achievement levels it is necessary to control for these other factors in order to discern the true effect of the public sector on the desired social outcome (i.e., lower crime rates or higher student achievement). Summers and Wolfe take a single equation process analysis approach to this issue, while Votey and Phillips both take the two-equation approach common in the economics of crime literature. This difference in approach raises an important issue which needs to be considered when modeling social outcomes. Should we see the public organization as directly producing the desired social outcome, or should we see the direct output of the public organization (e.g., school days, arrests) as one type of factor affecting the level of desired social outcome? The Summers and Wolfe paper takes the former approach,[6] whereas the papers by Votey and Phillips take the latter. The correct approach will vary with the type of public production being analyzed[7] and the nature of the policy issue being considered.[8] Elsewhere (Grizzle and Witte, 1981; see also Grizzle, et al., 1982) we have argued that the two-equation approach provides insights not possible with a single-equation approach when factors outside the public agencies control have a major effect on the desired social outcome.

In many ways, the Votey paper is much closer in spirit to the Summers and Wolfe paper, being concerned primarily with drawing policy-relevant conclusions, than to the paper by Phillips. Phillips's main focus is with modeling rather than policy issues. Specifically Phillips develops an approach to analyzing public processes and social outcomes which is dynamic.[9]

The Votey paper analyzes the effect of the activities of the Swedish criminal justice system (conviction rates and sentence lengths), and social and economic factors on crime rates using pooled cross-section (counties) and time-series (1975–1978) data. In his analysis Votey is careful to adjust for many of the weaknesses in the existing deterrence literature (e.g., spurious correlation; certain simultaneity issues). In addition, he is able to include many variables in his specifications which have been missing from models estimated using U.S. data (e.g., information on broken families and alcohol consumption levels) because of the extensive nationwide data bases maintained in Sweden. Votey's analysis of motoring offenses may be of particular interest given the recent extensive attention paid to drunken driving in this country.

In contrast to Summers and Wolfe, Votey uses aggregate rather than individual data; thus, his work is subject to aggregation bias of unknown nature. However, he does estimate separate equations for different crime types. Like Summers and Wolfe, Votey carefully compares his work to other work before drawing policy conclusions and notes which results are robust. The degree to which Votey's deterrence results using Swedish data are similar to results obtained using U.S. data is surprising and gives one far more confidence in the existence of a deterrent effect than would any single study, or indeed a simple comparison of results for the United States.

Votey's use of information and insights provided by Swedish government officials when interpreting his results is noteworthy, greatly strengthening the credibility of his conclusions. Such close interaction between researchers and public officials can serve to markedly improve our understanding of the way in which public agencies operate.[10]

One of Votey's more interesting findings is that in allocating police resources Swedish officials do not appear to have been much influenced by efficiency considerations. This is consistent with a number of empirical findings for different types of public agencies in the United States[11] and suggests that in modeling such agencies it is necessary to carefully consider the nature of the goals being pursued.[12] While cost minimization may be one of the goals, it appears to be only one among many. Note that we previously suggested that the extent to which cost minimization is pursued will be one factor determining the usefulness of tradition economic constructs. Economic models which explicitly model inefficiency have recently been developed, and these models may be more appropriate for analyzing public agencies than are traditional production and cost function models which assume that output is produced efficiently.[13]

As noted earlier, the Phillips paper is quite different from the other two papers in this part. Phillips is interested in developing a dynamic model of offenses and community response. He does this by using a model which has the same formal structure as Forster's one-state variable optimal control model of the consumption–pollution trade-off. As is usually the case with such models, Phillips is forced to make a number of simplifying assumptions in order to ensure mathematical tractability. Future work seeking to develop dynamic models of criminal behavior and community response could usefully relax a number of assumptions while still allowing the models to be solved. Existing work on the operation of the criminal justice system and individual crime patterns provides useful guidance.

Phillips's model deals with only two aspects of the criminal choice in any detail: (1) "rehabilitation with time and maturity," and (2) general deterrence. As Phillips notes, the model could usefully be extended to incorporate incapacitation. It would also be useful to consider specific deterrent effects.

Phillips's model assumes a single deterrence variable, the probability of arrest, although he begins with the notion that it is the certainty, severity, and celerity of punishment which is important. Enrichment of the deterrence variables is badly needed.

In developing his model, Phillips assumes that the number of individuals that remain in offender status will decline exponentially and that the number of offenses is proportional to the stock of offenders. Current research suggests that both of these assumptions are too simplistic. Work which considers the factors affecting the length of time that an offender will remain crime free (i.e., survival analyses)[14] suggests that a negative exponential decay function with its implicit assumption of a constant probability of return to crime (i.e., constant hazard rate) probably does not provide an accurate reflection of the nature of criminal behavior. Models which assume that the probability that an individual will return to crime declines as the time that the individual has been crime free increases (i.e., a declining hazard rate) appear to describe criminal behavior more accurately. Research which carefully analyzes the nature of criminal careers[15] suggests that it is a relatively few serious offenders who commit most crimes, i.e., that the number of offenses may not be proportional to the stock of offenders.

Phillips also assumes constant cost technology in the production of deterrence. There is a good bit of research exploring the way in which the costs of criminal justice agencies vary with work load.[16] This literature provides a relatively easy way of making a dynamic model of crime more realistic in its representation of the nature of operation of the criminal justice system.

Phillips is very careful to garner as many insights as possible from his theoretical work when specifying and estimating his empirical model. This approach is very fruitful and could usefully be more frequently emulated in applied microeconomic work. Phillips's theoretical model suggests simultaneity between offense and arrest rates and also that the mutual effects of these two variables follow a negative distributed lag structure.

Phillips's empirical work uses a small sample (annual time-series data for California for the period 1945–1978) and sparse specifications. Thus, results should be considered only indicative. However, the results are intriguing.

Phillips's results for homicide, auto theft, robbery, and burglary are consistent with his dynamic model of deterrence, while his results for aggravated assault are not. His results suggest that the criminal justice system does not behave in a manner designed to achieve "optimal public safety." Our discussion earlier suggests that this was likely to be the case.

Phillips's work demonstrates the usefulness of dynamic models of criminal behavior. It also points up the need, as does Votey's work, to estimate separate models of crime commission for different types of offenses. Finally, his results reinforce the need to develop models of public sector operation which do not assume simple maximizing behavior on the part of the public agency. Phillips has ably achieved his goal: to show the usefulness of dynamic modeling of crime and to provide a "framework for further analysis."

With the above discussion in mind, it is hoped that the reader will view the papers which follow in two lights. First, the papers should be considered as making a contribution to the particular literature from which they came (i.e., the economics of education and the economics of crime). Second, and perhaps more importantly, the papers should be seen as creative attempts by able researchers to come to grips with the very difficult question of how we can best use economic theory and econometric techniques to analyze the way in which the level of complex, difficult-to-measure outcomes desired by the public is determined.

NOTES

1.   See Alesch and Dougharty (1971), Hanushek (1979), Hanushek (1981), Vernez (1976), and Witte (1980) for summaries of work in various areas.

2.   See Witte (1980) for a summary of the discussion at the session.

3.   Psychologists and sociologists have been active in developing analytical methods to compare the results of studies using various methodologies and data sets. For example, see Glass et al. (1981) and Hunter et al. (1982).

4.   For example, see Chow and Lin (1971), Chow (1976), and Doran (1974).

5.   A good deal of interesting work has been done recently on methods of handling missing data in sample surveys. For example, see Greenlees et al. (1982), Little (1982), and NAS Panel on Incomplete Data (1983).

6.   Alternatively their approach can be considered a reduced-form approach.

7.   For example with the degree to which the public agencies control the level of desired social outcome. It could be argued that schools control student achievement to a much larger degree than police and other criminal justice agencies control crime rates.

8.   For example, the deterrence issue and the effect of legitimate opportunity on crime rates are central to the economics of crime literature, while the effect of school inputs is a major issue considered when analyzing student achievement.

9.   The approaches of Summers and Wolfe and of Votey are both basically static, although Votey does consider lagged effects and Summers and Wolfe's dependent variable is change in achievement over time.

10.   This belief is reinforced by our own recent experience in working closely with personnel of the U.S. Internal Revenue Service to develop models of tax compliance. See Witte and Woodbury (1983).

11.   For example, see Carlson (1972) for education, Phillips (1978) for police, and Grizzle and Witte (1983) for corrections.

12.   The literature on bureaucracy is relevant to this modeling effort. See Orzechowski (1977) for a survey.

13.   See Førsund et al. (1980) for a survey of models incorporating inefficiency. Grizzle and Witte (1983) explicitly model and estimate the level of inefficiency in large-scale prisons.

14.   Witte and Schmidt (1977) provide an example of early work in this area, and Schmidt and Witte (1983) provide a recent survey.

15.   See Wolfgang et al. (1972) for early work. Much of the more recent work has been done by the Rand Corporation. For a survey of criminal career research see Petersilia (1980).

16.   For an example of work in the police area, see Darrough and Heineke (1978). Gillespie (1977) and Weller and Block (1979) have considered judicial costs. Trumbull and Witte (1981/82) consider correctional costs.

REFERENCES

Alesch, D. J., and L. A. Dougharty, *Economies-Of-Scale Analysis in State and Local Government*. Santa Monica, CA: Rand, R-748-CIR, 1971.

Carlson, Daryl, "The Production and Cost Behavior of Higher Educational Institutions." Paper P-36 of the Ford Foundation Program for Research in University Administration. Berkeley, CA: University of California, 1972.

Chow, G. C., "Best Linear Unbiased Estimation of Missing Observations in an Economic Time Series." *Journal of the American Statistical Association* 71(September 1976):719–721.

Chow, G. C. and A. Lin, "Best Linear Unbiased Interpolation, Distribution, and Extrapolation of Time Series by Related Series." *Review of Economics and Statistics* 53(November 1971):372–375.

Doran, H. E., "Prediction of Missing Observations in the Time Series of an Economic Variable." *Journal of the American Statistical Association* 69(June 1974):546–554.

Darrough, M. N., and J. M. Heineke, "The Multi-Output Translog Production Cost Function: The Case of Law Enforcement Agencies." In J. M. Heineke (ed.), *Economic Models of Criminal Behavior*. Amsterdam: North Holland, 1978.

Førsund, Finn R., C. A. Knox Lovell, and Peter Schmidt, "A Survey of Frontier Production Functions and of Their Relationship to Efficiency Measurement." *Journal of Econometrics* 13(1980):5–25.

Gillespie, R. W., *Judicial Productivity and Court Delay: An Exploratory Analysis of the Federal District Court*. Washington, DC: National Institute of Law Enforcement & Criminal Justice, Law Enforcement Assistance Administration, U.S. Department of Justice, 1977.

Glass, G., B. McGaw and M. L. Smith, *Meta-Analysis in Social Research*. Beverly Hills, CA: Sage, 1981.

Greenlees, J. S., W. S. Reece and K. D. Zieschang, "Imputation of Missing Values When the Probability of Response Depends on the Variable Being Imputed." *Journal of the American Statistical Association* 77(June 1982):251–261.

Grizzle, G. A., et al., *Basic Issues in Corrections Performance*. Washington, DC: U.S. Department of Justice, 1982.

Grizzle, G. A. and A. D. Witte, "Issues in Measuring the Performance of Public Organizations." *Journal of Public & International Affairs* 2(Spring/Summer 1981):122–136.

Grizzle, G. A. and A. D. Witte, "Efficiency in Corrections Agencies." In G. L. Whitaker and C. Phillips (eds.), *Evaluating Performance of Criminal Justice Agencies*. Beverly Hills, CA: Sage, 1983, pp. 265–300.

Hanushek, Eric A., "Conceptual and Empirical Issues in the Estimation of Educational Production Functions." *Journal of Human Resources* 14(3 1979):351–388.

Hanushek, E., "Throwing Money at Schools." *Journal of Policy Analysis and Management* 1(Fall 1981):19–41.

Hunter, J. E., F. L. Schmidt and G. B. Jackson, *Meta-Analysis: Cumulating Research Findings Across Studies*. Beverly Hills, CA: Sage, 1982.

Little, R. J. A., "Models for Nonresponse in Sample Surveys." *Journal of the American Statistical Association* 77(June 1982):237–250.

NAS Panel on Incomplete Data, *Incomplete Data in Sample Surveys*, 3 Vols. New York: Academic Press (1983 forthcoming)

Niskanen, W. A., *Bureaucracy and Representative Government*. Chicago, IL: Aldine, 1971.

Orzechowski, W., "Economic Models of Bureaucracy: Survey, Extensions, and Evidence." In T. E. Borcherding (ed.), *Budgets and Bureaucrats: the Sources of Government Growth*. Durham, NC: Duke University Press, 1977.

Petersilia, Joan, "Criminal Career Research: A Review of Recent Evidence." In N. Morris and M. Tonry (eds.), *Crime and Justice: An Annual Review of Research,* Vol. 2. Chicago, IL: University of Chicago Press, 1980.

Phillips, L., "Factor Demand in the Provision of Public Safety." In J. M. Heineke (ed.), *Economic Models of Criminal Behavior.* Amsterdam: North-Holland, 1978.

Schmidt, Peter and Ann D. Witte, *An Economic Analysis of Crime and Justice: Theory, Methods and Applications.* New York: Academic Press (1984 forthcoming).

Summers, A. and B. Wolfe, "Do Schools Make a Difference?" *American Economic Review* 67(4 1977):639–652.

Trumbull, W. and A. D. Witte, "Determinants of the Costs of Operating Large Scale Prisons with Implications for Correctional Standards." *Law and Society Review,* 16(1 1981/82):115–137.

Vernez, George, *Delivery of Urban Public Services: Production, Cost and Demand Functions, and Determinants of Public Expenditures for Fire, Police and Sanitation Services.* Santa Monica, CA: Rand, P-5659, 1976.

Weller, Dennis, and Michael K. Block, "Estimating the Cost of Judicial Services." In Charles M. Gray (ed.), *The Costs of Crime.* Beverly Hills, CA: Sage, 1979.

Witte, Ann D., "Economics of Public Service Delivery Systems," Summary of Round Table Discussion at the Special National Workshop on Research Methodology and Criminal Justice Program Evaluation, Baltimore, MD, March 18, 1980.

Witte, A. D. and P. Schmidt, "An Analysis of Recidivism, Using the Truncated Lognormal Distribution." *Journal of the Royal Statistical Society: Series C (Applied Statistics* 26(3 1977):302–311.

Witte, A. D. and D. F. Woodbury, "The Effect of Tax Laws and Tax Administration on Tax Compliance." Working Paper, Department of Economics, University of North Carolina, Chapel Hill, 1983.

Wolfgang, Marvin E., R. M. Figlio, and T. Sellin, *Delinquency in a Birth Cohort.* Chicago, IL: University of Chicago Press, 1972.

IMPROVING THE USE OF EMPIRICAL RESEARCH AS A POLICY TOOL:
REPLICATION OF EDUCATIONAL PRODUCTION FUNCTIONS

Anita A. Summers and Barbara L. Wolfe

ABSTRACT

A major underutilized tool in the use of empirical research for policy purposes is replication. We explore the replication process in attempting to shed light on the question: Which school resources help the learning of junior high school students? Three forms of replication are used to test the "theory" derived from an initial mining of the data on 553 eighth-grade students in 42 schools in Philadelphia. We conclude that education production coefficients can contribute more to the policy reviews associated with budget cutbacks and declining enrollments if efforts are made to improve their reliability by using pupil-specific, longitudinal data and by replicating.

Advances in Applied Micro-Economics, Volume 3, pages 199–227.
Copyright © 1984 by JAI Press Inc.
All rights of reproduction in any form reserved.
ISBN: 0-89232-398-1

I. INTRODUCTION

The process by which knowledge is accumulated in economics is not clear. As in other fields, different, equally competent researchers give different answers to policymakers. Why do the answers differ so? In many research areas—education, fertility, and history are examples—the existing body of theory does not carry the investigators very far. With a set of priors which are not firmly established, the researcher goes to an examination of the data to further illuminate relationships. The data are mined, which means, of course, that standard errors and t-statistics do not really provide discriminatory guidelines for distinguishing the stable relationships. Such relationships can only be established by documenting their robustness— by replication. Despite references to replication in standard texts, however, it remains a greatly underutilized tool.[1] There is a need to encourage its use and explore the techniques and interpretation of multiple sets of results.

The objective of this paper is to consider some aspects of both the methodology and practice of replication in the area of educational production function analysis. The documentation of the profusion of conflicting results in this field is readily available: Hanushek (1981) has concluded that the variability in results in the large number of studies which he reviewed precludes any assertion that additional resources devoted to education will yield net benefits. Mullin and Summers (1983) have reviewed the results of the compensatory education programs and have extensively documented the substantial variability in the evaluations.

Our interest, therefore, is to demonstrate that educational production functions can be made more useful by stressing the criterion of robustness of results by means of replication. Replication improves the scientific characteristics of the inquiry into educational processes and, as a result, has implications for the policy recommendations that flow from the inquiry. The fact that policymakers receive empirical results that are less than firmly rooted explains, in part, why the world frequently does not behave as predicted when policies are implemented. And disaffection for empirical research, appropriately enough, sets in.[2]

In this article, therefore, we explore the process of replication using a student population from one school system. This allows us to abstract from locational and system-wide institutional differences. While the control over these differences is improved by using one location, there would clearly be much to be learned by another type of replication—one across school districts. If smaller classes helped low achievers in Boston, they should also be helping low achievers in Chicago.

Specifically, data for a large number of junior high school students in the Philadelphia School District are explored with the development of a hypothesized relationship and three replications. Even though the study is limited to one school district over one period of time, compromises with the data are required to allow for comparisons among the replications—and these are described. The results are compared statistically, and the differences in the policy recommendations flowing from the pre-replication and postreplication results are detailed.

Section II decribes the samples, data compromises, and model estimation procedures for the initial experiment with a pupil-specific[3] data set and for three forms of replication. A comparison of the major findings from these four experiments is presented in Section III. The differences in policy recommendations—the winnowing effect of replication—are discussed in Section IV. Some concluding remarks constitute Section V.

II. DESCRIPTION OF SAMPLES AND MODEL ESTIMATION PROCEDURES

All of the data used in this study are drawn from 1970/71 pupil files for eighth-grade pupils in the Philadelphia School District. These pupils attended junior high, K-8, and middle schools.[4] A two-year education history was compiled for each pupil, including achievement test scores in the sixth and eighth grades, and schools attended. Socioeconomic information was collected, including race and sex; and an estimated family income was assigned to each pupil by using his or her address.[5] The dependent variable chosen is the change in a composite achievement test score (Iowa Test of Basic Skills) over the two-year period spanning the sixth to the eighth grades. The equation is of the form:

$$\Delta A = F(GSES, TQ, SQ, PG), \tag{1}$$

where   A = achievement;
     GSES = genetic endowment and socioeconomic status;
     TQ = teacher quality;
     SQ = school quality (nonteacher);
     PG = peer group characteristics.

Four separate data sets were used to explore the replication process:[6] (A) Sample A—a relatively small, pupil-specific data set; (B) Sample B— a larger sample with limited pupil-specific data; (C) Sample C—a second randomly drawn sample with limited pupil-specific data; and (D) Sample B with estimators substituted for the non-pupil-specific data (these data were treated as a variant of the missing data problem). The level of detail, particularly teacher quality and attendance information, varies significantly by sample. In each case, Eq. (1) is estimated, though some of the variables differ in level of aggregation. The use of (A) to form the hypothesized relationships, which are then tested by (B), (C), and (D), is an attempt to accommodate the standard scientific procedure to the realities of the discipline.

A.   Sample A: A Small, Pupil-Specific Sample

The initial results are based on data for 553 eighth-grade pupils who attended 42 schools (Sample A). The schools were randomly selected and the pupils were randomly selected from these schools. Detailed data were obtained from files kept within the school; these included individual pupil attendance records, test scores, family backgrounds, and the specific teachers each pupil had. This information was then matched to a teacher file, so that each pupil's data file has, for his or her individual English, math, and social studies teachers,[7] a fairly detailed set of measurable characteristics of quality: a rating of the undergraduate institutions attended,[8] National Teachers Examination (NTE) scores, levels of education completed, and years of experience as a teacher. The pupil information was also matched to information on the school(s) attended: this included information on the principal's characteristics, racial composition, percentage of high and low achievers, enrollment, age and condition of the facilities, and class size by grade.

Sample A is the "ideal" one in terms of data. It is the one on which 453 regressions were run to arrive at the equation of "best fit" and also the one which, in the absence of an agreed-upon body of theory to test, provides the hypothesized relationship against which replications can be checked. The calculated results of the best-fit equation, our choice of the appropriate specification, are listed in Table 1, Column (2). A number of functional forms for each of the variables have been examined. Dummy variables and other nonlinearities were explored. Interactions between pupil characteristics and school inputs (the relationship between class size and pupil's family income, for example) were extensively examined, consistent with the generally accepted theory of educators that students of different abilities react differently to the characteristics of their schools, their peers, their teachers, and their programs. The empirical results of the interaction analyses must, of course, be read from Table 1 by *combining* the coefficients of the intercept and interaction terms. For example, lines 11 and 12 should be read thusly: for students whose sixth-grade score was considerably above grade level (= 80), each residential move was associated with a significant decline in test score growth of 4.3 months [2.12 + (−.08 × 80)]. The unnumbered lines in the table are examples of the results for selected values of the interaction terms; the terms in parenthesis are the matched tests of statistical significance.

All the findings were checked and rechecked against alternative specifications for robustness. Only those variables that remained strong throughout the mining process—the variables which had significant coefficients in virtually all of the alternative specifications—were retained. Normally, this is the sort of equation from which policy conclusions flow. However, we regard these results as Step 1: the development of a *hypothesized* relationship between the change in achievement from sixth to eighth grades and many inputs.

B.   Sample B: A Sample with Limited Pupil-Specific Data

Sample B was randomly drawn from the Philadelphia School District's computerized record files; after 130 observations were discarded because of incomplete data, the sample consisted of 1541 eighth-grade pupils in 52 schools. Step 2 involved attempting to fit the hypothesized relationship established in Step 1 to these virgin data.

In many respects, the data were of the same quality: Information on individual pupil test scores was matched to data that were available on tapes of individual records. These included data on sex, race, address (to match family income estimated with block income estimates), and schools attended. As in the small sample, these data were matched with characteristics of the schools and their principals.

However, some data differed and compromises had to be made. Information about the teachers each pupil had was not available on the tapes. Instead, each pupil was assigned the averages of the teachers in the school in the relevant grade and subject. Thus, Mary Smith's scores could not be matched with the number of years of experience of Mr. Jones, her eighth-grade math teacher (the detail of data available in the Sample A), but with the average years of experience of the eighth-grade math teachers in her school. Pupil-specific data on attendance were also unavailable: Mary Smith's scores could not be matched with her unexcused absences, but only with the average daily attendance of her school(s).

An equation, paralleling the best-fit equation of Sample A, is reported in Table 1, column (3): the best directly available substitutes for pupil-specific data were used and the variables with nonsignificant coefficients were dropped.

C.   Sample C: A Second Sample with Limited
Pupil-Specific Data

Typically, investigators of educational production functions randomly select one group of students in a school district to analyze. Sample B might be such an example. But what would be the results if the random selection produced another group of students? Would the policy recommendations flowing each of the data anlyses be the same?

Sample C is a second random sample drawn from the same population

Table 1. Regression Results for Four Eighth-Grade Samples of Philadelphia School District Students, 1969–1971[a]

(t-values in parentheses)

Variables (1)	Sample A: Pupil-Specific Data (2)	Sample B: Limited Pupil-Specific Data (3)	Sample C: Second Sample With Limited Pupil-Specific Data (4)	Tests of Equality (3) and (4) (5)	Sample B With Estimators (6)	Modified Sample A (7)	Tests of Equality (6) and (7) (8)
1. Sex	.63 (.73)	.58 (1.22)	1.20 (1.24)	.57	.67 (1.36)	.42 (.48)	−.25
2. (1) × Low Achievement Low Ach. = 1	−2.77 (−2.41)	−1.54 (−2.31)	−2.80 (−2.11)		−1.11 (−1.37)	−2.38 (−2.04)	
3. 2nd Generation Native Born	−2.14 (−2.58) 4.52 (2.13)	−.96 (−1.78) —[b]	−1.60 (−1.61) —[b]	−.56	−.44 (−.65) —[b]	−1.97 (−2.33) —[b]	−1.40
4. Third-Grade Score	.52 (2.41)	—[b]	—[b]		—[b]	—[b]	
5. (4)^2	−.004 (−1.49)	—[b]	—[b]		—[b]	—[b]	
6. Sixth-Grade Score	−.38 (−2.38)	.04 (1.26)	.07 (1.15)	.43	−.01 (−.03)	−.32 (−1.93)	−1.21
7. Race (Black = 1)	−.36 (−.12)	−1.39 (−2.62)	−.66 (−.61)	.61	.40 (.12)	.27 (.09)	−.03
8. Income	−.21 (−1.10)	.28 (3.10)	.44 (2.37)	.77	.17 (1.49)	−.15 (−.77)	−1.40
9. Unexcused Absences[c,f]	.30 (1.54)	.10 (1.86)	.11 (1.06)	.13	.18 (.53)	.33 (1.71)	
10. (9) × (6)[f]	−.01 (−2.69)	—[e]	—[e]		−.004 (−.63)	−.01 (−2.84)	
(6) = 30	−.02 (−.20)				.06 (.35)	.0003 (.004)	−.30
(6) = 50	−.23 (−5.15)				−.03 (−.25)	−.22 (−4.96)	−1.76
(6) = 80	−.54 (−4.16)				−.15 (−.68)	−.56 (−4.23)	−1.58
11. Residential Moves	2.12 (.69)	—[e]	—[e]		−.35 (−.24)	3.55 (1.15)	
12. (11) × (6)	−.08 (−1.27)	—[e]			.002 (.08)	−.11 (−1.72)	
(6) = 30	−.31 (−.24)				−.28 (−.38)	.24 (.19)	−.35
(6) = 50	−1.92 (−3.04)				−.24 (−.55)	−1.97 (−3.05)	−2.22√
(6) = 80	−4.35 (−2.01)				−.18 (−.22)	−5.28 (−2.42)	−2.19√

204

13. Rating of Social Studies Teacher's College[f]	−3.06 (−1.50)	—[e]			−.58 (−.22)	−3.49 (−1.68)	
14. (13) × (6)[f]	.06 (1.59)				.02 (.46)	.07 (1.82)	−.81
(6) = 30	−1.28 (−1.27)				.04 (.03)	−1.42 (−1.39)	−.46
(6) = 50	−.09 (−.17)				.45 (.48)	−.05 (−.09)	−.46
(6) = 80	1.69 (1.50)				1.07 (.77)	2.02 (1.77)	.52
15. Rating of English Teacher's College[d,f]	−2.10 (−3.02)	−1.13 (−1.70)	1.78 (1.49)	2.13 √	−.24 (−.28)	−1.99 (−2.81)	
16. (15) × (6)[d,f]	.04 (3.53)	.03 (5.02)	.02 (1.88)		.03 (4.03)	.04 (3.21)	
(6) = 30	−.96 (−2.07)	−1.14 (−.25)	2.49 (2.44)	2.25 √	.62 (.85)	−.94 (−1.98)	−1.78
(6) = 50	−.21 (−.53)	.51 (.94)	2.96 (3.08)	2.21 √	1.20 (1.76)	−.24 (−.59)	−1.82
(6) = 80	.93 (1.93)	1.50 (2.67)	3.66 (3.69)	1.90	2.06 (3.16)	.82 (1.68)	−1.53
17. English Teacher's Experience[d,f]	−.54 (−.78)	−3.70 (−2.72)	−5.29 (−1.92)	−.52	−.31 (−.17)	−1.05 (−1.56)	−.38
18. English Teacher's Experience, >3[d,f]	.14 (.18)	4.15 (2.97)	6.19 (2.20)	.65	.82 (.44)	1.13 (1.55)	.15
19. English Teacher's Experience, >10	3.93 (2.50)		—[b]			—[b]	
20. Math Teacher's Experience[d,f]	.16 (1.34)	.60 (3.76)	.12 (.40)	1.40	.16 (.57)	.19 (1.60)	.10
21. Social Studies Teacher's NTE Score[d]	.11 (2.01)	—[e]	—[e]		.02 (.27)	.11 (1.84)	.91
22. Math Teacher's Education Beyond B.A.[d]	—[e]	−2.69 (−3.69)	−.79 (−.52)	1.13	—[e]	—[e]	
23. Math Teacher's Race = Pupil's Race[f]	1.85 (1.89)	—[e]	—[e]		3.85 (1.10)	1.17 (1.18)	−.74

(continued)

Table 1. (Continued)

Variables (1)	Sample A: Pupil-Specific Data (2)	Sample B: Limited Pupil-Specific Data (3)	Sample C: Second Sample With Limited Pupil-Specific Data (4)	Tests of Equality (3) and (4) (5)	Sample B With Estimators (6)	Modified Sample A (7)	Tests of Equality (6) and (7) (8)
24. Percentage of Black Teachers	-.17 (-3.72)	—[e]	—[e]		-.01 (-.34)	-.16 (-3.54)	-2.76√
25. Remedial Education Expenditures	.03 (1.77)	.02 (4.26)	.03 (2.90)	.72	.02 (3.06)	.03 (1.61)	
26. (25) × Low Achievement Low Ach. = 1	-.04 (-1.72)	—[e]	—[e]		-.002 (-.15)	-.04 (-1.87)	-1.43
27. Class Size ≥ 32	-8.29 (-3.12)	—[e]	—[e]		1.95 (1.11)	-8.37 (-3.11)	-3.21√
28. (27) × (8)	.66 (2.10)				-.23 (-1.32)	.60 (1.88)	
(8) = 5	-4.99 (-4.05)				-.79 (.85)	-5.37 (-4.30)	(-3.95)√
(8) = 10	-1.69 (-1.74)				-.36 (-.77)	-2.37 (-2.42)	(-1.86)
(8) = 15	1.62 (.70)				-1.51 (-1.45)	.63 (.27)	.84
29. Attending a K-8 School	4.52 (3.28)	3.31 (3.54)	6.83 (3.39)	1.58	4.36 (5.00)	4.80 (3.43)	-.26
30. Percentage of Black Students	.07 (1.66)				.01 (.42)	.07 (1.56)	
31. (7) × (30)	-.04 (-.51)				.03 (.59)	-.08 (-.95)	
(7) = Black	.03 (.50)				.04 (.93)	-.01 (-.08)	-.58
32. Percentage of Black Students ≥ 50	-.21 (-1.99)	—[e]	—[e]		-.02 (-.20)	-.24 (-2.21)	
33. (7) × (32)	.32 (2.34)				-.06 (-.66)	.40 (2.89)	2.08√
(7) = Black	.11 (1.19)				-.08 (-1.13)	.16 (1.75)	

34. Relative Income Change in School Feeder Area, 1960–1970	—[e]	-8.71 (-2.39)	-22.66 (-3.07)	-1.70	—[e]
35. School Enrollment	—[e]	-.08 (-1.83)	-.03 (-.31)	.58	—[e]
Constant	13.59	9.00	-3.32	27.80	-2.54
$\bar{R}^2$	.32	.32	.30	.29	.35
$\hat{F}$	9.03	42.73	12.93	8.94	30.65
N	553	1541	465	553	1541

Notes: Dependent Variable: Eighth-Grade Iowa Test of Basic Skills (Composite) Minus Sixth-Grade Score.

[a] Sources of data are listed in the Appendix. The interpretation of interaction terms is described in the table of results, Table 2 (in Section III, below).

[b] Variable not available.

[c] In the samples described by columns (3) and (4), the variable used is average daily attendance in the pupil's school.

[d] In the samples described by columns (3) and (4), the variables used are the average quality characteristic of the relevant group of teachers in the pupil's school.

[e] Individual variable not significant at the t = .05 level.

[f] Variables for which estimators were developed.

√ Null hypothesis test reveals significantly different results.

as Sample B. It is made up of 465 eighth-grade pupils from 50 schools; 36 observations were discarded because of incomplete data. The data had the same limited pupil-specific characteristics as Sample B. The hypothesized relationship developed from the pupil-specific data of Sample A was fitted to these data, as it was on the 1541 observations of Sample B. Since both samples B and C had the same pupil-specificity characteristics, the variables, of course, are defined identically. The results of this replication are shown in Table 1, column (4).

D. Sample B with Estimators

The pupils included in this sample are the same as those in Sample B, but another form of data compromise was used. Correction factors were developed for the non-pupil-specific data. As an alternative to using aggregate data, estimators of pupil-specific data for teacher qualities and attendance were calculated using the information available from Sample A. This makes the not unreasonable assumption that the underlying relationships are the same for Samples A and B.

This approach can be thought of as a way to deal with missing data, a problem common to many multivariate analyses, and one virtually certain to be a problem in replication exercises. One standard approach is to eliminate missing data using either listwise deletion or pairwise deletion (methods of moments).

Another approach, and the one used here, is to estimate (replace) missing data. Replacing missing values by sample averages (means) is a well-known way of estimating missing values, though it can result in inconsistent estimates. For Samples B and C, however, even this was not feasible, since pupil-specific data for many variables were not available. Instead, and preferably, the missing variables can be regressed on the available variables.

More specifically, the problem in this study was to estimate an equation of the form:

$$A = Y\phi + X\beta + \epsilon, \tag{2}$$

where A = achieving (eighth-grade score minus sixth-grade score);
   Y = vector of variables not common to Samples A and B (and C);
   X = vector of variables common to Samples A and B (and C);
   ϕ = coefficients of the Y vector;
   β = coefficients of the X vector;
   ϵ = error term.

The problem was that there were missing data on Y. However, there was a data set (Sample A) which had information on Y for pupils in that sample. So, for each of these Y variables, using the data from Sample A, we estimated an "auxiliary regression" of the form:

$$Y = X\beta + Z\gamma + V, \tag{3}$$

where   Z = vector of variables common to Sample A and Sample B (and C) not used in Eq. (2);

γ = coefficients of the Z vector;

V = error term.

The Y vector, or vector of dependent variables for which estimators are generated, includes: unexcused absences of pupils; rating of undergraduate institutions attended by the social studies and English teachers; experience of the pupil's English and math teachers; scores of each pupil's social studies teacher on the NTE; and a match-up of the race of pupil and math teacher.

The X vector contains a set of variables describing socioeconomic characteristics (e.g., sex of student), school characteristics (e.g., enrollment of school), and student body characteristics (e.g., proportion of black students). The Z vector contains two types of variables: (1) match-up variables to the Y variables (the average experience of eighth-grade English teachers in a school matches up with the experience of each pupil's English teacher, for example); (2) additional variables available in both Samples A and B. The X and Z vectors are assumed to be functionally related to the Y vector.

These "auxiliary regressions" all had the same right-hand variables. The selection criteria for the set used were the R^2 values and the t-statistics. (The R^2 values are reported in the Appendix for the relevant variables.) To check further on the fit of the "auxiliary regressions," the estimators were substituted into the modified Sample A data set reported in Table 1, column (7)—modified because there were some data (third-grade score and country origin) for which no reasonable surrogate was available. The coefficients using the estimators, with one exception, were very similar to the coefficients using the pupil-specific data.[9] (The one exception occurred when a comparison of the school-wide racial composition of students to teachers was matched to the comparison of each student's race to his or her math teacher's race.)

In order to be confident that using the estimators in Eq. (2) (as independent variables) did not introduce multicollinearity into the achieving equation, a test for the degree of collinearity was made. This involved testing the usual assumption that the $E(V\epsilon) = 0$. If only one estimation was to be created, ϵ would simply be regressed against V from the auxiliary regression to test for collinearity. Since there are 11 estimators, there was a problem of aggregating the V's in order to conduct the collinearity test. This involved combining them into a scalar using appropriate weights: the weighting scheme employed used the coefficients of these variables (ϕ) from Eq. (2) [Table 1, column (7)] to calculate an appropriate scalar for this test; the adjusted R^2 for the equation $\epsilon = \alpha + b(W)$, where $W = V\phi$, was $-.0017$. It was legitimate to assume, therefore, that $E(V\epsilon) = 0$; that is, that there was no covariance between the error terms.

The auxiliary regressions were used to create estimators for each of these Y variables for each pupil in Sample B. These were then used as substitutes for the missing pupil-specific data in Sample B. Equation (2) was then run using these estimators to test the hypothesized relationships developed for Sample A. In order to permit better evaluation of the "auxiliary regression" procedure, a small adjustment[10] was made for the additional variance that resulted from this procedure. The results are in Table 1, column (6).

III. SUMMARY OF FINDINGS

To illustrate the practical and methodological problems of a replication procedure, the theories that some school and teacher inputs help learning growth and that the inputs have different impacts on different types of students were tested in one exploratory analysis and three replications involving Philadelphia junior high school students. Did the "answers" differ? Interestingly enough, most "answers" were consistent throughout the replications. Some, however, were only similar, and some differed substantially. These conclusions clearly emerge:[11] school resources help learning; organizational and teacher characteristics affect learning growth; and the negative effects of race and income can be traced through their impact on the student's ability to absorb particular pupil-specific school inputs.

The "answers" emerging from each experiment are laid out in Table 1 in columns (2), (3), (4), (6), and (7) in the form of coefficients and t-statistics.[12] Equality of coefficient tests [columns (5) and (8)] were performed to test whether or not answers from the different experiments differed.[13] Comparisons that failed the test are checked. But these significance tests do not, of course, provide anywhere near perfect guidance for interpreting the results. Sample A, the pupil-specific sample that we used to develop our hypothesis, is a "worked-over" sample, so the t-statistics in column (2) should be read with the recognition that they are overstated, reflecting the understatement of the standard errors. The t-statistics for the remaining samples are more consistent with the underlying assumptions of significance tests, however. The tests of equality [columns (5) and (8)] need to be interpreted with the recognition that the standard errors of the samples will differ because of differences in sample sizes. (Thus, the square root of the ratio of the Samples B and C sizes is 1.8, and the standard errors of the coefficients of Sample C vary around 1.8 times the coefficients of Sample B.)

To translate these statistical results into policy requires an intermediate step. That is, a pragmatic regression strategy calls for using all the results of the replications, with the appropriate caveats, in the final interpretations. These are laid out in Table 2, where the findings from the first experiment (Sample A), with pupil-specific data, are compared with the findings from the three replications.

Most of the estimates of the effects of genetic and socioeconomic inputs appear to be robust. At the junior high school ages, only the low-achieving males have slower achievement growth than their female counterparts. When an early achievement measure is included (third-grade score), the impact of the end-of-elementary-grades score (sixth-grade score) shows regression toward the mean; where all earlier achievement is reflected in one score only (sixth-grade score), the effects cancel out. The theory that pupils from different economic and racial backgrounds respond differentially to school and teacher inputs is confirmed:[14] being black is associated with less achievement growth, but where the effects of being black are traced through interactions with other inputs, no residual effect remains; similarly, students from higher-income families have more achievement growth, but where the effects of income are traced through interactions with other inputs, no residual effect remains. Motivation (the number of unexcused absences is the surrogate measure) is clearly associated with achievement growth.

Certain qualities of teachers—using a rating of undergraduate institutions, years of experience, score on NTEs, and amount of graduate education as quality measures—have a clear bearing on the achievement growth of students. The evidence suggests (1) that high-achieving students benefit most from being taught by English and social studies teachers who received their undergraduate degrees from higher-rated institutions; (2) that students benefit from being taught by more experienced English and math teachers; (3) that the NTE scores are not associated with student learning, except for social studies teachers; (4) that more graduate education for teachers is not associated with achievement growth in any of the subjects; and (5) that a match of race between pupil and teacher is not reflected in more or less learning. It is possible to conjecture, of course, that "good" teachers choose to teach "good" pupils. This level of freedom of choice, however, is not descriptive of the Philadelphia School District.

There are a number of clear associations and nonassociations between aspects of the school other than its teachers and junior high school student

Table 2. Comparison of Findings of Pupil-Specific Sample with Three Other Samples of Philadelphia Eighth-Grade Students, 1969–1971

Inputs	Sample A: Pupil-Specific Sample[a]	Replications: Samples B, C, and B with Estimators[b]
Genetic and Socioeconomic Inputs		
Sex[c]	Low-achieving males have lower achievement growth than low-achieving females; higher-achieving males and females show no difference.	*Same findings.*
Sixth-Grade Score	Starting score shows regression toward the mean.	*Same findings from equations with pupil specificity.* (No evidence of regression toward the mean in equations without pupil specificity.)
Race	Race of the pupil is not directly associated with achievement growth, though it does interact with school inputs.	*Same findings from equations with pupil specificity.* (Being nonwhite is negatively associated with achievement growth in equation without pupil specificity.)
Income	Income of the pupil is not directly associated with achievement growth, though it does interact with school inputs.	*Same findings from equations with pupil specificity.* (Income is positively associated with achievement growth in equations without pupil specificity.)
Unexcused Absences[c]	Unexcused absences are negatively related to achievement growth—the higher the achiever, the greater the loss.	*Same findings from equations with pupil specificity.* (Different variable—average daily attendance—supports results in equations without pupil specificity.)
Residential Moves[c]	More residential moves are associated with less achievement growth for middle and high achievers; low achievers were unaffected.	*Dissimilar findings:* More residential moves are not associated with achievement growth of low, middle, or high achievers.

School Inputs: Teacher Quality

Rating of Teacher's College		
Social Studies Teacher[c]	Being taught by a social studies teacher who attended a higher-rated college is associated with greater achievement growth for higher achievers; middle and low achievers were unaffected.	*Same findings from equations with pupil specificity.* (No association in equation without pupil specificity.)
English Teacher[c]	Being taught by an English teacher who attended a higher-rated college is associated with greater achievement growth for high achievers, less achievement growth for low achievers. Middle achievers were unaffected.	*Same findings for high achievers:* Dissimilar findings for middle and low achievers.
Math Teacher	Being taught by a math teacher who attended a higher-rated college is not associated with achievement growth.	*Same findings.*
Years of Experience		
English Teacher	More experience is associated with higher achievement growth (the significant association is with teachers with 10 or more years of experience).	*Similar findings:* Same general finding, but data did not permit exploring impact of 10 or more years of experience.
Math Teacher	Being taught by a math teacher with more experience is associated (though not strongly) with higher achievement growth.	*Similar findings:* Same general finding, but stronger findings from equation without pupil specificity.
Social Studies Teacher	Being taught by a social studies teacher with more experience is not associated with achievement growth.	*Same findings.*
Score on National Teachers Exam (NTE)		
Social Studies	Being taught by a teacher who scored higher on an NTSSE is associated with higher achievement growth.	*Same findings from equations with pupil specificity.* (No association in equation without pupil specificity.)

(continued)

213

Table 2. (Continued)

Inputs	Sample A: Pupil-Specific Sample[a]	Replications: Samples B, C, and B with Estimators[b]
English	Being taught by a teacher who scored higher on an NTEE is not associated with achievement growth.	Same findings.
Math	Being taught by a math teacher who scored higher on an NTME is not associated with achievement growth.	Same findings.
Common	Being taught by a teacher who scored higher on an NTE is not associated with achievement growth.	Same findings.
Graduate Education Math Teacher	Being taught by a math teacher with more graduate education is not associated with achievement growth.	Same findings from equations with pupil specificity. (Negative association in equations without pupil specificity.)
Social Studies Teacher	Being taught by a social studies teacher with more graduate education is not associated with achievement growth.	Same finding.
English Teacher	Being taught by an English teacher with more graduate education is not associated with achievement growth.	Same finding.
Race of Pupil = Race of Math Teacher	Being taught by a math teacher of the same race is positively associated with a pupil's achievement growth.	Dissimilar findings. No evidence of association in other equations.
Race of Pupil = Race of English Teacher	Being taught by an English teacher of the same race is not associated with achievement growth.	Same finding.

Race of Pupil = Race of Social Studies Teacher	Being taught by a social studies teacher of the same race is not associated with achievement growth.	*Same finding.*
Percentage of Black Teachers	A higher percentage of black teachers is negatively associated with achievement growth.	*Dissimilar findings.* No evidence of association in other equations.
School Inputs: Non-Teacher School Quality		
Remedial Expenditures per Low Achiever[c]	More remedial expenditures were associated with higher growth for middle and high achievers but were not related to achievement growth for low achievers.	*Similar findings.* Positive association with learning for middle and high achievers confirmed, but positive association for low achievers found in all other samples.
Class Size ≥ 32[c]	Being in a class with 32 or more pupils is most negatively associated with achievement growth for lower-income pupils; higher-income pupils were unaffected.	*Dissimilar findings.* Lower-income pupils showed no association between learning and class size, as did higher-income pupils.
K-8 Elementary School	Attending eighth grade in a K-8 school is associated with much greater achievement growth.	*Same findings.*
School Size	Size of school has no association with achievement growth.	*Same findings from pupil-specific samples.* (Negative association in samples without pupil specificity.)
Experience and Education of Principals	Additional experience, degrees, and credits of education of principals are not associated with achievement growth.	*Same findings.*
Physical Condition of School	Attending a school with fewer pupils per lab, in better physical condition, or newer is not associated with achievement growth.	*Same findings.*

(continued)

215

Table 2. (Continued)

Inputs	Sample A: Pupil-Specific Sample[a]	Replications: Samples B, C, and B with Estimators[b]
Peer Group Effects Percentage of Black Pupils[c]	An increasing percentage of black pupils in a school up to 50% has no association with achievement growth for blacks or nonblacks.	*Same findings.*
	An increasing percentage of black pupils in a school from 50% to 100% has no clear association with achievement growth for blacks but a negative association for nonblacks.	*Dissimilar findings.* No association found for blacks or nonblacks.
Change from 1960 to 1970 in Relative Income of Feeder area	Attending a school with a higher relative income change is not associated with achievement growth.	*Same findings from pupil-specific samples.* (Negative association in samples without pupil specificity.)

Notes:

[a] Summary of results in Table 1, column (2).

[b] Summary of results in Table 1, columns (3)–(8).

[c] Variables with interaction specification. Coefficients cannot be read directly from Table 1, but should be calculated by adding the coefficient of the intercept term to the coefficient of the interaction term multiplied by the relevant values of that term. For example, for students whose sixth-grade score was considerably above grade level (=80), each move of residence was associated with a significant reduction in test score growth of 4.3 months [2.12 + (−.08)(80)]; for those below grade level (=30), each move was associated with a nonsignificant reduction of .3 months [2.12 + (−.08)(30)]. Thus, the unnumbered lines in Table 1 provide these calculations for selected values of the interaction terms.

216

achievement growth: a positive one between remedial education expenditures and learning for students with high ability; a positive one between attending a K-8 school and achievement growth; none between additional experience, degrees, and credits of education of principals and student learning; and none between the measurable physical conditions of the school and learning. This study does little to resolve the class-size debate:[15] while the sample with the most ideal data shows that classes larger than 32 are negatively associated with the achievement growth of low-income pupils, the other replications do not support this finding. The only consistent finding on class size in these samples is that higher-income students are unaffected by the class size.

Finally, we find over the four samples, the consistent result that variations between 0 and 50 percent black in the racial mix of the schools were not associated with learning changes for blacks or nonblacks; neither was there a discernible relationship for blacks in the range of 50–100 percent black; for nonblacks in the more than 50 percent black schools, no robust finding emerged.

It is clear, in this sorting out of robust findings, that whether or not the sample has pupil-specific data is a major determinant of whether or not a result is replicated. When the school inputs are pupil specific, either obtained originally or estimated (columns [2], [6], and [7]) most of the findings are repeated. The exceptions are the ones relating to the impact of the number of residential moves, the percentage of black teachers, class size for low-income pupils, and more than 50 percent black pupils in a school. When pupil-specific data are not used, more findings fall away. Most strikingly, if the school inputs are not specified in terms of the pupil, the results concerning socioeconomic status are significantly altered: being nonwhite or poor assumes excessive importance.

It is equally clear, as one might expect, that while we gain in certainty as the replication procedure develops, we lose in the number of conclusions we can be confident about.

IV. POLICY IMPLICATIONS

What policies are suggested by exploratory analysis of the pupil-specific data set? What policies remain after the replications? The empirical results of Table 1 and the interpretation of the results of Table 2 are translated into suggested policies in Table 3. Column (1) lists the prereplication advice and column (2) the postreplication advice for helping to maximize achievement growth between the sixth and eighth grades. An additional type of replication is grafted on to this table; in it we have noted the results from our previous study (Summers and Wolfe, 1977a) of third- to sixth-grade student achievement growth in the Philadelphia School Dis-

Table 3. Pre- and Postreplication Policy Suggestions for Improving Sixth- to Eighth-grade Achievement Growth in the Philadelphia School District

Prereplication	Postreplication
* Use the number of unexcused absences of a pupil as a trouble signal.	* *Same.*
√ Rearrange assignments or hire teachers of the "softer" subjects so that those from higher-rated colleges are placed with the high-achieving pupils.	√ *Same.*
√ Higher pay for more experienced English and math teachers is warranted in terms of productivity.	√ *Same.*
Use the NTSSE score as a predictor of teacher ability to improve overall achievement growth. The common and other subject exam scores are not useful indicators.	*Same.*
* Differential pay for teachers who have education beyond the B.A. is not warranted.	* *Same.*
* Policies in teacher placement should not include matching teacher's race to pupil's race.	* *Same.*
Allocate the black teachers in a school system evenly among schools, if the objective is to give each student body an equal impact of racial balance of staff.	* Use criteria other than achievement as the basis for allocating black teachers.

* The evidence that the experience and amount of education beyond the B.A. of principals has no payoff for student achievement growth should be borne in mind in determining hiring and salary criteria.	* *Same.*
Efforts to reach the low-achieving target group should be increased, because remedial expenditures are not helping those for whom they are intended.	*Same,* but remedial expenditure help low achievers, too.
√ As school systems try to cope with declining enrollments, an important finding is that having an eighth grade as part of the elementary school is the most productive form of organization.	√ *Same.*
√ Have class sizes less than 32 in schools with many low-income students, and large classes in schools with many high-income students.	√ Larger classes do not have a negative effect.
Impact on achievement growth is not a useful criterion for determining school size.	√ Smaller schools might have a positive effect on pupil achievement growth.
√ Integration levels of schools do not seem to affect achievement.	Assign students to schools without regard to racial mix.
* Additional expenditures on plant and equipment are not warranted in terms of pupil learning.	* *Same.*

* Duplicated in a study of Sixth-grade students by Summers and Wolfe (1977a).   √ Partially duplicated in a study of Sixth-grade students by Summers and Wolfe (1977a).

219

trict. An asterisk in Table 3 indicates that this elementary school study had results leading to the same policy suggestions; a check mark indicates that the elementary school study had results leading to similar policy suggestions.

So—it seems appropriate to generate some enthusiasm for action in a policy suggestion which has a *Same* in column (2) and asterisks or checks in both columns. Such a finding has weathered a fair number of storms. There are a good number of such findings on the list, relating to pupil motivation, teacher qualities, class size, qualifications of the principal, and physical characteristics of the school.

Any enthusiasm for action, of course, must be confined to the Philadelphia School District. Whether or not such policies would emerge from studies of other school districts is an item in a research agenda, not a known piece of information.

V.   CONCLUDING REMARKS

In education, as in several other areas of socioeconomic policy, econometric analyses have produced widely different results measuring the effectiveness of input measures on output measures. In this paper we have sought to explain some of the data issues, replication procedures, and problems of the aggregation of results that are involved in using replication to reduce the variance in such results. A sample of junior high school students in the Philadelphia School District were analyzed.

First, we conclude that data compromises are likely to have to be made, even when one location and time period is used for all the replication samples. In the sample of pupils we used—where it is well established that pupil-specific data are essential to illuminating the relationships between inputs and learning—we found that using a small sample of pupil-specific data to develop pupil-specific proxies for a larger sample of aggregated data provided a cheap and productive way of moving toward disaggregation.

Second, we conclude that there is a small group of results (in Philadelphia at least) in which we have enough confidence to warrant marginal policy changes: sixth- to eighth-grade learning is significantly affected by the experience of teachers, by the quality of the undergraduate institutions teachers attended, by the grade organization of the school, and by remedial expenditures; the number of unexcused absences is a useful sign of trouble; there are a number of costly items that do not have a payoff in learning growth—education of teachers beyond the B.A., small classes for most students, experience and education beyond the B.A. for principals, and physical characteristics of the school.

Third, we conclude that encouragement needs to be given—in education, as in other fields where large quantities of public resources are spent—to developing large, uniform, easily available data bases which are disaggregated, longitudinal, and have wide geographic coverage, so that the benefits of replication can be reaped.

APPENDIX

The definitions, $\overline{X}$'s, and σ's of each of the variables in Table 1 are listed here with the corresponding row numbers. The $\overline{X}$'s and σ's are presented for the independent variables of Samples A, B, and C and for the estimators of Sample B (EST). The bracketed letters following SS and LS are key letters to the sources listed at the end. The R^2 values and F-statistic for the "auxiliary regressions" are reported for the EST variables.

The $\overline{X}$'s and σ's for the dependent variable, the difference between the eighth-grade and sixth-grade scores, are as follows: A[A]: $\overline{X} = 11.72$, $\sigma = 8.53$; B[A]: $\overline{X} = 13.04$, $\sigma = 8.91$; C: $\overline{X} = 12.88$, $\sigma = 9.16$.

1. Sex: Dummy variable, 0 = female, 1 = male. A[B]: $\overline{X} = .46$, $\sigma = .50$; B[A]: $\overline{X} = .49$, $\sigma = .50$; C: $\overline{X} = .47$, $\sigma = .50$.

2. (1) × Low achievement: Interaction of Sex with dummy variables. 0 = non–low achiever; 1 = low achiever (sixth-grade score ≤ 5.1).

3. Second Generation Native Born: Dummy variable, 0 = no, 1 = yes. A[C]: $\overline{X} = .98$, $\sigma = .15$.

4. Third-Grade Score: Score on Iowa Test of Basic Skills given at the end of third grade. A[B]: $\overline{X} = 32.26$, $\sigma = 8.35$.

5. Square of Third-Grade Score.

6. Sixth Grade Score: Score on Iowa Test of Basic Skills given at the end of the sixth grade. A[B]: $\overline{X} = 53.21$; $\sigma = 13.26$; B[A]: $\overline{X} = 57.08$, $\sigma = 14.72$; C: $\overline{X} = 55.95$, $\sigma = 14.44$.

7. Race: Dummy variable, 0 = nonblack, 1 = black. A[B]: $\overline{X} = .69$, $\sigma = .46$; B[A]: $\overline{X} = .63$, $\sigma = .48$; C: $\overline{X} = .66$, $\sigma = .47$.

8. Income: Estimated family income (in thousands). A[D,E]: $\overline{X} = 8.07$, $\sigma = 2.35$; B[D,E]: $\overline{X} = 9.22$, $\sigma = 3.00$; C: $\overline{X} = 9.03$, $\sigma = 2.89$.

9. Unexcused Absences: Average of annual number of unexcused absences over two years, 1969/70–1970/71. A[F]: $X = 6.25$, $\sigma = 7.86$; EST: $\overline{X} = 4.37$, $\sigma = 5.62$, $R^2 = .20$, F = 4.66. Or Average

Daily Attendance: Average for two years, 1969/70–1970/71, of the percentage of average daily attendance in pupil's school. B[G]: $\overline{X}$ = 83.21, σ = 4.58; C: $\overline{X}$ = 83.11, σ = 4.23.

10. (9) × Sixth-Grade Score: Interaction of sixth-grade score with unexcused absences; EST: R^2 = .14, F = 3.50.

11. Residential Moves: Total number of residential moves of pupil between 1969 and 1971. A[B]: $\overline{X}$ = .20, σ = .52; B[A]: $\overline{X}$ = .36, σ = .70; C: $\overline{X}$ = .34, σ = .67.

12. (11) × Sixth-Grade Score: Interaction of sixth-grade score with number of residential moves.

13. Rating of Social Stdudies Teacher's College: Gourman rating of eighth-grade social studies teacher's undergraduate college. A(H,I): $\overline{X}$ = 415.8, σ = 61.3; EST: $\overline{X}$ = 414.0, σ = 34.7, R^2 = .15, F = 3.57. Or school $\overline{X}$ of ratings of social studies teachers' undergraduate colleges: School average of Gourman ratings of all social studies teachers' undergraduate colleges. B[H,I]: $\overline{X}$ = 433.9, σ = 35.0; C: $\overline{X}$ = 435.2, σ = 36.4.

14. (13) × Sixth-Grade Score: Interaction of sixth-grade score with rating of eighth-grade social studies teacher's college. Or interaction of sixth-grade score with school $\overline{X}$ of ratings of social studies teachers' colleges; EST: R^2 = .78, F = 53.30.

15. Rating of English Teacher's College: Gourman rating of eighth-grade English teacher's undergraduate college. A[H,I]: $\overline{X}$ = 421.7, σ = 82.9; EST: $\overline{X}$ = 406.5, σ = 47.7, R^2 = .17, F = 4.09. Or school $\overline{X}$ of ratings of English teachers' colleges: School average of Gourman ratings of all English teachers' undergraduate colleges. B[H,I]: $\overline{X}$ = 430.2, σ = 33.9; C: $\overline{X}$ = 432.5, σ = 42.3.

16. (15) × Sixth-Grade Score: Interaction of sixth-grade reading score with rating of eighth-grade English teacher's college. Or interaction of sixth-grade reading score with school $\overline{X}$ of ratings of English teachers' colleges; EST: R^2 = .67, F = 31.90.

17. English Teacher's Experience: Eighth-grade English teacher's experience, in years up to 11. A[I]: $\overline{X}$ = 5.51, σ = 3.13; EST: $\overline{X}$ = 6.08, σ = 2.13, R^2 = .32, F = 7.86. Or school $\overline{X}$ of English teachers' experience: School average of all English teachers' experience (in years up to 11). B[I]: $\overline{X}$ = 5.78, σ = 1.95; C: $\overline{X}$ = 5.56, σ = 1.84.

18–19. English Teacher's Experience > 3 > 10: Two additional pieces of a three-piece linear function (spline) of eighth-grade English teachers' experience with corner points at 3 and 10 years. (18) = maximum (0, years of experience − 3). (19) = maximum (0, years of experience − 10). Or school $\overline{X}$ of English teachers' experience − 3: Additional piece of a two-piece linear function (spline) of the school average of all English teachers' experience, set to equal maximum (0, average years of experience − 3); EST: R^2 = .33, F = 8.23.

20. Math Teacher's Experience: Eighth-grade math teachers' experience, in years up to 11. A[I]: $\overline{X}$ = 5.26, σ = 3.10; EST: $\overline{X}$ = 5.58, σ = 1.98, R^2 = .32, F = 8.15. Or school $\overline{X}$ of math teachers' experience (in years up to 11). B[I]: $\overline{X}$ = 5.36, σ = 1.97; C: $\overline{X}$ = 5.56, σ = 1.84.

21. Social Studies Teacher's NTE Score: Eighth-grade social studies teacher's score on the NTSSE. A[I]: $\overline{X}$ = 64.58, σ = 5.96; EST: $\overline{X}$ = 64.15, σ = 4.18, R^2 = .34, F = 8.78. Or school $\overline{X}$ of social studies teachers' NTSSE score: School average of social studies teachers' scores on the NTSSE. B[I]: $\overline{X}$ = 63.90, σ = 3.17; C: $\overline{X}$ = 63.98, σ = 3.14.

22. Math Teacher's Education Beyond B.A.: Number of additional credits beyond the B.A. of the eighth-grade math teacher. A[I]: $\overline{X}$ = 1.41, σ = .53. Or school $\overline{X}$ of eighth-grade math teachers' education beyond B.A.: School average of eighth-grade math teachers' extra credits beyond the B.A. B[I]: $\overline{X}$ = 1.44, σ = .36; C: $\overline{X}$ = 1.40, σ = .33.

23. Math Teacher's Race = Pupil's Race: Eighth-grade math teacher's race is same as pupil's race, 0 = no, 1 = yes. A[I]: $\overline{X}$ = .38, σ = .49; EST: $\overline{X}$ = .45, σ = .40, R^2 = .57, F = 20.82. Or difference between percentage of black students and percentage of black teachers: Absolute value of the percentage of black pupils minus percentage of black teachers in pupil's school. B[J,K]: $\overline{X}$ = 33.85, σ = 17.54; C: $\overline{X}$ = 34.45, σ = 18.74.

24. Percent Black Teachers: Average percentage of black teachers in schools pupils attended, 1969/70–1970/71. A[K]: $\overline{X}$ = 35.7, σ = 16.7; B[K]: $\overline{X}$ = 33.33, σ = 18.10; C: $\overline{X}$ = 34.38, σ = 18.42.

25. Remedial Education Expenditures: Expenditure in pupil's school on remedial education per low-achieving pupil. A[L]: $\overline{X}$ = 38.58, σ = 24.06; B[L]: $\overline{X}$ = 47.05, σ = 38.02; C: $\overline{X}$ = 46.45, σ = 36.91.

26. (2) × if Low Achiever: Interaction of remedial expenditure per low achiever with dummy variable; 0 = non–low achiever, 1 = low achiever sixth-grade score ≤ 5.1).

27. Class Size $\geq$ 32: Average number of pupils per classroom unit reporting attendance in pupil's seventh and eighth grade. Dummy variable: 0 = class size < 32, 1 = class size $\geq$ 32. A[G]: $\overline{X}$ = .29, σ = .45; B[G]: $\overline{X}$ = .33, σ = .47; C: $\overline{X}$ = .35, σ = .48.

28. (27) $\times$ Income: Interaction of income with class size $\geq$ 32.

29. Attending a K-8 school: Dummy variable, 0 = attending eighth grade not in an elementary school, 1 = attending an eighth grade in an elementary school. A[M]: $\overline{X}$ = .09, σ = .29; B[A]: $\overline{X}$ = .06, σ = .24; C: $\overline{X}$ = .04, σ = .20.

30. Percentage of Black Students: Average percentage of black students in school pupil attended, 1969/70–1970/71. A[J]: $\overline{X}$ = 65.64, σ = 36.04; B[J]: $\overline{X}$ = 60.20, σ = 39.31; C: $\overline{X}$ = 64.37, σ = 38.03.

31. (30) $\times$ Race: Interaction of pupil's race with percentage of black students in school.

32. Percent Blacks in School $\geq$ 50: Second piece of a two-piece linear function (spline) of percent black students in school with corner at 50 percent; set to equal maximum (0, percent black $-$ 50).

33. (32) $\times$ Race: Interaction of pupil's race with percentage of black students in school ($-$ 50).

34. Relative Income Change in School Feeder Area, 1960–1970: Income of student's school feeder area in 1960 relative to $\overline{X}$ income of Philadelphia $\div$ same ratio for 1970. A[E]: $\overline{X}$ = .03, σ = .06; B[E]: $\overline{X}$ = .06, σ = .08; C: $\overline{X}$ = .05, σ = .08.

35. School Enrollment: Number of pupils enrolled in school. A[G]: $\overline{X}$ = 1632.54, σ = 585.07; B[G]: $\overline{X}$ = 1676.44, σ = 532.96; C: $\overline{X}$ = 1704.20; σ = 514.29.

Sources: [A] School District of Philadelphia (SDP) Pupil History Files; [B] Individual Pupil Records, Form EH-7; [C] Individual Admission Application Form, EH-40; [D] SDP 1960–70 Pupil Address File; [E] Summers and Wolfe (1978); [F] SDP Roll Sheets; [G] SDP October Monthly Reports; [H] Gourman Report; [I] SDP Permis File; [J] Enrollment, Negro and Spanish-Speaking in the Philadelphia Public Schools; [K] Summary of Personnel in the Philadelphia Public Schools; [L] Detail of Proposed General Fund School Operating Budget; [M] Forms E-83 and E-84.

ACKNOWLEDGMENTS

The authors wish to thank Lawrence H. Summers for his many suggestions and his interest, the School District of Philadelphia for its willingness to allow access to the detailed data, and Arthur S. Goldberger for his insightful and helpful comments.

NOTES

1. Theil (1971, p. 603) suggested that "a plea can be made to divide the available observations into three parts, the first of which is used for the choice of the specification, the second for the estimation, and the third for conditional prediction based on the estimated equation in order to verify whether the method actually works." And Christ (1966, p. 548) observed that "in time-series studies the two main virtues of prediction tests—extending the number of observations with which a model is confronted, and doing so in a way that prevents us from choosing the model in the light of knowledge of the data with which it is to be confronted—can be attained by fitting the model to all the data in question just as well as they can be attained by fitting to some of the data and predicting the rest." But, he continued, "In cross-section studies the situation may be different. Here the sample is typically very much larger than in time-series studies. We can therefore divide an available sample into two parts, each containing hundreds or thousands of observations, one part to be used initially to help suggest the form of the model and the other part to be used later as a test of the predictive ability of the model chosen. It is not difficult to make that division so as to prevent our knowledge of the entire sample from influencing our choice of the model."

2. In the landmark *Hobson* v. *Hansen* case, Circuit Judge J. Skelly Wright of the District Court "held that Superintendent and Board, in operation of public school system in District of Columbia, unconstitutionally deprived Negro and poor public school children of their right to equal educational opportunity with white and more affluent public school children" [269 F. Supp. 401 (1967), p. 401, D.D.C. 1967]. In the follow-up suit Judge Wright conveyed his disaffection with the opposing testimonies of expert witnesses: "the unfortunate if inevitable tendency has been to lose sight of the disadvantaged young students on whose behalf this suit was first brought in an over-grown garden of numbers and charts and jargon. . . . The reports by the experts—one noted economist plus assistants for each side— are less helpful than they might have been for the simple reason that they do not begin from a common data base, disagree over crucial statistical assumptions, and reach different conclusions" [327 F. Supp. 844 (1971), p. 859, D.D.C. 1971]. Also, see Summers and Wolfe (1976, 1977b) and Berk (1977) for an exchange on the use of statistics in the courtroom.

3. Some of the data, such as test scores and sex, are unambiguously specific to the pupil. Other data, such as the class size and teacher background, are treated as uniform for all students in the classroom. If students in the same class are handled differently—receiving more or less of the teacher's time, for example—the data are not then literally specific to the pupil.

4. The present authors did a study on 1970/71 elementary school pupils in the Philadelphia School District (Summers and Wolfe, 1977a) in which general comparisons were made with other studies, but no precise replication was attempted. The implementation efforts associated with that study are what gave rise to this one.

5. We have developed a procedure described in a paper (Summers and Wolfe, 1978) using 1970 Philadelphia Census data for estimating block income which were generated from data on block mean housing values, block mean contract rental values, tract distribution of block contract rental values, and tract distributions of income values.

6. Definitions, $\overline{X}$'s, σ's, and sources of the data are in the Appendix.

7. These were the subjects all students were required to take.

8. The Gourman rating, published in *The Gourman Report* (Phoenix, Arizona: The Continuing Education Institute, 1967) was used. It is a rating based on the undergraduate programs of nearly all colleges and universities in the United States, with information drawn

from professional societies, commercial publications, foundations, etc., as well as the in-stitutions themselves.

9.   The coefficients of the modified Sample A equation using the estimators which are to be compared with the results in Table 1, column (7), are these: row 9, .50; row 10, −.02; row 13, −7.75; row 14, .12; row 15, −1.08; row 16, .03; row 17, −1.42; row 18, 1.69; row 20, −.32; row 21, .11; row 23, 7.65.

10.   The adjustment factor was based on the ratio of the variance of the Sample A equation S_ϵ^2 [Table 1, column (7)] to the variance of the same equation using estimators, $S_{\epsilon\phi v}^2$. This scalar was used to adjust the variance–covariance matrix and generate new standard errors. This procedure assumes $E(V\epsilon) = 0$. (See preceding paragraph).

11.   See Summers and Wolfe (1977a). The same general conclusions were reached for elementary school students.

12.   For interaction variables, the t-statistics in the table indicate only whether or not there is a significant difference in the impact of each input among different types of students. Tests of the form

$$\theta = \frac{\hat\alpha + \hat\beta_{y^*}}{\sqrt{\hat\sigma_\alpha^2 + \hat\sigma_\beta^2 y^{*2} + 2\hat\sigma_{\alpha\beta}y^*}}$$

were used to determine the significance of specific values (y*) of the interaction terms. The θ values for a full range of these interaction term values are shown in Table 1.

13.   For the variables without interaction the test took the form:

$$\tilde\theta = \frac{\hat\beta_1 - \hat\beta_2}{\sqrt{\hat\sigma_1^2 + \hat\sigma_1^2}} \ ,$$

where $\hat\beta_1$ is the coefficient of the base sample; $\hat\beta_2$ is the matching coefficient of a replication sample; $\hat\sigma_1$ is the standard error of the coefficient of base sample; and $\hat\sigma_2$ the standard error of the coefficient of the sample. For variables with interactions, the test was of the form:

$$\tilde\theta = \frac{(\hat\alpha_1 + \hat\beta_1 y^*) - (\hat\alpha_2 + \hat\beta_2 y^*)}{\sqrt{[\hat\sigma_{\alpha_1}^2 + \hat\sigma_{\beta_1}^2 y^{*2} + 2\text{cov}(\hat\alpha_1\hat\beta_1)] + [\hat\sigma_{\alpha_2}^2 + \hat\sigma_{\beta_2}^2 y^* + 2\text{cov}(\hat\alpha_2\hat\beta_2)]}} \ ,$$

where the terms with 1 as a subscript refer to the base sample; the terms with 2 as a subscript refer to the replication sample; and y* refers to specific values of the interaction terms.

14.   Interpretation of the interaction term coefficients is described in footnote c of Table 2.

15.   A detailed review of the results on class size in a recent Educational Research Service study (1978, p. 68) concludes: "There is general consensus that the research findings on the effects of class size on pupil achievement across all grade levels are contradictory and inconclusive."

REFERENCES

Berk, R., "A Comment on Summers and Wolfe." *Journal of Human Resources* 12(3 1977):401–5.

Chamberlain, G. and Z. Griliches, "Unobservables with Variance-Components Structure: Ability, Schooling, and the Economic Success of Brothers." *International Economic Review* 16(2 1975):422–50.

Christ, C., *Econometric Models and Methods*. New York. John Wiley and Sons, Inc., 1966.

Educational Research Service, Inc., "Class Size: A Summary of Research." *Research Brief*, Virginia, 1978.

Frane, J., "Some Simple Procedures for Handling Missing Data in Multivariate Analysis." *Psychometrika* 41(3 1976):409–15.

Gourman, J., *The Gourman Report,* Phoenix, 1967.

Hanushek, E., "Throwing Money at Schools." *Journal of Policy Analysis and Management* 1(Fall 1981).

Heckman, J., "The Common Structure of Statistical Models of Truncation, Sample Selection and Limited Dependent Variables and a Simple Estimator for Such Models." *Annals of Economic and Social Measurement* 5(4 1976):475–92.

Mullin, S. and Summers, A., "Is More Better? An Analysis of the Evidence on the Effectiveness of Spending on Compensatory Education." *Phi Delta Kappan* 64(January 1983).

Summers, A. and B. Wolfe, "Intradistrict Distribution of School Inputs to the Disadvantaged: Evidence for the Courts." *Journal of Human Resources* 11(1976):328–42.

Summers, A. and B. Wolfe, "Do Schools Make a Difference?" *American Economic Review* 67(4 1977a):639–52.

Summers, A. and B. Wolfe, "Reply." *Journal of Human Resources* 12(3 1977b):406–9.

Summers, A. and B. Wolfe, "Estimating Household Income from Location." *Journal of the American Statistical Association* 73(362 1978):288–92.

Taubman, P., *Sources of Inequality of Earnings.* Amsterdam: North-Holland, 1977.

Theil, H., *Principles of Econometrics.* New York. John Wiley and Sons, Inc., 1971.

CRIME IN SWEDEN:

CAUSALITY, CONTROL EFFECTS, AND ECONOMIC EFFICIENCY

Harold L. Votey, Jr.

I. INTRODUCTION

This paper reports on an econometric analysis of social and economic factors thought to influence crime and the effects of resources applied by the Swedish authorities to control it. An important aspect of the analysis is a test of whether law enforcement resources are allocated in accordance with rules that will yield economic efficiency across communities and crime categories. Crime is viewed both in the aggregate and broken down by broad offense categories: personal crimes, crimes against property, and motoring offenses. The data base for the analysis is a cross-section of 24 Swedish counties for the years 1975 through 1978. Modeling is similar to previous studies evaluating variation in deterrence or control effects that stem from variations in conviction probabilities and penalties. That

Advances in Applied Micro-Economics, Volume 3, pages 229–265.
Copyright © 1984 by JAI Press Inc.
All rights of reproduction in any form reserved.
ISBN: 0-89232-398-1

approach has been criticized, most notably by Blumstein et al. (1978), for a number of reasons. The empirical validity of some of their criticisms is subject to test. This study, in addition to providing a test of efficiency and an entirely new data base for comparison with earlier results for the United States, thus provides an opportunity to evaluate those criticisms in the light of new data.

This study has the added advantage that it can test hypotheses about the effects of potential causal variables that typically haven't been included in U.S. studies, in part because beliefs that such variables are causally important may be held more strongly in Sweden than in the United States and in part because the Swedish penchant for recording such data in a systematic and easily accessible fashion is greater than that in the United States. Social and economic factors that are investigated for crime-inducing effects are broken family relationships, alien population, and alcohol consumption levels, as well as lack of employment opportunities. Highway accidents, an outcome of motoring offenses, are perceived to stem from the level of driving, traffic density, and other factors reflecting the driving environment as well as from such illegal behavior as drunken driving.

Econometric results lend support to economic decision theory and neoclassical criminological theory predicting that criminal behavior will be deterred by the threat of sanctions. These results are consistent with an earlier aggregate time-series study of Sweden by the author investigating similar effects at the national level. Acknowledging the criticisms of deterrence studies by Blumstein et al. (1978), one cannot claim that these results establish unambiguous evidence of a deterrence effect; however, they provide strong evidence of a control effect, a necessary condition for the establishment of cost-effective crime control efforts.

II.   THE DATA

As noted, the data are composed of annual information on 24 Swedish counties (*län*) for the years 1975 through 1978. All data have been provided by Swedish national data-collection sources. Most are published or provided by the National Central Bureau of Statistics, although some come directly from the responsible agency—for example, alcohol consumption data have been provided, in part, by the Alcohol Bureau. Virtually all data that are compiled about individuals, even though aggregated, are based on national files where the unit of observation is the individual and where the data may be aggregated over county (*län*), municipality (*kommun*), or police district (*polisdistrikt*). Individual data of different categories, e.g., income, education, birth, marriage, accident, and health data, are linked for an individual by a *personnumber* issued at birth. The aggregation is conducted with centralized computer facilities which, in theory, make it possible to have a complete file on all aspects of an individual's life from birth. In practice, the files are strictly segregated and extreme care is used to protect the privacy of information for individuals. The system can, however, yield highly accurate aggregate data on any desired level. Considerable care is taken to see that reporting is uniform across the country, since the collection and processing of any one class of data is done centrally by persons employed by the state rather than the local community. In general, local community preferences do not enter separately into decisions about how carefully or completely data shall be collected. In Sweden, careful data tabulation has been the rule for much annual economic data for more than a century, and birth, death, and marriage records go back to the early 1700s. Thus, the data for this study are probably as accurate a representation of the nature of a particular community or county as could be produced in any country.

An alleged problem with much crime data has been that it may vary in quality across jurisdictions. This is less likely to be true in Sweden than in the United States because the police are organized, trained, and assigned at the national level. This does not mean that there are no local differences, but these tend to be minimized because transfers between communities are possible and standards and training are uniform across police districts. Some kinds of training are conducted at the national level. The criminal code does not vary across districts and judicial appointments are not a local decision. Corrections facilities are largely a matter for the national authorities as well. Thus, the kinds of problems that worry researchers when using cross-section data in the United States, particularly across states, are not a matter of concern with Swedish data.

Swedish crime data and behavior are of particular interest because of a number of similarities with those of the United States. Police procedures in Sweden follow a pattern very similar to that in the United States. Sweden has tended to emulate U.S. criminal justice and law enforcement procedures to a considerable degree. For example, police are normally armed as they are in the United States; they use virtually the same technology for patrol, communications, and detection; and corrections procedures are also very similar. While Swedish law has evolved more from Roman law, with nothing like the English common law tradition that is the basis for U.S. law, this appears to have little impact in creating differences in the likelihood of conviction, or the nature of sentencing. Although the decision on what to record as a crime may vary somewhat between Sweden and the United States, the uniformity of that decision across jurisdictions in Sweden is likely to be high.

Sweden is, of course, very similar to the United States in terms of average living standards, educational techniques and levels, health care, and attitudes toward work and leisure. Consequently, it provides an ideal for comparison with U.S. studies, with the advantage of providing a more uniformly high quality of data for statistical evaluation that can be found elsewhere. This is not to say that Swedish crime data are without flaws. Sweden has a considerable amount of unreported crime, just as in the United States, and with less independent survey information on which to base estimates of the extent of underreporting. There is no reason to believe, however, that this problem is greater than in the United States, nor that patterns of crime have changed over the time period or across jurisdictions of this study. Thus the Swedish data provide an ideal candidate for evaluation.

One characteristic of Sweden that differs from the United States is that of density of population. Sweden is a sparsely populated country, still largely involved in agriculture, forestry, or fisheries over much of the land area, with manufacturing concentrated in a few urban locations of modest size. There are only three cities with populations greater than 240,000: Stockholm, Göteborg, and Malmö. Crime in Sweden, as in the United States, tends to be an urban phenomenon, but Sweden's urban areas are minimal and most of the country corresponds more in terms of population distribution to the rural United States. This may have some bearing on why violent crime rates, on the average, tend to be lower in Sweden than in the United States. The distribution of cities by size is shown in Table 1. A comparison of typical Swedish and U.S. crime variables is presented in Table 2. In general, crime levels and their rates of growth are lower in Sweden than in the United States, with the exception of reported property offenses. The fact that the latter are higher in Sweden could be a consequence of differences in the level of unreported crime or differences in police recording of offenses. There is no way to evaluate either possibility.

Table 1. Distribution
of Municipalities by
Size

Population	Number
≥500,000	1
250,000–499,999	1
150,000–249,999	1
100,000–149,999	8
50,000–99,999	23
25,000–49,999	61
0–24,999	178

Source: Statistisk årsbok 1977.

Table 2. Comparative Crime Statistics for Sweden and the United States, 1977

Country	Offenses	Crime Mix (%)	Rate per 100,000 pop.	Growth Reported Offenses 1968–1977 (%)	Clearance Ratio (%)
Sweden	Violent	5.5	380.2	36.4	36
	(Homicide)	(0.6)	(4.8)	(73.8)	(56)
	Property	90.6	6320.8	55.8	15
	Drunken Driving	3.9	269.4	39.3	—
		100.0			
United States	Violent[a]	8.3	466.6	56.4	51.2
	(Homicide)	(.16)	(8.8)	(38.6)	(75.5)
	Property[b]	81.3	4588.4	62.1	18.9
	Drunken Driving	10.4	585.4	110.2	—
		100.0			

Notes:
[a] These include murder, forcible rape, robbery and aggravated assault.
[b] These include burglary, larceny–theft, and motor vehicle theft.
Sources: Sweden—*Rättsstatistisk årsbok 1978*; United States—FBI, Uniform Crime Reports, 1977.

Another characteristic of Sweden recommends cross-section analysis using the county (*län*) as the unit of observation. Not only is income distributed quite uniformly across the Swedish population relative to that of most countries, the population is distributed geographically in such a manner as to minimize the likelihood of statistical problems associated with spillover effects. Examination of the dispersal of population with regard to urban clustering and county boundaries suggests that, since crime tends to be an urban phenomenon, it will tend to focus inward away from county boundaries rather than move across county boundaries. That is, if one were to think of setting up a gravity model to explain crime based on the populations associated with denser, urban populations, one would expect to get the same distribution of crime as if county boundaries defined the population borders. This, at least, would be the conclusion from analyzing population dispersal by county and major cities, noting the distance from population centers to county borders and to the next adjacent population center in contiguous counties. The data to do so are presented in Table 3. Examination of the distribution of population county by county shows that on the average 47.3 percent of the population resides in an urban area central to the county, averaging 36.8 km from the county border and 84.6 km from the closest urban area of more than 15,000 population in the next adjacent county. No major cities lie close to county

Table 3. Characteristics of Population Concentration Counties (*län*)

	Main City	Pop. Density	Percentage of Total län	Aver. Pop. Density of län	Air Dist. Pop. Ctr. to Closest Border (km)	Air Dis. Pop. Ctr. to Next Closest Pop. Ctr. in Adjacent län (km)
AB	Greater Stockholm	3551	55	231	30	55
C	Uppsala	56	60	33	18	55
D	Nyköping-Oxelösund	30	31	41	18	48
E	Linköping-Norrköping	80	62	236	20	50
F	Jönköping	72	36	30	25	70
G	Växjö	37	37	20	26	92
H	Kalmar-Nybroborgholm	55	35	21	52	72
I	Visby	17	100	17	105	105
K	Karlskrona	57	39	53	23	70
L	Kristionstad-Hässleholm	54	42	45	25	70

M	Malmö-Lund	1562	43	150	32	58
N	Halmstad	73	34	40	30	70
O	Göteborg-Bohus	992	69	139	12	57
P	Borås	88	25	36	29	57
R	Mariestad	40	46	33	32	68
S	Karlstad	62	42	16	50	98
T	Örebro	63	53	32	36	72
U	Surahammar-Västeras	123	45	41	25	72
W	Falun-Borlänge	78	42	10	25	82
X	Gävle	54	55	16	44	82
Y	Härnösand-Sundsvall	29	45	12	25	165
Z	Östersund	24	41	2	62	165
AC	Umeå	32	63	4	60	98
BD	Luleå	11	36	2	50	200
	Whole country		$\bar{x} = 47.3$ $\sigma = 16.4$	$\bar{x} = 20$	$\bar{x} = 36.8$ $\sigma = 19.5$	$\bar{x} = 84.6$ $\sigma = 38.3$

235

borders. Thus, while one would expect what is known in the trade literature as cross-hauling along borders, there is no reason to expect any systematic flow of criminals residing in one county and committing crimes in another. Causal inquiry suggests that the Swedish National Police believe spillovers are negligible, as would be expected based on U.S. studies in which spillovers tend to be limited largely to traffic between proximate urban areas, certainly less than 40 or 50 km apart.

III. MODELING CRIMINAL BEHAVIOR

Criminal behavior has been examined extensively from a theoretical perspective in recent years, beginning with the landmark article by Becker (1968) that was a revitalization and extension of the early work of the Utilitarians, including the Marchese di Beccaria and Jeremy Bentham. A nonexhaustive list of notable studies include Ehrlich (1973), Block and Heineke (1975), and Heineke (1978). Empirical studies built on this framework include those of Ehrlich (1973), Carr-Hill and Stern (1973), Sjoquist (1973), and Phillips and Votey (1975). In these models, the behavior that generates individual crime levels is thought to be a response to lack of economic opportunities and to other social and economic forces that contribute to antisocial behavior. Such behavior is moderated by the threat of imposition of real costs on the perpetrator through loss of freedom, fines, and other sanctions. These models imply that crime levels or rates will be responsive to the individual's subjective probabilities of sanctions being imposed and, in the aggregate, are expected to be related to the objective probability of apprehension and conviction. Additionally, the expected costs of illegal behavior are influenced by the severity of the sentence imposed. Typically, studies have found that to a substantial degree these two forces alone explain the levels of crime that prevail.

Economists hardly believe that the process of crime generation can be completely described by the latter sparse specification, and most studies capture a part of the impact of other social factors by including unemployment and labor force participation rates or poverty indices to reflect legitimate earnings opportunities or their lack. Ethnic variables are often included to capture effects expected to fall more heavily on ethnic minorities. These are captured by a relation of the form

$$OF_i = g(CR_i, SV_i, SE, \ldots), \qquad i = 1, \ldots, n, \qquad (1)$$

where OF_i represents aggregate crime rates for each of n crime categories; CR_i represents the probability of apprehension or conviction; SV_i represents the statutory penalty prescribed for offenders; and SE represents a vector of social and economic factors that influence individual criminal behavior.

It is not appropriate to estimate this crime generation relationship in isolation because, as has been noted in numerous studies, arrest and conviction variables and perhaps sanction variables are jointly determined with the level of offenses.[1] Thus, to avoid simultaneity bias, one must account for the way apprehension probabilities are determined, i.e., take account of the process of crime control.

A criticism of this specification, noted by Blumstein et al. (1978), is that the estimation of a formulation in which the independent variable is the denominator of a key explanatory variable will create a spurious negative relationship, thus confusing a test of causality.[2] The existence of that effect is tested by an appropriate reformulation of the estimation form as is reported with the estimation results.

IV. CRIME CONTROL

Crime control is generally viewed as a production process in which law enforcement inputs interact with the offense load on the system to generate convictions and hence conviction probabilities. In the case of Sweden, the criminal justice system's control effort can be determined by the relation

$$CR_i = (OF_i, L_i, \ldots), \tag{2}$$

in which CR_i and OF_i have already been defined, and L_i represents the amounts of law enforcement inputs allocated to the control of each crime classification. Some studies, e.g., that of Ehrlich (1973), include environmental variables in this relation to help differentiate among police districts for differences in the law enforcement environment or operating procedures that might affect output. In the Swedish case this was not felt to be necessary since the police are a national force, uniformly trained, and operating under common policy directives. Heineke (1978) and Phillips (1978) test more sophisticated models of police productivity than that tested here, including tests of appropriate functional form, factor substitutionality, and returns to scale, using a cost function approach to estimation. For this study, in view of the lack of data on inputs other than police manpower, such sophistication is simply not feasible. As has been noted in other studies, however, police manpower generally represents as much as 85 percent of law enforcement inputs.[3] The focus here has been on the role of law enforcement, in general, in controlling crime, rather than on factor substitution. Darrough and Heineke (1978) argue for the exclusion of OF as a load factor largely on the basis that the output elasticity with respect to load in other studies is insignificantly different from 1, an assumption for his own data set that simplifies the analysis, but one he does not test. Here the role of OF in the simultaneous relationship makes its inclusion more important.

A potential weakness of this specification from an econometric perspective is that, since CR is a ratio of convictions to offenses, there will be a negative correlation between the dependent variable and OF, independent of any causal link in terms of load on the system. Thus, the parameter estimate may not measure what it purports to in the model, and test statistics may be biased in favor of the hypothesis with respect to the effects of load. However, it should be noted that in earlier studies, estimates derived using an alternative specification where OF did not serve as the denominator of the dependent variable yielded identical coefficients to the case where the ratio form was used. Moreover, the parameter estimates remained highly significant.[4]

The need for conceiving of the problem as one of simultaneous estimation follows from the fact that the offense rate OF is the output of crime generation and at the same time an input (load variable) for the criminal justice production function. Similarly, CR, the level of output of the criminal justice system, is a deterrent force affecting crime generation. Taking account of the joint determination of OF and CR requires that a simultaneous estimation technique be used.

There is another potential simultaneity that should be considered. As noted by Blumstein et al. (1978), it is possible that the level of law enforcement inputs is not exogenous to the system but is jointly determined in a demand–supply interaction along with the offense rate and the conviction ratio.[5] If this interaction is a simultaneous one, it can be captured by presuming a supply function for law enforcement inputs in which

$$L_s = s(w), \tag{3}$$

i.e., the supply of law enforcement inputs is a function of their wage w.

With respect to demand, two possibilities might be considered. One is that society through its agents, the authorities in the criminal justice system, will act to minimize the social costs of crime. In this case they would want to minimize a social cost function of the form

$$SC = \sum_i r_i OF_i + w \sum_i L_i, \tag{4}$$

where r_i is the average loss rate per offense in each offense class. The process of social cost minimization incorporated into the simultaneous relationships of Eqs. (1), (2), and (3) will yield an equilibrium level of law enforcements inputs L of the form

$$L = h(OF_i, r_i, w_i, Y), \tag{5}$$

i.e., a function of offense levels, the loss rate per offense (r_i), input prices (w_i), and community income levels (Y). The express derivation of the estimating form will follow Phillips and Votey (1975), Phillips et al. (1976), and Votey (1982). Details for this model are in the Appendix.

A simpler hypothesis is that while society may allocate funds to crime control, rather than 'to other potential recipients of national funds, on the basis of some vague notion of rising crime costs, law enforcement authorities do not allocate across jurisdictions on the basis of variation in offense levels. In this event, the overall magnitude of L may depend upon the loss rate in the sense that political pressure for public safety efforts will depend upon overall costs of crime, but allocation across communities will be responsive to income levels simply because they represent ability to tax, and tax revenues in turn reflect power to demand services from the criminal justice establishment. In this event, variations in offense levels across communities would not be good predictors of community law enforcement allocations.

It also seems plausible that law enforcement input demand is recursive rather than simultaneous, if one considers how criminal justice budgets are determined. Since law enforcement is a public enterprise with budgets established annually for the coming year, a plausible alternative would be to assume that in estimating with annual data all the variables on the right-hand side of Eq. (5) should be lagged by one year to account for the budgetary process. Then there would be no need to take into account Eq. (5) when estimating Eqs. (1) and (2). With these possibilities in mind, we can proceed to the specifications of relationships for estimation, taking into account data availability.

V. IMPLEMENTATION OF THE MODEL

A. Offense Generation

The offense generation relationship Eq. (1) is estimated in two forms: (i) as an aggregate, and (ii) disaggregated to consider separately personal (violent) crimes, property offenses, and motoring offenses within the systems framework. One of the reasons for doing so is that there are sound reasons to expect that different types of crimes are motivated by different causal factors. For example, one would be likely to expect the motive for property offenses to be economic gain, whereas personal crimes are more likely to be generated by frustrations and deteriorating interpersonal relationships, some of which might, of course, be aggravated by economic hardship. It is often alleged, in Scandinavia in particular, that alcohol use may be a contributing factor to crime by reducing inhibitions to illegal behavior and by inciting individuals to be less rational, perhaps more violent. The presence of a greater number of aliens in the population is thought by some to be associated with higher crime levels. This may be a consequence of a higher incidence of social instability related to lack of economic opportunity, in which case we might expect crime to be predicted better by economic indicators than by the level of alien population. On the other hand, the higher crime levels may be a consequence of more complex problems associated with the assimilation of people into an alien culture. A specification that investigates crime generation by distinguishing, even to a limited extent, among crime classes should help to generate insights into underlying causal relationships.

In the case of motoring offenses, the analysis becomes additionally complex, since the crime loss in the case of motoring offenses stems from the social cost of accidents. To deal with this, a complete specification requires the inclusion of an accident relationship.[6] The consideration of motoring offenses adds a further complication to the analysis because of the way such crimes are recorded. Unlike personal and property crimes, motoring offenses are not generally reported to the police by victims or persons observing the offense. Rather, they are almost invariably the result of traffic or preventive patrol and show up on the record first as arrests, rather than as offenses reported to the police. To see how this problem must be dealt with, it is useful to specify the disaggregated model in greater detail.

B.　The Disaggregated Model

The model to be used for estimation is composed of eight equations, as follows:

$$OFV = V \cdot CRV^{\gamma_v} ATSV^{\sigma_v} ALIEN^{\eta_v} DIV^{\delta_v} UP^{\mu_v} ALC^{\phi_v} \epsilon_V \tag{6}$$

$$OFP = P \cdot CRP^{\gamma_p} ATSP^{\sigma_p} ALIEN^{\eta_p} DIV^{\delta_p} UP^{\mu_p} ALC^{\phi_p} \epsilon_P \tag{7}$$

$$OFM = M \cdot CRM^{\gamma_m} ATSM^{\sigma_m} ALC^{\phi_m} KD^{\kappa_m} VM^{v_m} \epsilon_m \tag{8}$$

$$CRV = v \, OFV^{\omega_v} L_v^{\beta_v} \epsilon_v \tag{9}$$

$$CRP = p \, OFP^{\omega_p} L_p^{\beta_p} \epsilon_p \tag{10}$$

$$CRM = m \, OFM^{\omega_m} L_m^{\beta_m} \epsilon_m \tag{11}$$

$$AC = a \, OFM^{\theta} KD^{\kappa_A} VM^{\gamma_A} \epsilon_A \tag{12}$$

$$L = n \, OF^{\rho} AC^{\tau} Y^{\lambda} \epsilon_L. \tag{13}$$

Variables are defined in Table 4. (For a further discussion, see the Appendix.)

Additional relationships needed to complete the system are the identities

$$L \equiv L_V + L_P + L_M + kL \tag{14}$$

Table 4. The Variables Defined

OF	Offenses reported to the police (per capita)
OFV	Personal offenses reported (per capita)
OFP	Property offenses reported (per capita)
OFM	Motoring offenses based on arrests (per capita)
CR	Total convictions/total offenses
CRV	Personal crime convictions/personal offenses
CRP	Property crime convictions/property offenses
CRM	Motoring offense convictions/motoring offenses
AC	Fatal and serious injury accidents (per capita)
L	Law enforcement manpower per capita; when associated with specific crimes, inputed values assigned to those crimes
ATS	Average time served per conviction; when associated with specific crime classes time served is for that class of crime
ALIEN	Non-Swedish population/population
DIV	Divorces and legal separations/population
UPM	Unemployed males/male working age population
ALC	Consumption of pure alcohol/population 15 years of age and older
KD	Index of kilometers driven
VM	Two-wheeled vehicles/total vehicles
Y	Median real income (per capita)
r	Loss rate per offense
w	Factor price: average wage to law enforcement personnel
ϵ_i	Stochastic error terms

and

$$OF \equiv OFV + OFP + OFM, \qquad (15)$$

where k is the proportion of law enforcement manpower that is devoted to activities other than dealing with crime control, presumed to be proportional to the total resources available.

There are still a number of problems that need to be resolved before the model can be estimated. In particular, it was previously noted that motoring offenses are not recorded in a way comparable to other offenses. It would be possible to estimate Eq. (8) using the reported figures for arrests, but this would mean that Eqs. (6), (7), and (8) would not be receiving parallel treatment, since personal and property crimes are measured by offenses reported to the police. An alternative would be to consider the real target of social intervention into a criminal behavior of reducing the social cost of that behavior. If we regard accidents as the target, it need not be a matter of concern that we cannot properly measure OFM or CRM.[7] By substitution, the accident relationship of Eq. (12) can be written

$$AC \equiv a^* L_M^{\beta_A} ATSM^{\alpha_A} KD^{\kappa_A} VM^{\gamma_A} \epsilon_A^*. \qquad (16)$$

Since L, and hence L_M, are perceived as potentially endogenous to the system, Eq. (16) should still be estimated in a simultaneous framework. However, if law enforcement labor is determined recursively based on the previous period's magnitudes for the explanatory variables, Eq. (16) can be thought of as a reduced-form relationship in which L_M is exogenous.

The concern that a spurious result insofar as causation is concerned will be the consequence of regressing offenses on a probability in which the denominator is the offense level can be dealt with in the formulation of Eqs. (6) and (7) by estimating the form

$$OF_i = C_i^{1/(1+\gamma)} CON_i^{\gamma/(1+\gamma)} ATS_i^{\alpha/(1+\gamma)}$$
$$\cdot ALIEN^{\eta/(1+\gamma)} DIV^{\delta/(1+\gamma)} UP^{\mu/(1+\gamma)} ALC^{\phi/(1+\gamma)} \epsilon_i^{1/(1+\gamma)}. \quad (17)$$

The results of this estimation are reported for comparison with the model estimated directly with the equations as specified by Eqs. (6) and (7). This test was not applied to Eq. (8) since that equation was not estimated with comparable data to (6) and (7) and the results of estimating Eq. (16) were considered more meaningful. The formulation of Eq. (16) avoids the potential criticism, in any event.

Another potential problem stemming from lack of observable data relates to the breakdown of law enforcement labor among the various activities included in Eq. (14). One alternative is to assume that this allocation is determined by the police maximizing their preference function with respect to convictions or crimes cleared by arrest, permitting, under appropriate assumptions, the substitution of L for the L_i in the production relations Eqs. (9), (10), and (11).[8] A second alternative is to assume that police minimize a social cost function of the form of Eq. (4).

To test the hypothesis of cost minimization with respect to allocating police manpower across offense classes, i.e., to minimize the sum of perceived losses to crime and law enforcement resources requires taking account of the first-order conditions with regard to manpower allocation derived from the minimization calculation. This is a procedure that has been used effectively by Phillips and Votey (1975), Phillips et al. (1976), and Votey (1982). For such a test there are no data on the loss rates (r_i). Consequently, in the estimation these variables are captured by the constant term or are assumed to be a function of income levels. Given the short time period over which the study is conducted, this should not be a serious concern, since what is relevant is whether the ratio of r_i/r_j changes over the estimation period, rather than the absolute levels of r_i. Changes in law enforcement wages are presumed to be linked to income, since in Sweden, as elsewhere, salaries of civil service workers tend to move with national income levels. Thus, the test comes down to whether the crime generation relationships are improved by specifying manpower per crime class in the general form

$$L_i = M_i \frac{OF_i}{\sum a_i OF_i} L, \qquad i = 1, 3. \tag{18}$$

(The details of this result are supplied in the Appendix.)

The only point in the estimation in which the inclusion of this variable makes a difference is in relations (9), (10), and (11). Taking account of relation (18) implies that a term $L/\sum a_i OF_i$ will replace L as an explanatory variable in those equations. The interpretation of the coefficient will be modified in the process of excluding the OF_i and $\sum a_i OF_i$ from the right-hand side of the equations since these are endogenous to the system.

The first test that has been applied to the data has been to estimate the so-called covariance model in which it is assumed that each cross-sectional unit and each time period has its own intercept. This was done estimating the model using two-stage least squares. For a typical offense generation equation this required the estimation of 32 coefficients, including the constant term. Not surprisingly, no significant coefficients were produced by these estimates, but a number of the variables specified in Eqs. (6)–(13) tended to show greater significance than did the regional and time dummies. One exception was that a dummy for region 13 tended to show some significance, suggesting that it be included in a reduced set of parameter estimates in which other regional and time dummies were excluded.

A number of statistical concerns have been taken into account in establishing the subsequent procedure for estimation. An obvious concern when dealing with cross-section data is the presence of heteroscedasticity. To consider that possibility in any practical sense requires us to have some notion of what the source of heteroscedasticity might be. One possibility is that crime varies over counties for reasons not fully accounted for by the variables included in the explanatory set. This could be a consequence of size alone, since it is an observed fact that urban crime rates in the United States vary positively with city size. All nonratio variables have been standardized by population, and all variables are expressed in their natural logarithms to minimize this effect; but, of course, if crime varies other than log-linearly with population, this will not be a sufficient correction unless the set of explanatory variables contains sufficient information to explain why crime rates vary with community size. Crime may vary with population density, but—with population already included in expressing offenses in terms of crime rates—adding population density would be including a variable likely to be negatively collinear with the others since it would represent the county's population divided by a constant.

Income variations by county could have an influence on crime rates. In estimating the cost minimization model, incomes enters in the reduced-form equations and should thus reduce the likelihood of heteroscedasticity if the relationship varies approximately log-linearly with income. Tests of the regression results will allow conclusions to be drawn in this regard.

The possibility of crime spillovers is a potential concern in estimating the offense generation equations with cross-section data. It is conceivable that offenses recorded in one jurisdiction could be a consequence of differentials in expected returns to crime because of differences among jurisdictions in opportunities for gain or in expected costs to the criminal because of differences in apprehension rates and penalties among jurisdictions. Studies of spillovers for the United States have tended to focus on two classes of causal forces in association with arrest or conviction probabilities (Fabrikant, 1979; Hakim et al., 1979). These causes are income or wealth differentials among jurisdictions, and distance. The most complete effort in terms of specification is that of Fabrikant, who takes into account distance, wealth differentials, the degree of competition among criminals in the location of residence, and differentials in arrest probabilities. He finds both wealth and distance to be significant, but by far the most important factor is distance. The implication of his study of data for the Los Angeles area is that the proportion of crimes committed outside a criminal's own Census tract falls to less than 1 percent in approximately 16 miles. Furthermore, geographic barriers such as freeways form an almost impenetrable barrier insofar as spillovers are concerned. That such an effect could be important for Sweden is further reinforced by Hägerstrand (1967), who in a study of communication across space makes explicit reference to the severely limiting effects of water barriers to both migration and communication. These results, combined with the previous discussion of the distribution of population among Swedish counties, would suggest that spillovers should not be a major concern in estimating crime relationships with county data. Nonetheless, to the extent that this possibility can be tested as a hypothesis, it should be. The effect would be spatial autocorrelation and the potential biasing of parameter estimates as a consequence of violating the assumption that error terms are uncorrelated, in this case, across the cross-sections.

A further problem worth considering is the possibility of time-series autocorrelation for the time-series observations of each of the counties in the data set. The data set covers a short time horizon and therefore provides a limited empirical basis for judging the extent of serial correlation. Nonetheless, it is a possibility that should not be ruled out in establishing an estimation procedure.

An appropriate procedure for estimation would be to specify a cross-sectionally correlated and time-wise autoregressive model. Such a procedure, discussed in Kmenta (1971), would test in a single estimating procedure for heteroscedasticity, mutual correlation of cross-sectional error terms, and autoregression over time. With appropriate data sets, this procedure can be applied using SAS–TSCSREG for single-equation estimation. That procedure was undertaken here for the reduced form equations for the offense generation equations. Unfortunately the results were not especially encouraging. Apparently multicollinearity among the set of explanatory variables prevented the estimation of precise individual coefficients.[9] As a consequence, other estimating techniques have been undertaken to conduct a piecemeal test of heteroscedasticity and serial correlations over space and time.

The literature discussing the problem of spatial interaction suggests a number of alternatives for dealing with it.[10] A typical procedure would involve the calculation of a weighting function based on the factors that are the most important in generating the interactions—in this case, crime spillovers. For Sweden, where wealth and income vary very little across jurisdictions as broad as counties, the most likely candidate would be distance. The possibility for variations in crime commission costs clearly exists if there is sufficient variance in conviction probabilities for them to be a significant determinant of variations in offense levels.

The likelihood of crime spillovers where the unit of observation is the county will be quite small, however, if the distance effects are similar to those in the Fabrikant (1979) study. In that study, analysis of the raw data indicated that spillovers across unpopulated areas were virtually nil. In Sweden, urban areas across county lines are separated by extensive agricultural and/or forest areas and in a number of cases by large bodies of water. Population centers in the northern counties are separated by very large distances (see Table 3), but even in the more populous south virtually every separation would exceed the 16 miles noted above for communities greater than 3000 or 4000 persons. In Sweden, where there is considerably greater use of public transportation and less reliance on private automobiles then in the United States, one would expect spillovers to become negligible at even smaller distances. Nonetheless, the hypothesis should be tested that spatial autocorrelation could exist, i.e., that error terms are correlated for contiguous counties across whose borders spillovers could take place.

The geographic distribution of Swedish counties lends itself to a simplified estimation procedure for testing the hypothesis of spatial interaction using the autoregressive model for the error terms as discussed in Ord (1975). The approach involves taking note of the natural barriers to criminal transactions between counties when criminals are accustomed to operation within a limited radius of their residential location. If one focuses upon the main transportation links and the physical layout of

Swedish counties, it is possible to construct an organization of the counties that places contiguous counties in a linear continuum in which the major communication links would be along that continuum and any links off the linear continuum would entail physical barriers such as lakes, forests, and/or agricultural areas where distances would exceed the limit beyond which interactions would become minimal.

An ordering of counties with these factors taken into account is presented in Table 5. The geographic location of counties is shown in Figure 1. The counties are ordered in such a way as to place adjacently in the continuum the counties that are most closely connected by highways between municipalities of greater than 5000 persons. Minimum distances between such communities are indicated in column 2 along with the name of the next closest community in the adjacent county to one in the county under consideration. Contiguous counties are noted which are joined along the coast where population is more concentrated than in the interior agricultural/forest areas.

In the case of crime spillovers, it would be appropriate to assume the weights between noncontiguous counties to be zero, since spillovers are virtually ruled out in any meaningful statistical sense. Similarly, between counties not in direct contiguity along the continuum, in view of the natural barriers, it would be appropriate to assume weights of zero. This leaves weights to be chosen for contiguous counties along the continuum. If one makes the simplifying assumption that spillovers all along the continuum are equally likely, then the appropriate weights would all be 1. This yields the standard model for the analysis of time-series autocorrelation in which the autoregressive parameter, ρ, is estimated by an iterative regression procedure. Such an approach is particularly fortunate in the case of the problem at hand, in which simultaneity among structural equations is expected to be of the utmost importance because the model can be estimated by a two-stage Cochrane–Orcutt estimation technique. That procedure has been adopted here to test the hypothesis of spatial interaction along the continuum representing the primary intercounty economic activity and hence also the most likely path of crime spillovers.

VI.   EMPIRICAL RESULTS

To deal with simultaneity the model is initially estimated by two-stage least squares, with the data ordered as supplied by Swedish sources, i.e., not in a manner to explicitly check for the possibility of serial correlation across counties. This is the ordering of Table 3. The results of the estimation are shown in Table 6 for the aggregate model and in Table 7 for the disaggregated approach.

One point that stands out from these results is the lack of sensitivity

Table 5. Ordering of Counties to Test for Spatial Autocorrelation

County		Closest Municipality by Highway	Bordering Coastal Counties	Farm, Forest Open Country Separation	Water Barrier Separation
C	Uppsala	Gävle, X (20) Sigtuna, AB (30)	AB	U	D,X
AB	Stockholms	Uppsala, C (30) Nyköping, D (70)	C,D		
D	Södernanlands	Södertälje, AB (70) Norrköping, E (58)	AB,E		C,U,T
E	Östergötlands	Nyköping, D (58) Tranås, F (30)	D,H	F,T	I,R
I	Gotlands	(Island in Baltic)			E,H
H	Kalmar	Kisa, E (40) Karlskrona, K (58)	E,K	F,G	
K	Blekinge	Emmmaboda, H (58) Kristianstad, L (30)	H,L	G	
L	Kristianstads	Sölvesborg, K (30) Ystad, M (40)	K,M,N	G	
M	Malmöhus	Kristianstad, L (25) Ängelholm, L (35)	L		
N	Hallands	Ängelholm, L (35) Kungsbacka, O (22)	L,O	F,G,P	
G	Kronoborgs	Värnamo, F (42) Karlskrona, K (42)		H,K,L,N,F	
F	Jönköpings	Ljungby, G (42) Tranemo, P, (26)		N,G,H,E,P	R
P	Älvsborgs	Göteborg, O (45) Gislaved, F (26)		N,F,O,R,S	
O	Göteborg och Bohus	Trollhättan, P (28)	N	P	
R	Skaraborgs	Jönkoping, F (20) Vårgårda, P (28)		T	E,F,S
S	Värmlands	Karlskoga, T (22)		P,T,W	R
T	Örebro	Arboga, U (35) Vingåker, D (48)		R,S,U,W	E,D
U	Västmanlands	Enköping, C (44)		T,E,C,W,X	D
W	Kopparbergs	Hofors, X (38)		S,T,U,X,Z	
X	Gävleborgs	Sundsvall, Y (72)		U,W,Z,Y	C
Z	Jämtlands	Sundsvall, Y (110)		W,X,Y,AC	
Y	Västernorrlands	Ostersund, Z (110) Umeå, AC (79)		X,AC	Z
AC	Västerbottens	Piteå, BD (70) Örnsköldsvik, Y (99)	Y,BD	Z	
BD	Norrbottens	Skellefteå, AC (70)	AC		

AB Stockholms
C   Uppsala
D   Södermanlands
E   Östergötlands
F   Jönköpings
G   Kronobergs
H   Kalmar
I   Gotlands
K   Blekinge
L   Kristianstads
M   Malmöhus
N   Hallands
O   Göteborgs och Bohus
P   Älvsborgs
R   Skaraborgs
S   Värmlands
T   Örebro
U   Västmanlands
W   Kopparbergs
X   Gävleborgs
Y   Västernorrlands
Z   Jämtlands
AC Västerbottens
BD Norrbottens

Figure 1.   Counties and Provincial Capitals of Sweden

Source: Statistisk årsbok för Sverige 1978.

248

Table 6. Estimates for the Aggregate Model

Test	Dependent Variable	Constant	Coefficient on: CR	ATS	OF	L	DIV	ALIEN	UPM	ALC	MEDY	D-W	F (DF)
Exogenous Law Enforcement Resources													
I	OF	.050 (0.06)	−.789 (10.94)*	−0.000 (0.06)			.771 (6.15)*	−0.089 (2.13)*	0.027 (0.71)	−0.119 (2.99)*		2.01	87.94 (6,88)
	CR	3.03 (3.88)*			−1.08 (11.35)*	1.08 (11.10)*						2.38	334.86 (2,93)
Endogenous Law Enforcement Resources													
I	OF	0.14 (0.18)	−.812 (9.66)*	.002 (0.23)			1.778 (5.98)*	−.082 (1.93)*	.033 (0.87)	−.119 (2.99)*		2.02	88.81 (6,88)
	CR	5.11 (5.22)*			−1.17 (10.48)*	1.44 (10.36)*						2.39	253.09 (2,92)
	L	13.05 (11.75)*			−.030 (0.33)						1.44 (6.30)*	2.05	23.05 (2,92)

Note: Student's t-statistics (absolute value) are in parentheses.
* Significant at the .05 level (one-tailed test).

Table 7. Estimates for the Disaggregated Model

Test	Dependent Variable	Constant	CR	ATS	OF	L	DIV	ALIEN	UPM	ALC	MEDY	KD	VM	D-W	F (DF)
								Coefficient on:							
Exogenous Law Enforcement Resources															
II	OFV	-4.54 (4.58)*	-1.04 (7.62)*	.005 (0.06)			.240 (1.97)*	.097 (1.60)*	.060 (1.29)	.046 (0.80)				1.91	40.08 (6,89)
	OFP	1.03 (1.11)	-.819 (8.58)*	-.161 (1.26)			.616 (5.27)*	.153 (3.04)*	.047 (1.08)	.123 (2.55)*				1.60	45.26 (6,89)
	AC	-4.66 (3.26)*		-.049 (0.22)		-.267 (2.17)*				.089 (2.25)*		.507 (3.58)*	.210 (3.67)*	2.38	17.10 (5,90)
	CRV	-2.05 (2.54)*			-.709 (8.16)*	.534 (5.04)*								1.96	147.16 (2,93)
	CRP	2.01 (2.91)*			-.732 (8.60)*	1.03 (9.91)*								2.12	174.81 (2,93)
	CRM	-.841 (1.12)			-.906 (8.93)*	.721 (8.04)*								1.69	173.66 (2,93)

Endogenous Law Enforcement Resources

III	(1)	(2)	(3)	(4)	(5)	(6)	(7)	(8)	(9)	(10)	(11)	D-W	F
OFV	-5.07 (4.22)*	-1.29 (7.45)*	.036 (0.41)			.306 (2.07)*	.060 (0.81)	.065 (1.14)	.006 (0.08)			2.03	22.76 (6,89)
OFP	1.16 (1.01)	-1.19 (8.11)*	-.158 (0.99)			.797 (5.25)*	.149 (2.36)*	.094 (1.69)*	.089 (1.46)			2.10	23.71 (6,89)
AC	-6.97 (3.95)*		-.085 (0.36)		-.515 (3.13)*				.053 (1.23)	.438 (2.96)*	.192 (3.27)*	2.36	15.57 (5,90)
CRV	-2.91 (3.36)*			-.730 (8.67)*	.418 (3.43)*							2.02	148.48 (2,93)
CRP	1.74 (2.28)*			-.746 (8.94)*	.992 (8.18)*							2.12	177.59 (2,93)
CRM	-.874 (1.14)			-.979 (9.96)*	.773 (7.36)*							1.75	171.71 (2,93)
L	-12.61 (12.05)*			.035 (0.49)							1.38 (6.37)*	1.75	23.43 (2,93)

Note: Student's t-statistics (absolute value) are in parentheses.
* Significant at the .05 level (one-tailed test).

of the control variables to the degree of aggregation or model specification. The coefficient on the conviction ratio is of the same order of magnitude (-0.789 to -1.29) and always highly significant (at the .0001 level or better), whereas time served in jail is uniformly insignificant. In contrast to this result, it makes a difference whether the model is aggregate or disaggregated with regard to the implied effect of some of the causal variables. While divorces and separations are uniformly and positively related to offense rates irrespective of model specification or degree of aggregation, the proportion of alien population tends to be significantly negatively related to offense rates in the aggregate models but highly significantly positively related to property offense rates and somewhat less to personal offense rates when these crimes are estimated separately. Similarly, alcohol consumption is shown to be negatively related to aggregate offense rates and weakly positively related to property offenses when offense classes are estimated separately. The unemployment variable, which is defined here as the proportion of unemployed males to their component of the population, is weakly positively associated with offense rates. The level of significance, although still low, rises with disaggregation. Surprisingly, divorces and separations seem to have a bigger impact on property crimes than on personal crimes, both in terms of magnitude of the coefficients and statistical significance. The same is shown to be true for the variable representing alien population. The overall results, in conjunction with the information on the proportion of variance explained by the estimated relationships, based on F-statistics, lends support to the notion that property crimes are more likely to be rational, less impulsive acts than are personal crimes.

The accident relationship in the disaggregated model yields similar results with respect to enforcement resources, the latter having a significant and negative impact on accidents and presumably drunken driving. Once more, time served in jail is not shown to be significant and both these results are consistent irrespective of model specification. As might be expected, alcohol consumption levels are positively related to accidents, as is the index of distance driven and the proportion of two-wheel to four-wheel vehicles, consistent with other studies.[11] The outcome of specifying a relationship that takes account of the demand for law enforcement has been the finding that law enforcement manpower is not significantly related to offense levels contemporaneously but is strongly related to median family income levels across communities. This conclusion holds whether offenses are included by category (including accident levels) or as an aggregate. This suggests that, at least for the Swedish data, the concern expressed by Blumstein et al. (1978) in regard to an unspecified positive link between offense levels and manpower inputs biasing the estimated results for control effects is unfounded in this instance. Further, the reason was not found to be a recursive relationship, i.e., a consequence of a lag between budget setting and crime control operations, since estimating the relation with one-year lags on the explanatory variable does not improve the fit.[12]

The criticisms can be laid to rest that regressing offense rates on the probability of conviction (which necessarily incorporates offense levels in the denominator) will yield spurious results with regard to the effect of law enforcement on offenses, at least insofar as these data are concerned. The results of running the offense rate relations for the case in which law enforcement resources are endogenous (Test III) yields highly significant results for the coefficient on convictions (t = 3.44 and 3.02 for personal and property crime convictions respectively) and implied values for γ, the control effect, of -1.83 and -2.17 for personal and property offenses. These values compare favorably with the results of estimation of Eqs. (6) and (7) of -1.29 and -1.19, respectively, making it clear that the sign and magnitude of the effect do not depend upon a mechanical link of including the dependent variable in the denominator of the conviction probability.

The test of the social cost minimization hypothesis would seem to indicate that the police are not allocating manpower among tasks in a way consistent with cost minimization. That is, the statistical results on the labor input variable of the form of relation (18) yield coefficients hardly significant and of the opposite sign of that to be expected, indicating that the balance of enforcement activity among activities implied by the cost minimization hypothesis is not being maintained.[13] This is hardly surprising when it seems clear that allocations across communities are similarly not related to implied crime costs, the other part of the social cost minimization hypothesis tested here. Based on this result, one would have to conclude that the more complex modeling of cost minimization is not a superior approach for modeling crime control across Swedish counties.

The limited tests for spatial autocorrelation along the continuum outlined in Table 5 indicate that, when estimators are derived from an instrumental variables approach to two-stage estimation, the hypothesis of serial correlation over the cross-section cannot be rejected out of hand, with Durbin–Watson statistics either falling in the inconclusive range or that for accepting the hypothesis of serial correlation. When the Cochrane–Orcutt technique for two-stage least squares is applied, the effects of aliens and weak effects of alcohol on personal and property offenses become weaker, but all other relationships that were previously significant at substantial levels remain so.

The cross-sections have been estimated singly, year by year, to assess the effect of time-series autocorrelations. While significance falls for all variables, the conviction variables remain highly significant, as do divorces and separations for personal and property crimes. For accidents, there is no qualitative difference aside from moderately lower t-values.[14]

As to heteroscedasticity, by plotting the residuals for the offense generations equations against the log of population it becomes clear that expressing variables in per capita terms and in natural logs effectively eliminates any heteroscedasticity associated with population size.[15] Since the income distribution in Sweden is such that the more populous counties are also those with the higher median incomes, it is similarly unlikely that heteroscedasticity exists associated with income variation.

Three aspects of these results deserve additional comment which, while in some sense speculative, may shed light on why they have been found:

One is the result with respect to time served in jail. While some theoretical arguments suggest that severity of sentence should be less important than probability of apprehension in deterring crime, that theory does not predict a complete lack of significance.[16] One difficulty with using the Swedish data base over a short time period for such analysis is that, as has been noted previously, there is relatively little variance across jurisdictions with respect to sentencing. The weak result is precisely what was predicted by statisticians of the Swedish Central Bureau of Statistics, even though they had not conducted their own analyses of the data. It was not that they were not convinced that sentence length makes a difference. The conventional wisdom there is that Swedish sentencing, like the Swedish income distribution, is highly egalitarian. Thus, in the short run, there was not sufficient variance across counties to facilitate estimation of the effect. As will be discussed in comparisons with time-series results, it was found that, for the aggregate model over a longer time series, sentence length was negatively related to offense levels—a fact that lends support to their position, since there have been changes in sentencing policy over time. Such speculation is hardly science, however. At best, it suggests that other means should be developed to test hypotheses about impacts of sentencing.

A second point of concern is the result with respect to lack of employment opportunities. In Sweden, those people who are officially listed as unemployed are supported far better by their government than are citizens of almost every other nation. While the variable used to measure the extent of lack of employment was essentially the product of the unemployment and labor force participation rates so that it would tend to capture the effect of the discouraged worker hypothesis, that effect is likely to be weaker in Sweden than elsewhere. If lack of economic opportunities is the key, the population most likely to turn criminal in Sweden as a consequence of lack of employment are those youth who do not yet qualify for support payments because they have no work history. Employment experience for those persons will be captured imperfectly by a statistic that represents the proportion of officially unemployed males to the total male working age population. Thus, these results are an imperfect test of the hypothesis that lack of economic opportunities will be causally related to crimes and particularly property crimes.

Finally, comment is indicated in regard to the finding that police manpower deployment across counties is unrelated to offense rates but is related to income. Swedish authorities were not surprised with the former result, but highly skeptical of the latter one. In fact, they asserted that manpower deployment in Sweden is based on a formula that considers primarily urban population density and nothing else. They were not willing to accept the notion that ability to pay taxes, the relative valuation placed on losses that might vary with income, or political influence that might relate to income or the productivity of a given community could have anything to do with the allocation of police protection. Yet, it is certainly true that offense levels consistently show up as insignificant in the police manpower relation across all model variants tested whereas income continues to show up strongly positively related to manpower deployment. Further investigation would appear to be warranted on all three of these issues.

VII. COMPARISON WITH TIME-SERIES RESULTS

An interesting comparison can be made between the results of estimation based on the recent (1975–1978) cross-section–time-series data and the longer time-series data (1954–1977) for the country as a whole. These (latter) results are summarized in Table 8.[17] The most striking similarity is with respect to the control effect of increasing conviction probabilities and the limited ability to estimate significant effects for the time-served-in-jail variable. One should note, however, that in aggregate versions of the time-series model, time served in jail was statistically significant at the .01 level or better (using a one-tailed test). While there are some similarities with respect to the impacts of the causal variables for personal crimes and property crimes, there is a considerable difference in significance levels, no doubt due in part to the better quality of data for more recent years and the larger sample size for the pooled study. No meaningful comparison can be made for accident results, since accidents were separated between serious and fatal accidents, and estimation procedures were not fully comparable.

The results for police effectiveness show similarities with respect to the impact of load variables but not with respect to the effect of manpower resources. The results that accord with theoretical expectations in the cross-section study are probably attributable to the improved quality of data on police manpower. The series that was available for the annual

Table 8. Estimates from Time-Series Analysis: National Data, 1954–1977 (Endogenous Law Enforcement Resources)

Dependent Variable	Constant	CR	ATS	OF	L	DIV	ALIEN	UP	ALC	MEDY
						Coefficient on:				
OFV	-.284 (1.90)	-.898 (5.37)*	-.053 (0.54)			.190 (1.97)*	.264 (2.68)*		.199 (.095)	
OFP	-.052 (0.06)	-.655 (4.00)*	0.28 (0.34)				.175 (1.19)	.068 (1.11)		
AC	No comparable estimates									
CRV	-2.69 (6.21)*			-.386 (3.55)*	-.688 (2.37)*					
CRP	-1.92 (5.00)*			-1.09 (3.90)*	-.586 (0.68)					
CRD	No comparable estimates									

Notes: Student's t-statistics (absolute value) are in parentheses.
* Significant at the .05 level or greater.

aggregate study suffered from definitional changes that left serious doubt as to its being a reliable continuous series.

VIII. COMPARISONS BETWEEN RESULTS FOR SWEDEN AND COMPARABLE U.S. STUDIES

In view of the similarities between Sweden and the United States in terms of income levels, life-styles, criminal behavior, and enforcement, it is interesting to compare these results with those of similar studies for the United States. Results of such a comparison for the impact of law enforcement effectiveness on reported offenses is shown in Table 9 for studies that view the determination of crime levels and law enforcement effectiveness as a simultaneous process. One would hardly expect identical results in view of the differences in levels of aggregation and in model specifications. Even if the relationships in the two countries were identical, estimates might nonetheless differ for Sweden since the range of offense rates, except for property crimes, is lower than for the United States. Consequently, it is interesting to note that the elasticities for Sweden fall in the middle of the range of estimates for the United States.

It is also possible to compare estimates of the productivity of law enforcement manpower in determining control effectiveness. These comparisons are shown in Table 10. For these estimates, model specification differs to an even greater degree than is the case for offense generating functions; but, again, it is interesting to note that the results for Sweden do not differ qualitatively from similar estimates for the United States and tend to fall in the middle of the range of U.S. estimates.

It did not appear fruitful to attempt to compare results for other parameter estimates.[18] A number of similar studies show significant positive results for deteriorating economic opportunities and crime rates in the United States, but, as noted previously, the Swedish data available do not permit a direct comparison;[19] U.S. studies do not take account of effects of a high proportion of alien population since, in the past, this has not been thought to be a problem for most areas. On the other hand, when race variables are included in U.S. studies, they are typically significant depending on model specifications with respect to other causal variables.[20] This latter effect may be related to the role of aliens in Sweden. However, since this variable is not significant for most of the Swedish results, further discussion is not warranted.

IX. IMPLICATIONS FOR POLICY

The implications of these results for policy are that we still do not know enough about penalties to advocate a change one way or the other. How-

Table 9. Offense Elasticities With Respect to Measures of Law Enforcement Effectiveness: Comparison of Results for Sweden and the United States

	Class of Offenses	Law Enforcement Effectiveness Measure				Source
		Arrest Ratio	Clearance Ratio	Conviction Ratio	Imprisonment Ratio	
Sweden	Felonies			−.789 to −.812		Table 5
	Property			−1.04 to −1.19		Table 4
	Personal			−.819 to −1.29		Table 4
United States	Felonies				−.99	Ehrlich (1973)
	Homicide	−1.5				Ehrlich (1975)
	Robbery	−2.99				Mathieson and Passell (1976)
	Felonies		−1.95			Jackson (1980)
	Felonies			−.61		Phillips and Votey (1981)

258

Table 10. Police Effectiveness Elasticities with Respect to Offense Levels and Law Enforcement Manpower: Comparison of Results for Sweden and the United States

Class of Offenses	Measurement of Police Effectiveness	Elasticity with Respect to:		Source
		Offense Levels	Police Manpower	
Sweden				
Felonies	Conv. Ratio	−1.08 to −1.17	1.08 to 1.44	Phillips and Votey (1981) Table 5
Property	Conv. Ratio		.992 to .103	Table 4
Personal	Conv. Ratio		.418 to .534	Table 4
United States				
Felonies	Conv. Ratio	−1.45 to −1.60	2.24 to 2.32	Ehrlich (1973)[a,b]
Felonies	Imprisonment Ratio		.30	Chapman (1976)
Property	Arrest Ratio		.60	Mathieson and Passell (1976)[c]
Robbery	Arrest Ratio		.22	
Burglary	Clearance Ratio	−.814	.722	Votey and Phillips (1981)[a]
Larceny	Clearance Ratio	−.372	.405	Votey and Phillips (1981)[a]

Notes:
[a] These are ordinary least squares estimates.
[b] Ehrlich's estimate was insignificant.
[c] Manpower is measured relative to the number of offenses rather than per capita.

259

ever, with respect to law enforcement inputs, the impact of an increase is shown to be substantial. To illustrate this, one can calculate the output elasticities with respect to the personal crime rate, the property crime rate, and serious and fatal accidents by working through the structural equations using the estimates of Table 6. The results obtained from a 1 percent increase in law enforcement inputs (assuming a middle-range estimate of 1.0 for the two offense rates) for the elasticity of offense rates with respect to changes in the conviction ratio, and using the estimated values from Eq. (12), will be a 1.55 percent decrease in the personal crime rate, a 3.91 percent decrease for the property crime rate, and a .515 percent decrease for fatal and serious accidents. The cost effectiveness of such an expenditure will depend upon the resultant change in the number of offenses and the accidents, the appropriate loss rates per offense, and the marginal cost of the added resources; these calculations are easily made, given expenditure data for law enforcement and reasonable estimates for the social cost of the offenses prevented.

Such an outcome presumes that the allocation of resources among offenses remains as it has been over the period of the study. It may appear, however, that based on the loss rates perceived per type of offense, a different enforcement emphasis is indicated. Unfortunately, study at this level of aggregation does not provide insights into the relative effectiveness of internal reallocations in cases in which substantial changes are made in enforcement emphasis. The efficacy of such an internal reallocation depends upon the nature of the transformation curve among outputs in relation to loss rates for the offense categories.

X. SUMMARY AND CONCLUSIONS

These results should not be surprising for anyone familiar with econometric research on crime in the United States, if one is willing to believe that the Swedish population and their institutions do not differ in substantial degree from those of the United States. They tend to support the results of a number of U.S. studies and to allay some of the reasonable concerns of their critics.

Results in this study say more for the effects of law enforcement in the control of offenses and accidents than they do for other causal factors. Not only are the results statistically significant at substantial levels, they are largely consistent with previous time-series analyses. The results with respect to police effectiveness in using resources are also impressive in terms of the extremely high levels of significance. The findings in regard to allocative efficiency across communities and among crime classes are not what economists would hope to find, and so must indicate that law enforcement authorities have not been under pressure to concern themselves with crime mix or the efficiency of manpower allocations across communities. The results for the variables representing social and economic factors contributing to crime provide insights with respect to a number of factors thought to be contributing or influencing factors in crime.

With respect to policy implications, while it is not so clear how the information on causal variables can lead to policy improvement, it is quite clear that law enforcement activities have a substantial impact on accidents and offenses whose social value could be readily established with reasonable extensions of this research.

APPENDIX

Here we shall derive the relationships for estimating law enforcement manpower levels and allocation among activities based on social cost minimization.

It is presumed that the objective is to minimize Eq. (4), subject to crime generation relations (6) and (7), law enforcement productivity relations (9), (10), and (11), the relation for accidents (12), and the identity of (14). The results also depend upon the condition that the wage level for law enforcement personnel is a function of the general level of income in the community and that loss rates for crime tend to vary with income levels.

The Lagrangian function[21]

$$\Psi = r_1 AC + r_2 OF2 + r_3 OF3 + wL + \psi_1(L(1 - k) - L1 - L2 - L3)$$

$$+ \psi_2(OF2 - gCR2^{\gamma_2}) + \psi_3(CR2 - hOF2^{\omega_2}L2^{\beta_2}) \qquad (A1)$$

$$+ \psi_4(OF3 - mCR_3^{\gamma_3}) + \psi_5(CR3 - nOF3^{\omega_3}L3^{\beta_3})$$

$$+ \psi_6(AC - dL1^{\beta_1}) + \psi_7(w - sL^{\sigma})$$

yields the following first-order conditions:

$$\frac{\partial\Psi}{\partial AC} = r_1 + \psi_6 = 0 \qquad (A2)$$

$$\frac{\partial\Psi}{\partial OF2} = r_2 + \psi_2 - \psi_3\omega_2 \frac{CR2}{OF2} = 0 \qquad (A3)$$

$$\frac{\partial\Psi}{\partial OF3} = r_3 + \psi_4 - \psi_5\omega_3 \frac{CR3}{OF3} = 0 \qquad (A4)$$

$$\frac{\partial\Psi}{\partial CR2} = -\psi_4\gamma_3 \frac{OF3}{CR3} + \psi_5 = 0 \qquad (A5)$$

$$\frac{\partial\Psi}{\partial L} = w + \psi_1(1 - k) - \psi_7\sigma \frac{w}{L} = 0 \qquad (A6)$$

$$\frac{\partial \Psi}{\partial L1} = -\psi_1 - \psi_6 \beta_1 \frac{AC}{L1} = 0 \tag{A7}$$

$$\frac{\partial \Psi}{\partial L2} = -\psi_1 - \psi_3 \beta_2 \frac{CR2}{L2} = 0 \tag{A8}$$

$$\frac{\partial \Psi}{\partial L3} = -\psi_1 - \psi_5 \beta_3 \frac{CR3}{L3} = 0 \tag{A9}$$

$$\frac{\partial \Psi}{\partial w} = L + \psi_7 = 0. \tag{A10}$$

From the first-order conditions the result can be obtained that

$$L = \frac{1}{w(1 + \sigma)} (a_1 AC + a_2 OF2 + a_3 OF3), \tag{A11}$$

where $a_1 = r_1 \beta_1$; $a_2 = r_2 \gamma_2 \beta_2 / \gamma_2 \omega_2 - 1$; and $a_3 = r_3 \gamma_3 \beta_3 / \gamma_3 \omega_3 - 1$. If it is postulated that wages are related to community income levels

$$w = c(Y) \tag{A12}$$

and perceived loss rates vary with income levels

$$r_i = b_i(Y), \tag{A13}$$

then one can write

$$L = f(AC, OF2, OF3, Y), \tag{A14}$$

where one would expect

$$\frac{\partial L}{\partial AC}, \quad \frac{\partial L}{\partial OF2}, \quad \frac{\partial L}{\partial OF3}, \quad \text{and} \quad \frac{\partial L}{\partial r_i} \frac{\partial r_i}{\partial Y} > 0$$

and

$$\frac{\partial L}{\partial w} \frac{\partial w}{\partial Y} < 0.$$

In order to facilitate estimation in the simultaneous framework, it is assumed that this relationship can be approximated by the estimating form

$$L = nOFV^{pv} OFP^{pp} AC^{\tau} Y^{\lambda} \epsilon_L. \tag{A15}$$

To calculate relations for the L_i, note that (14) can be written in the typical form

$$L2 = \frac{L2(1 - k)}{L1 + L2 + L3} L. \tag{A16}$$

Note also that from the first-order conditions results for the L_i can be derived which, substituted into Eq. (A16), yield a set of results typified by

$$L1 = \frac{a_1(1 - k)AC}{a_1 AC + a_2 OF2 + a_3 OF3} L. \qquad (A17)$$

For estimation purposes this yields relations

$$L_i = M_i \frac{OF_i}{\Sigma a_i OF_i} L. \qquad (A18)$$

In estimating the model with Eq. (A18) in the production function, the effect of OF_i will be included in the coefficient on the load variable and the labor input will be represented by $L/\Sigma a_i OF_i$. Estimation of the a_i will have to be an iterative process. The initial estimation will presume the $a_i = 1$, i.e., that accidents (AC) will be counted equally with offenses as elements of the load.

ACKNOWLEDGMENTS

The author acknowledges the financial support of the Swedish National Council for Crime Prevention and the University of California–Santa Barbara's Committee on Research.

NOTES

1.   There is, by now, an extensive literature on the deterrence issue and crime generation. Surveys of this literature are in Blumstein et al. (1978), Cook (1977), and Palmer (1977).

2.   Blumstein et al. (1978), p. 24.

3.   Phillips, Votey and Howell (1976), p. 467.

4.   Votey and Phillips (1972), p. 438.

5.   See Blumstein et al. (1978), pp. 30–33.

6.   A more detailed theoretical and empirical analysis that focuses on the accident relationship and its control and the derivation of estimating relationships is in Votey (1982).

7.   For results of analyzing other data sets where this approach has been followed, see Votey (1982).

8.   This is the technique followed in Votey and Phillips (1972).

9.   This SAS program was "not supported by the author or SAS" so that the conclusion that collinearity among the instruments was the cause for the program's failure could only be deduced by general statements in SAS (1980) that collinearity would cause the program to fail and the knowledge that collinearity among the instruments was substantial.

10.   An excellent introduction to the subject of spatial autocorrelation is Cliff and Ord (1981).

11.   A number of such studies are cited in Votey (1982), p. 95.

12.   While the unlagged version is superior to that in the model specifying one year lags, difference between the two estimates for this equation are slight and only in significance level.

13.   Efforts to model law enforcement productivity as joint production using only a single

input measure are reported in Votey (1981). In general, the simple formulation used here, not assuming cost minimizing behavior by the authorities, proved to fit the data best.

14. For accidents, in all years estimated, time served in jail had the expected negative coefficient and, in fact, in two years it was statistically significant.

15. Not only was there no relationship between county population and the magnitude of residuals, but the counties with the largest urban population showed no special similar characteristics in terms of their residuals that were seemingly different from, say, the least populated county.

16. See Becker (1968), p. 171.

17. The time-series results have been presented in Votey (1980).

18. It is notable that for the effect of law enforcement resources on accidents, Norway has similar results to those given here, based on estimates presented in Votey (1982).

19. A number of such studies are reported in Phillips and Votey (1981). Efforts to link the lack of economic opportunities to crime with individual data have shown mixed effects. See, for example, Witte (1980) and Myers (1980). The Witte results show negative or insignificant effects on recidivism for the time in months to the first job for released prisoners, and Myers finds that the number of months a released prisoner has a job is negatively related to recidivism. The difficulty with attempting to compare such results with those reported here is that in an aggregate study such as this there is no distinction made between general and specific deterrence, and, for that matter, effects of incapacitation, whereas in individual studies only specific deterrence is measured. Behavior among persons without criminal experience is likely to differ extensively from that among persons who have already been apprehended and sanctioned at least once.

20. In Phillips and Votey (1975) an extensive list of potential causal forces was evaluated with county data for California. In those results ethnic variables became insignificant when economic opportunity variables were included in the set.

21. Note that in Eqs. (A1)–(A10) the causal variables are ignored for the purpose of the derivation since they have no bearing on the cost minimization process.

REFERENCES

Becker, Gary, "Crime and Punishment: An Economic Approach." *Journal of Political Economy* 78(2, 1968):169–217.

Block, Michael K. and J. M. Heineke, "A Labor Theoretic Analysis of Criminal Choice." *American Economic Review* 65(June 1975):314–25.

Blumstein, Alfred, Jacqueline Cohen, and Daniel Nagin, *Deterrence and Incapacitation: Estimating the Effects of Criminal Sanctions on Crime Rates.* Washington, D.C.: National Academy of Sciences, 1978.

Carr-Hill, R. A., and N. H. Stern, "An Econometric Model of the Supply and Control of Recorded Offenses in England and Wales." *Journal of Public Economics* 2(4, 1973):289–318.

Chapman, J. I., "Economic Model of Crime and Police: Some Empirical Results." *Journal of Research in Crime and Delinquency* 13(January 1976):48–63.

Cliff, A. D. and J. K. Ord, *Spatial Processes: Models and Applications,* London: Pion Ltd., 1981.

Cook, Philip J., "Punishment and Crime: A Critique of Current Findings Concerning the Preventive Effect of Punishment." *Law and Contemporary Problems* 41(Winter 1977):164–204.

Darrough, M. N. and J. M. Heineke, "The Multi-Output Translog Production Cost Function: The Case of Law Enforcement Agencies." In J. M. Heineke (ed.), *Economic Models of Criminal Behavior.* Amsterdam: North Holland, 1978, pp. 259–302.

Ehrlich, Isaac, "Participation in Illegitimate Activities: A Theoretical and Empirical Investigation." *Journal of Political Economy* 81(3, 1973):521–65.

———, "The Deterrent Effect of Capital Punishment: A Question of Life and Death." *American Economic Review* 65(June 1975):397–417.

Fabrikant, Richard, "The Distribution of Criminal Offenses in an Urban Environment: A Spatial Analysis of Criminal Spillover and of Juvenile Offenders." *The American Journal of Economics and Sociology* 38(1, January 1979).

———, "Interjurisdictional Spillovers of Urban Services: A Comment." *Southern Economic Journal* (January 1980).

Hägerstrand, T., *Innovation as a Diffusion Process*. Chicago: University of Chicago Press, 1967.

Hakim, Simon, Arie Ovadia, Eli Sagi and J. Weinblatt, "Interjurisdictional Spillover of Crime and Police Expenditure." *Land Economics* 55(2, May 1979).

Heineke, J. M., "Economic Models of Criminal Behavior: An Overview." In J. M. Heineke (ed.), *Economic Models of Criminal Behavior*. Amsterdam: North-Holland, 1978, pp. 1–33.

Jackson, J. J., "Juvenile and Adult Justice in California: An Economic Analysis of Control Effects." Unpublished, University of California, Santa Barbara, 1980.

Kmenta, Jan, *Elements of Econometrics*. New York: Macmillan Publishing Co., Dec. 1971.

Mathieson, D., and P. Passell, "Homicide and Robbery in New York City: An Econometric Model." *Journal of Legal Studies* 6(January, 1976):83–98.

Myers, Samuel L., Jr., "Employment Opportunities and Crime," Technical Report to the National Institute of Justice, December 1980.

Ord, Keith, "Estimation Methods for Models of Spatial Interaction." *Journal of the American Statistical Association.* 70, 349(March 1975).

Palmer, Jan, "Economic Analysis of the Deterrent Effect of Punishment: A Review." *Journal of Research in Crime and Delinquency* 14(January 1977):4–21.

Phillips, Llad, "Factor Demands in the Provision of Public Safety." Chapter 6 in J. M. Heineke (ed.), *Economic Models of Criminal Behavior*. Amsterdam: North-Holland, 1978.

Phillips, Llad, and Harold L. Votey, Jr., "Crime in California." *The Journal of Legal Studies* IV(2, 1975):327–49.

———, *The Economics of Crime Control*, Beverly Hills: Sage Publications, 1981.

Phillips, Llad, Harold L. Votey, Jr., and John Howell, "Handguns and Homicide: Minimizing Losses and the Costs of Control." *The Journal of Legal Studies* V(June 1976):463–478.

SAS, *Supplemental Library Users Guide*, Cary, NC: SAS Institute, Inc. (1980).

Sjoquist, D., "Property Crime and Economic Behavior: Some Empirical Results." *American Economic Review* 63(3, 1973):439–46.

Votey, Harold L., Jr., "Scandinavian Drinking–Driving Control: Myth or Intuition." *The Journal of Legal Studies* XI(1 1982):93–116.

———, "The Control of Crime in Sweden: An Econometric Analysis." Working Paper, Santa Barbara, CA: The Community and Organization Research Institute, June 1980.

———, "Alternative Analyses of law Enforcement Effectiveness: A Pooled Time Series–Cross Section of Sweden." Presented before the Annual Meeting of the Western Economic Assoc., International, San Francisco, CA, July 1981.

Votey, Harold L., Jr., and Llad Phillips, "Police Effectiveness and the Production Function for Law Enforcement." *The Journal of Legal Studies* 1(1972):423–436.

Witte, Ann Dryden, "Estimating the Economic Model of Crime with Individual Data." *The Quarterly Journal of Economics* 94(February 1980):57–84.

A DYNAMIC MODEL OF THE PROVISION OF PUBLIC SAFETY AND JUSTICE

Llad Phillips

I. INTRODUCTION

The economic analysis of crime and punishment has been static in nature, and empirical studies of the supply of offenses and the control activities of the criminal justice system have stayed within this framework.[1] To be sure, some empirical studies have incorporated lagged endogenous variables, often used as instrumental variables, but the conceptualization of the models has been static.[2] There have been few distributed lag formulations of the deterrent effect of the certainty or severity of punishment, and these have been ad hoc modifications to static models of constrained optimization.[3]

There are naturally dynamic aspects to criminal behavior and crime control. Over the life cycle the relative attractiveness of criminal activity

Advances in Applied Micro-Economics, Volume 3, pages 267–293.
Copyright © 1984 by JAI Press Inc.
All rights of reproduction in any form reserved.
ISBN: 0-89232-398-1

may diminish as an individual accumulates human capital through experience and learning, increasing the rewards of legitimate activity. The disutility of apprehension and punishment may increase over the life cycle as well, as people marry, raise families, and establish identities and reputations within a community. Time and maturity can be a major factor in rehabilitation. A young person who becomes an offender may, as the expected costs of engaging in criminal activity increase with age, relative to the benefits, return to nonoffender status as he or she grows older.

This notion of rehabilitation with time and maturity is modeled in this essay by assuming that the flow of individuals leaving offender status is proportional to the stock of offenders. This implies that if a cohort of young people of a given age become offenders in an initial period, their number remaining in offender status declines exponentially with time, as an increasing number return to nonoffender status as they age.

The flow entering offender status is presumed to decrease linearly with arrests, reflecting the impact of general deterrence on those tempted to allocate time to criminal activity. Together, this specification of the flow entering offender status and the specification of the flow leaving that status, as discussed above, determine the dynamic behavior of the stock of offenders. The flow of reported offenses, which is an observed variable, is presumed to be proportional to the stock of offenders, which is not observed.

Of course, there are other dynamic aspects to criminal behavior and crime control. Incarceration intrinsically involves time, as individuals are apprehended and removed from offender status but then may return to that status after they serve their time, depending upon whether they have been rehabilitated or not. Deterrence may not only diminish the number of new offenders but may shorten the time, on average, that offenders remain in that status before maturing and engaging in socially acceptable activities. These additional features are not pursued in this essay, but the dynamic model that is developed provides a framework for further analysis.

A static model of the supply of offenses and the production of crime control activities, such as arrests, is specified to provide a basis for understanding the steady-state behavior of the dynamic model. The special feature that the introduction of the dynamic behavior of the stock of offenders provides is the implication that offenses will be a negatively weighted exponential distributed lag of arrests. Thus an explicit dynamic specification of the supply of offenses is deduced from the assumptions about the dynamic behavior of the stock of offenders.

The introduction of considerations of optimal behavior for a community involves a choice of allocating production, taken as exogenous, between consumption or expenditures on arrests to reduce offenses. A community preference function for consumption and offenses is presumed. In the static model, the community chooses consumption to maximize utility. In the dynamic model, the community chooses the time path of consumption to maximize discounted future utility. The special feature that optimizing behavior provides is the response of expenditures on crime control to reported offenses. In the dynamic optimal control model, optimizing behavior implies that arrests will be a distributed lag of offenses.

This optimal control model of crime and punishment has the same formal structure as Forster's one-state variable optimal control model of the consumption–pollution trade-off.[4] The economic choice between more of a good or less of a bad is of course similar for pollution and crime. It is interesting that the dynamic equations of motion relating the control variable, consumption, to the state variable, crime or pollution, prove to be similar in form as well. Of course there are differences between the two models in the conceptual formulation of this dynamic behavior.

This optimal control model of crime and punishment implies that offenses will be a negatively weighted exponential distributed lag of arrests and, in trurn, that arrests will be a negatively weighted distributed lag of offenses and will vary positively with exogenous variables that increase the flow of new offenders. Thus causality is mutual or runs both ways as a function of lag for arrests and offenses. These implications are investigated for five felony offenses in California—homicide, robbery, auto theft, burglary, and aggravated assault—using annual time series for the period 1945 through 1978. For each crime, the offense rate is related to the probability of imprisonment. Autoregressive integrated moving average (ARIMA) models are estimated for these two variables, and the resulting estimated innovations or error processes are cross-correlated as a function of lag. The cross-correlation functions imply that offense rates are negatively weighted geometric distributed lags of the probability of imprisonment, except for assault, where the probability of imprisonment is a distributed lag of offenses. The distributed lags implied by the cross-correlation analysis and ARIMA models are corroborated by estimating transfer functions. The results for homicide and assault are reported as examples. Except for assault, there is no evidence that the probability of imprisonment is a distributed lag of offenses. This implies that there is no optimizing behavior and that the response of criminal justice system authorities to offense rates is weak at best.

II. THE STATIC MODEL

The likelihood that an individual will commit an offense will vary with the costs and benefits perceived to be associated with the offense, and the supply of offenses, OF, will vary with variables affecting cost such as certainty, CT, severity, SV, and celerity, CY, of punishment, as well as a set of other variables, x, that affect benefits:

$$OF = OF(CT, SV, CY, x). \tag{1}$$

One of the variables that will affect the certainty of punishment is the probability of arrest, P_A, and if we emphasize this variable separately from the rest of the certainty variables, CT^*, we have

$$OF = OF(P_A, CT^*, SV, CY, x). \tag{2}$$

The probability of arrest can be defined as the ratio of arrests A to offenses OF:

$$P_A = \frac{A}{OF}. \tag{3}$$

Equation (3) can be used to eliminate the probability of arrest from Eq. (2), and combining these two equations we have

$$OF = g(A, CT^*, SV, CY, x), \tag{4}$$

where the supply of offenses will vary inversely with arrests A, i.e.,

$$\frac{\partial OF}{\partial A} < 0.$$

This can be understood intuitively by referring to the graphic depiction of the supply of offenses, Eq. (2), and the probability of arrest, Eq. (3), in Figure 1. An increase in resources allocated to producing arrests will shift the probability of arrest function to the right, shifting the equilibrium from point A to point B. The result of increasing arrests is to reduce offenses.[5] Hence the specification of the supply of offenses with arrests will imply that the supply of offenses slopes downward as arrests increase, provided the offense is controllable by means of increasing the certainty of punishment.

The cost of the criminal justice system, K, will vary with the production of the activities determining the certainty, severity, and celerity of punishment, and with the prices of resources such as police manpower and patrol cars denoted by the set of prices, w:

$$K = K(A, CT^*, SV, CY, w). \tag{5}$$

If the marginal cost of producing an additional arrest, $\partial K/\partial A$, is a constant, K_A,

$$\frac{\partial K}{\partial A} = K_A, \tag{6}$$

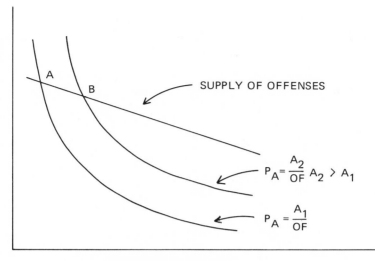

Figure 1. The Effect on the Offense Rate of Increasing Expenditures to Produce Arrests

then the costs of producing arrests will be proportional to the number of arrests, and if we denote the resources devoted to this activity by E, we have

$$E = K_A A. \tag{7}$$

Production, ϕ^{∞}, is presumed exogenous and, holding other criminal justice system activities constant, at resource cost equal to $\phi^{\infty} - \phi^{\circ}$, we have the remaining resources, ϕ°, equal to expenditures, E, and consumption, C:

$$\phi^{\circ} = E + C. \tag{8}$$

The supply of offenses, Eq. (4), expenditures on arrests, Eq. (7), and the constraint on resources, Eq. (8), can be combined to express offenses as a function of consumption:

$$OF = g\left(\frac{\phi^{\circ} - C}{K_A}, CT^*, SV, CY, x\right) \equiv G(C), \tag{9}$$

where, holding the other arguments constant, this is defined as the function $G(C)$. The relationship between $G(C)$, and the three functions from which it is derived is depicted in Figure 2. The supply of offenses as a

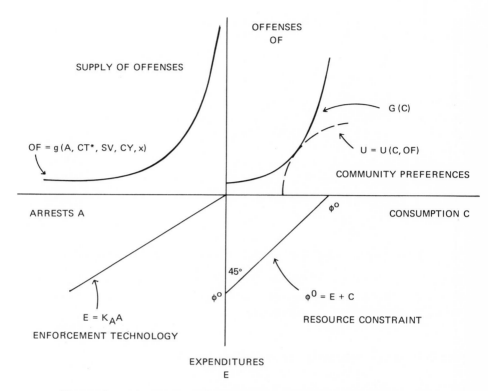

Figure 2. The Variation of Offenses with Consumption, G(C).

function of arrests is in quadrant II, expenditures as a function of arrests in quadrant III, and the resource constraint in quadrant IV.

Community preference or social welfare is measured by a strictly concave utility function of consumption and offenses:[6]

$$U = U(C, OF). \qquad (10)$$

An optimal level of consumption will maximize social welfare, Eq. (10), subject to the constrained trade-off between offenses and consumption represented by Eq. (9). The assumption that the marginal utility of consumption approaches infinity as consumption approaches zero,

$$\lim_{C \to 0} \frac{\partial U}{\partial C} = \infty, \qquad (11)$$

ensures that the optimal policy will not be zero consumption. If a sufficiently large number of arrests could drive offenses to zero, the assumption that the marginal disutility of crime approaches zero as crime approaches zero,

$$\lim_{OF \to 0} \frac{\partial U}{\partial OF} = 0, \tag{12}$$

ensures that the optimal policy will not lead to a crime-free society. Relaxation of this assumption may lead to an optimal solution which is crime free, but it is also still possible that there may be an interior solution (OF > 0).

Referring to Eq. (9), and the function G(C), an optimal policy of consumption equal to disposable resources, ϕ°, is ruled out if the function G(C) has a slope, dG/dC, that approaches infinity as consumption approaches ϕ°.

III. THE DYNAMICS OF THE OFFENDER POPULATION

The net rate of change of the offender population is equal to the inflow of new offenders, N(t), minus the outflow from that status, which is presumed proportional to the stock,

$$\dot{\Omega}(t) = N(t) - \lambda\Omega(t), \tag{13}$$

where the differential operator D is defined as

$$Dx(t) \equiv \frac{d}{dt} x(t) = \dot{x}(t). \tag{14}$$

The assumption that the number leaving offender status is proportional to the stock of offenders reflects the notion that with increasing age, maturity, and job experience, youthful offenders will tend to find crime increasingly less attractive. The expected psychic costs of apprehension and punishment will tend to increase over the life cycle as individuals marry, raise families, and establish reputations and social connections in a community. The earnings from allocating time to legitimate work will rise as human capital accumulates through experience and learning over the life cycle.

To see the implications of the assumption that the outflow from offender status is proportional to the stock of offenders, consider the solution to Eq. (13), where the inflow, N(t), is presumed constant at N°:

$$\Omega(t) = \frac{N^\circ}{\lambda} + \left[\Omega(0) - \frac{N^\circ}{\lambda} \right] e^{-\lambda t}. \tag{15}$$

Suppose that the flow of new offenders at time zero is a cohort of young people of a given age, which is a fraction α of the population at that age, $Y(0)$,

$$N(0) = \alpha Y(0), \tag{16}$$

and the flow of new offenders is zero after that,

$$N(t) = 0, \qquad t > 0. \tag{17}$$

Then the stock of offenders at time zero will be the number of youth in the cohort

$$\Omega(0) = \alpha Y(0), \tag{18}$$

and the number that remain in offender status will decay out exponentially as the youths age with time and advance in their life cycle:

$$\Omega(t) = \alpha Y(0)e^{-\lambda t}. \tag{19}$$

Thus the assumption that the outflow from offender status is proportional to the stock of offenders is consistent with the strong dependence of observed arrest rates on age.

For a steady flow of new offenders, $N°$, the steady-state solution for the stock of offenders as t grows large is

$$\Omega(\infty) = \frac{N°}{\lambda}, \tag{20}$$

i.e., the steady-state stock of offenders is the product of the constant flow of new offenders, $N°$, times the mean time in offender status, $1/\lambda$.[7]

General deterrence is presumed to operate by diminishing the flow of new offenders, affecting at the margin individuals in nonoffender status who are making the choice between allocating their time to legal or illegal activities. Tightening enforcement by increasing arrests, $A(t)$, and hence the probability of apprehension, increases the expected cost of engaging in criminal behavior, discouraging new offenders, and is presumed to decrease their number, $N(t)$. This can be represented by a linear approximation,

$$N(t) = a - bA(t), \tag{21}$$

where a and b are positive parameters. The flow of offenses, $OF(t)$, is presumed to be proportional to the stock of offenders, $\Omega(t)$,

$$OF(t) = k\Omega(t). \tag{22}$$

Equations (13), (21), and (22) can be combined to express the differential equation for offenses in terms of arrests,

$$\dot{OF} = ka - kbA(t) - \lambda OF(t), \tag{23}$$

or, equivalently, offenses can be expressed as an exponential distributed lag of arrests:[8]

$$OF(t) = \frac{ka}{\lambda} - \frac{kb}{\lambda} \int_0^\infty \lambda e^{-\lambda u} A(t - u) \, du. \tag{24}$$

Consider a community with a constraint on resources, as given by Eq. (8), where the expenditure of resources $\overline{E}$ on arrests is exogenous and possibly nonoptimal. For the constant cost technology described by Eq. (7), the level of arrests, $\overline{A}$, will equal $\overline{E}/K_A$. The steady state level of offenses, where the rate of change of offenses, $\dot{OF}$, is zero, is from Eq. (23) or (24):

$$OF(\infty) = \frac{ka}{\lambda} - \frac{kb}{\lambda} \overline{A}. \tag{25}$$

Thus the steady state supply of offenses is a linear approximation to the supply of offenses function in the static model, illustrated in quadrant II of Figure 2. Expressing steady state offenses as a function of consumption, where $\overline{E} \equiv \phi^\circ - \overline{C}$,

$$OF(\infty) = \frac{ka}{\lambda} - \frac{kb}{\lambda} \frac{(\phi^\circ - \overline{C})}{K_A}, \tag{26}$$

which is a linear approximation to the function $G(C)$ illustrated in quadrant I for the static model.

IV. AN OPTIMAL CONTROL MODEL OF DETERRENCE

For a community with a resource constraint given by Eq. (8), enforcement technology given by Eq. (7), and a dynamic supply of offenses given by Eq. (23), the rate of change of offenses as a function of consumption can be expressed as

$$\dot{OF} = ka - \frac{kb}{K_A} [\phi^\circ - C(t)] - \lambda OF(t), \tag{27}$$

which is the equation of motion relating the state variable, offenses, to the control variable, consumption. This is a linear approximation to

$$\dot{OF} = Z(C) - \lambda OF(t), \tag{28}$$

where $Z(C)$ is presumed to have a slope, $dZ/dC \equiv Z'$, that approaches infinity as consumption approaches ϕ°:

$$\underset{C \to \phi^\circ}{Z'}(C) = \infty \tag{29}$$

This would be the case if new offenders increase at an increasing rate as consumption increases and expenditure on arrests decrease.

If social welfare is measured by the strictly concave utility function given by Eq. (10), then the rational agency planning problem is to choose the time path of consumption to maximize discounted future utility,

$$\max_{C} \int_{0}^{\infty} e^{-\rho t} U(C, OF) \, dt, \tag{30}$$

subject to Eq. (28), to the initial level of offenses, OF(0), and to nonnegativity constraints on offenses and crime control expenditures.

This problem has the same formal structure as Forster's model of the consumption–pollution trade-off, where the solution is examined in detail. The conditions (11), (12), and (29) ensure an interior solution, i.e., $OF > 0$ and $0 < C < \phi^{\circ}$.

The Hamiltonian is

$$H = e^{-\rho t} U(C, OF) + \Psi^{*}[Z(C) - \lambda OF], \tag{31}$$

where Ψ^{*} is the discounted shadow price of offenses or costate variable and the current price is

$$\Psi = e^{\rho t} \Psi^{*}. \tag{32}$$

The Lagrangian incorporating the nonnegativity constraints on offenses and crime control expenditures is

$$L = H + r^{*}[Z(C) - \lambda OF] + q^{*}[\phi^{\circ} - C], \tag{33}$$

where to ensure that offenses are nonnegative we note that if offenses are zero over an interval then $\dot{OF}$ must be constrained to be nonnegative and r^{*} is the multiplier on this constraint.

Setting the derivative of the Lagrangian with respect to the control variable equal to zero,

$$e^{-\rho t} \frac{\partial U}{\partial C} + \Psi^{*} Z'(C) + r^{*} Z'(C) - q^{*} = 0, \tag{34}$$

or in terms of current prices,

$$\Psi + r = \frac{q - \partial U / \partial C}{Z'(C)}. \tag{35}$$

Note that for an interior solution,

$$OF > 0, \qquad 0 < C < \phi^{\circ},$$

the shadow prices on the constraints, r and q respectively, must be zero and hence we obtain

$$\Psi = -\frac{\partial U/\partial C}{\partial Z/\partial C} \cdot \tag{36}$$

Note that the shadow price of offenses, Ψ, is negative and is governed by the differential equation obtained from the first-order condition

$$\dot{\Psi}* = -\frac{\partial L}{\partial OF} \cdot \tag{37}$$

Evaluating this condition,

$$\dot{\Psi}* = -e^{-\rho t}\frac{\partial U}{\partial OF} + \Psi*\lambda + r*\lambda \tag{38}$$

or

$$e^{\rho t}\dot{\Psi}* = -\frac{\partial U}{\partial OF} + \Psi\lambda + r\lambda = \dot{\Psi} - \rho\Psi, \tag{39}$$

and for an interior solution ($r = 0$), we obtain

$$\dot{\Psi} = (\rho + \lambda)\Psi - \frac{\partial U}{\partial OF} \cdot \tag{40}$$

Equation (36) can be used to express consumption as a function of the shadow price and offenses,

$$C = C(\Psi, OF), \tag{41}$$

where $\partial C/\partial \Psi > 0$ and $\partial C/\partial OF < 0$.[9]

The phase diagram can be used to illustrate the dynamic behavior of the shadow price Ψ and offenses, OF. The loci of $\dot{OF} = 0$ [from Eq. (28)] and $\dot{\Psi} = 0$ [from Eq. (40)] are represented by solid lines in Figure 3. From Eq. (28), when $\dot{OF} = 0$,

$$OF = \frac{Z(C)}{\lambda}, \tag{42}$$

and as OF approaches zero, C approaches C_0, the level of consumption where $Z(C) = 0$, i.e., the net inflow to crime is zero. In addition, from Eq. (36), the loci of $\dot{OF} = 0$ at $OF = 0$ will have, for an intercept, the shadow price,

$$\Psi_{C_0} = -\frac{\partial U/\partial C(C_0, 0)}{\partial Z/\partial C(C_0)}, \tag{43}$$

as indicated in Figure 3. To determine the slope of the loci $\dot{OF} = 0$, starting

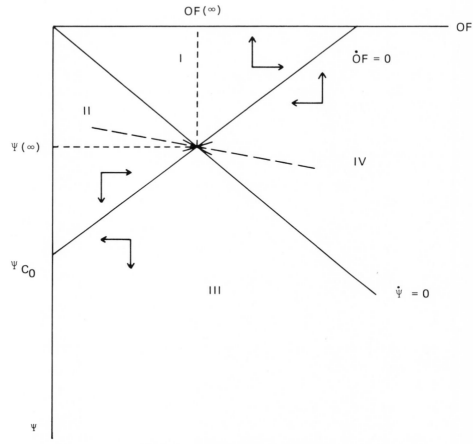

Figure 3. Phase Plane Diagram

from the intercept Ψ_{C_0}, note that as offenses increase, consumption increases, i.e, from Eq. (42):

$$\frac{dC}{dOF} = \lambda \left/ \frac{dZ}{dC} \right. > 0, \tag{44}$$

and differentiating Eq. (36) with respect to OF, we can use condition (44) to show that $d\Psi/dOF$ is monotonically increasing.[10] Recall from Eq. (41) that for Ψ constant, $\partial C/\partial OF < 0$, and hence from Eq. (28) as OF increases, $\dot{OF}$ is decreasing and thus $\dot{OF} > 0$ to the left of $\dot{OF} = 0$ and $\dot{OF} < 0$ to the right, as indicated by the solid arrows in Figure 3.

To investigate the properties of the loci of $\dot{\Psi} = 0$, we have from Eq.

(40), when $\dot{\Psi} = 0$,

$$\Psi = \frac{\partial U/\partial OF}{\rho + \lambda}, \tag{45}$$

and from Eq. (12), as OF approaches 0, Ψ approaches 0, as indicated in Figure 3. Equations (36) and (45) both specify Ψ as a function of C and OF, and they can be differentiated and solved for $d\Psi/dOF$, showing that the slope of the loci $\dot{\Psi} = 0$ is monotonically decreasing.[11] Evaluating Eq. (40) for OF constant, as Ψ increases, recalling from Eq. (41) that $\partial C/\partial \Psi > 0$, $\dot{\Psi}$ increases, and hence $\dot{\Psi} < 0$ below the loci $\dot{\Psi} = 0$ and $\dot{\Psi} > 0$ above, as indicated by the solid arrows in Figure 3. The optimal trajectory will lie in regions II and IV as illustrated by the dotted line in Figure 3. Paths in regions I and III move away from the equilibrium given by the intersection of the loci $\dot{OF} = 0$ and $\dot{\Psi} = 0$.

The intersection of the loci $\dot{OF} = 0$ and $\dot{\Psi} = 0$ determine the steady-state optimal values $OF(\infty)$ for offenses and $\Psi(\infty)$ for its shadow price, as illustrated in Figure 3, which in turn, using Eq. (41), gives a value for steady-state optimal consumption, $C(\infty)$. Evaluating Eq. (42) at this equilibrium, we obtain steady-state offenses,

$$OF(\infty) = \frac{Z(C(\infty))}{\lambda} \simeq \frac{ka}{\lambda} - \frac{kb}{\lambda}\frac{(\phi° - C(\infty))}{K_A}, \tag{46}$$

which can be contrasted with the nonoptimal steady-state solution, given by Eq. (26), with $\overline{C} \neq C(\infty)$. There are two expressions for the shadow price, Eq. (36),

$$\Psi(\infty) = -\frac{\partial U/\partial C}{\partial Z/\partial C}, \tag{47}$$

and Eq. (45),

$$\Psi(\infty) = -\frac{\partial U/\partial OF}{\rho + \lambda}, \tag{48}$$

implying that

$$-\frac{\partial U/\partial C}{\partial U/\partial OF} = \frac{dZ/dC}{\rho + \lambda}, \tag{49}$$

i.e., the marginal rate of substitution equals the present value of the increase in crime from an increment in consumption.

V. THE COMMUNITY RESPONSE TO CRIME

Equation (41) expresses optimal community consumption as a function of the shadow price and offenses. Taking a linear Taylor series expansion around the equilibrium values $\psi(\infty)$ and $OF(\infty)$,

$$C = C[\psi(\infty), OF(\infty)] + \frac{\partial C}{\partial \psi} [\psi(\infty), OF(\infty)][\psi - \psi(\infty)]$$

$$+ \frac{\partial C}{\partial OF} [\psi(\infty), OF(\infty)][OF - OF(\infty)], \quad (50)$$

where, we recall, $\partial C/\partial \psi > 0$ and $\partial C/\partial OF < 0$, and differentiating with respect to time,

$$\dot{C} = \frac{\partial C}{\partial \psi} (\infty)\dot{\psi} + \frac{\partial C}{\partial OF} (\infty)\dot{OF}. \quad (51)$$

Using Eq. (27) to substitute for $\dot{OF}$,

$$\dot{C} = \frac{\partial C}{\partial \psi} (\infty)\dot{\psi} + \frac{\partial C}{\partial OF} (\infty) \left[ka - \frac{kb\phi^{\circ}}{K_A} \right]$$

$$+ \frac{\partial C}{\partial OF} (\infty) \frac{kb}{K_A} C(t) - \frac{\partial C}{\partial OF} (\infty)\lambda OF(t), \quad (52)$$

and defining the parameters β_i,

$$\beta_0 = \frac{\partial C}{\partial \psi} > 0, \qquad\qquad \beta_1 = \frac{\partial C}{\partial OF} \left[ka - \frac{kb\phi^{\circ}}{K_A} \right],$$

$$\beta_2 = - \frac{\partial C}{\partial OF} \frac{kb}{K_A} > 0, \qquad \beta_3 = - \frac{\partial C}{\partial OF} \lambda > 0,$$

we can express Eq. (52) as

$$\dot{C} = \beta_0\dot{\psi} + \beta_1 - \beta_2 C(t) + \beta_3 OF(t). \quad (53)$$

Equivalently, consumption can be expressed as the sum of exponential distributed lags of the rate of change of the shadow price, $\dot{\psi}$, and the level of offenses, OF:

$$C(t) = \frac{\beta_1}{\beta_2} + \frac{\beta_0}{\beta_2} \int_0^{\infty} \beta_2 e^{-\beta_2 u} \dot{\psi}(t - u) \, du$$

$$+ \frac{\beta_3}{\beta_2} \int_0^{\infty} \beta_2 e^{-\beta_2 u} OF(t - u) \, du. \quad (54)$$

This expression of consumption as a positive distributed lag of offenses is consistent with the phase plane diagram where, for example, taking a point on the optimal trajectory in region II of Figure 3, we note that $\dot{\psi} < 0$ and $\dot{OF} > 0$. Differentiating Eq. (41) with respect to time, we find $\dot{C} < 0$ if $\dot{\psi} < 0$ and $\dot{OF} > 0$. Since $\dot{OF}$ is inversely related to OF, $\dot{C}$ and OF will be positively related, as in Eq. (53). Intuitively, for low levels of offenses below the steady-state optimum, the rate of change of offenses is positive and the community must cut back on consumption and increase expenditures on deterrence to diminish the flow of new offenders. If offense levels are above the steady-state optimum, the rate of change of offenses is negative and the community can afford to increase consumption. It is important to note, however, that this argument abstracts from exogenous shifts in new offenders, which would be reflected by changes in the parameter a. Consumption will be negatively related to the parameter a, as indicated in Eq. (52), and hence will decrease if there are changes in exogenous variables which increase the number of new offenders, thereby increasing the steady-state equilibrium level of offenses, OF(∞), as given by Eq. (46).

Since arrests are inversely related to consumption, arrests will be a negatively weighted exponential distributed lag of offenses and also of the rate of change of the shadow price, but arrests will increase with exogenous factors increasing the flow of new offenders. The causality between offenses and arrests is two-way, or mutual, with negative correlation. Arrests lead offenses in Eq. (24), reflecting deterrence, and as implied by Eq. (54) offenses lead arrests, reflecting optimizing behavior on the part of the community. This continuous deterministic optimal control model is the basis of the expectations about the nature of the lag structure that might link the observed stochastic discrete crime and sanction variables.

VI. EMPIRICAL ANALYSIS

To test for the possible two-way causality between crime rates and sanction variables, with each a negative distributed lag of the other, Box–Jenkins time-series methods were employed.[12] The probability of imprisonment was the sanction variable available, and it was utilized in the analysis. To avoid spurious correlations between the offense rate and the probability of imprisonment, ARIMA models were estimated for each of these variables and then their white noise residuals were cross-correlated.

The stochastic model motivated by the optimal control model of deterrence specifies the offense rate, OF(t), as a negative distributed lag of the probability of imprisonment, P(t), plus an error process, $\mu_1(t)$, representing exogenous factors affecting the flow of new offenders:

$$OF(t) = -\sum_{i=0}^{\infty} m_i P(t-i) + \mu_1(t) = -\sum_{i=0}^{\infty} m_i Z^i P(t) + \mu_1(t)$$

$$= -M(Z)P(t) + \mu_1(t), \tag{55}$$

where the lag operator Z is defined as

$$Z^n x(t) = x(t - n) \tag{56}$$

and $M(Z)$ is a polynominal in Z. The probability of imprisonment is specified as a negative distributed lag of the offense rate plus a constant of proportionality, v, times the error process, $\mu_1(t)$, representing the exogenous factors affecting the flow of new offenders:

$$
\begin{aligned}
P(t) &= - \sum_{i=0}^{\infty} n_i OF(t - i) + v\mu_1(t) = - \sum_{i=0}^{\infty} n_i Z^i OF(t) + v\mu_1(t) \\
&= - N(Z)OF(t) + v\mu_1(t).
\end{aligned}
\tag{57}
$$

The offense rate and probability of imprisonment were each specified as ARIMA models of the white noise innovations $e_1(t)$ and $e_2(t)$, respectively:

$$A(Z)OF(t) = B(z)e_1(t) \tag{58}$$

and

$$C(Z)P(t) = D(Z)e_2(t). \tag{59}$$

Equations (58) and (59) can be used to substitute for $OF(t)$ and $P(t)$ in terms of $e_1(t)$ and $e_2(t)$, respectively, in Eqs. (55) and (57) yielding $e_1(t)$ as a negative distributed lag of $e_2(t)$,

$$e_1(t) = - M(Z) \frac{A(Z)D(Z)}{B(Z)C(Z)} e_2(t) + \frac{A(Z)}{B(Z)} \mu_1(t), \tag{60}$$

and $e_2(t)$ as a negative distributed lag of $e_1(t)$,

$$e_2(t) = - N(Z) \frac{B(Z)C(Z)}{A(Z)D(Z)} e_1(t) + v \frac{C(Z)}{D(Z)} \mu_1(t). \tag{61}$$

Thus the cross-correlation function for $e_1(t)$ and $e_2(t)$ is expected to be possibly two-sided with negative correlations at both positive and negative lags.[13]

These estimated cross-correlation functions between the white noise innovations and the estimated ARIMA models were used to infer the distributed lag weights relating the probability of imprisonment and the offense rate. Transfer function models of the distributed lag linking these variables were estimated, following the Box–Jenkins procedure. If the dynamic model of deterrence were correct, the offense rate should be a negatively weighted geometric lag of the sanction variable, the probability of imprisonment. If the community was acting to optimally allocate resources to crime control, the probability of imprisonment would be a negatively weighted geometric lag of the offense rate. A time-series measure of the shadow price of offenses was not available for inclusion in the empirical analysis, but some other sanction variables and the unemployment rate for youths were included in the transfer function analysis of homicide.

VII. FELONY CRIME IN CALIFORNIA

Annual time series were available in California for the period 1945 through 1978 for reported offenses and commitments to prison for the felony crimes of homicide, auto theft, burglary, robbery, and aggravated assault. The ratio of prison commitments to reported offenses was used as a measure of the probability of imprisonment, $P(t)$. The lag relationship between the offense rate per capita, $OF(t)$, and the probability of imprisonment, $P(t)$, was investigated by fitting ARIMA models to each of the series, and then cross-correlating the white noise innovations. The cross-correlation functions for homicide, auto theft, robbery, and burglary all exhibit a significant negative peak only at lag zero as reported in Table 1 and illustrated for homicide in Figure 4, and suggest a model between the residuals of the form:[14]

$$e_1(t) = -me_2(t) + \mu(t). \tag{62}$$

Substituting in Eq. (62) for the innovations from the estimated ARIMA models, Eq. (58) and (59),

$$\frac{A(Z)}{B(Z)} OF(t) = -m \frac{C(Z)}{D(Z)} P(t) + \mu(t), \tag{63}$$

and the weights of the imputed transfer function

$$\theta(Z) = 1 + \theta_1 Z + \theta_2 Z^2 + \cdots = -m\frac{B(Z)C(Z)}{A(Z)D(Z)} \tag{64}$$

can be calculated from the estimates. These are illustrated in Figure 5 for homicide, auto theft, and robbery, and these crimes plus burglary exhib-

Table 1. Cross-Correlations Between Residuals $e_1(t)$ and $e_2(t)$

Crime	$\rho_{e2,e1}(0)$	Std. Dev.	$\rho_{e1,e2}(1)$	Std. Dev.
1. Homicide	$-.569$	.18		
2. Robbery	$-.479$	.18		
3. Auto theft	$-.597$	.17		
4. Burglary	$-.544$	.17		
5. Aggravated assault			$-.440$	.18

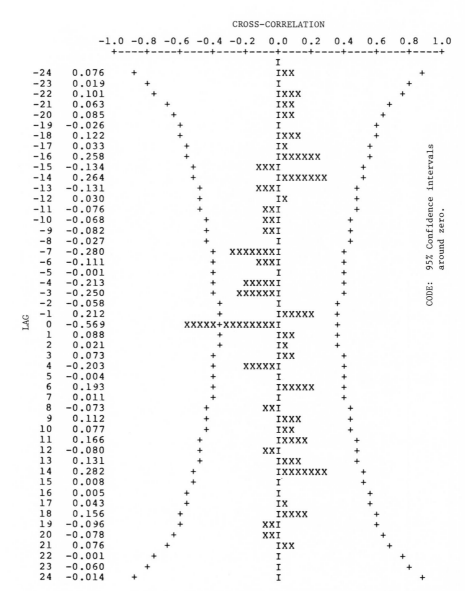

Figure 4. Cross-Correlation between the Innovations of the Homicide
Offense Rate and the Probability of Imprisonment

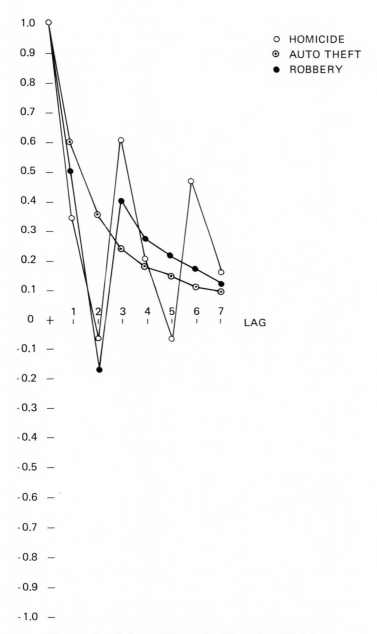

Figure 5.   Inferred Transfer Function Weights

ited a declining geometric lag structure consistent with the model of deterrence.

Using the Box–Jenkins technique, a transfer function model was estimated for homicide, with the offense rate and the probability of imprisonment in differences, $\Delta = (1 - Z)$, and with the transfer function specified in geometric lag form

$$m(Z) = \sum_{i=0}^{m} m_i Z^i = (1 - m) \sum_{i=0}^{m} m^i Z^i = \frac{(1 - m)}{(1 - mZ)},$$

resulting in the following parameter estimates:

$$\Delta OF(t) = \underset{(t=4.24)}{1.0857} - \frac{\overset{(t=6.72)}{2.9963}}{\underset{(t=39.45)}{[1 - 0.9407Z]}} \Delta P(t) + \frac{e(t)}{\underset{(t=4.57)}{[1 + 0.6668Z]}}, \quad (65)$$

where the constant term represents a trend in homicide rates and e(t) is the residual. The residual mean square is .0759. The mean lag in this bivariate model is approximately 16 years. Various other variables were introduced into the model, as reported by Phillips and Ray (1982). The variables *median time served for imprisonment for homicide* and the *unemployment rate for 18- and 19-year-old males* were insignificant when the variables were expressed in differenced form as in Eq. (65). The best forecasting model adds another term to Eq. (65), a distributed lag on the variable *probability of receiving the death sentence given commitment for murder in the first degree* (PD1):

$$\Delta OF(t) = \underset{(t=3.7)}{0.428} - \frac{\overset{(t=4.7)}{8.72\,\Delta P(t)}}{\underset{(t=1.9)}{[1 - .209Z]}} - \frac{\overset{(t=4.8)}{1.81\,\Delta PD1(t)}}{\underset{(t=13.4)}{[1 - .931Z]}} + \frac{e(t)}{\underset{(t=2.1)}{[1 + 430Z]}}, \quad (66)$$

with a residual mean square of .074. Note that the mean lag on the probability of imprisonment is now approximately a quarter of a year, whereas the mean lag on receiving the death sentence given conviction for first-degree murder is 13.5 years. The elasticity of the homicide rate with respect to the probability of imprisonment at lag zero is $-.48$, calculated at the means, and the elasticity for all lags is $-.61$. The corresponding short-run and long-run elasticities for the probability of receiving the death sentence are $-.07$ and -1.1. It is interesting to note the long lags in both Eqs. (65) and (66), which may reflect the slow decay with age from offender status [the parameter λ in Eq. (24)].

The cross-correlation function for aggravated assault showed a significant negative peak at lag 1 with, however, offense rates leading the probability of imprisonment, as illustrated in Figure 6 and reported in Table

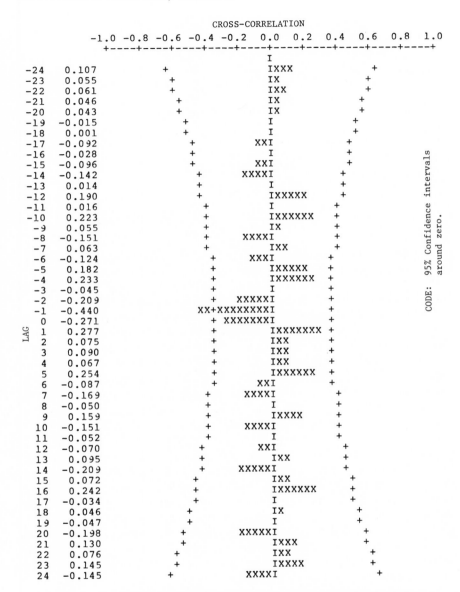

Figure 6.   Cross-Correlation between the Innovations of the
Aggravated Assault Offense Rate and the Probability of Imprisonment

1. The imputed transfer function weights for the model between the innovations

$$e_2(t) = -ne_1(t - 1) + \mu(t) \tag{67}$$

is illustrated in Figure 7 (but not multiplied by the negative coefficient $-n$).

The estimated transfer function model for assault is

$$
P(t) = \underset{(t=8.1)}{0.0127} - \frac{\overset{(t=3.5)}{70.18[1 - Z]}}{\underset{(t=3.7)}{(1 - 0.5896Z)}} OF(t)
$$
$$
+ \frac{1}{[1 - \underset{(t=4.3)}{0.551Z} - \underset{(t=2.5)}{0.319Z^5}]} e(t) \tag{68}
$$

with a residual mean square 2.06×10^{-6}. If the assault rate is not changing, the probability of imprisonment has a homeostatic tendency toward .0127, close to the average value of .0121 for the period 1949 through 1966, before the assault rate began to trend upward rapidly.

The probability of imprisonment is a negatively weighted geometric lag of the change in the offense rate, rather than of the offense rate. Hence this is different than expected for the community response. There was no evidence that the offense rate was a distributed lag of the probability of imprisonment. Attempts to estimate a transfer function with the probability leading the offense rate resulted in insignificant parameters. Thus, for aggravated assault, neither the dynamic model of deterrence nor the model of optimal community response seems appropriate.

However, there is another possibility. Perhaps the assault rate is a proxy for the shadow price. The community response, as represented in Eq. (54), shows consumption as a positive exponential distributed lag of the change in the shadow price, and hence arrests would be a negative exponential distributed lag of the change in the shadow price. Recall that the shadow price is negative, and if, for example, the assault rate is positively correlated with the shadow price, then as the assault rate increases, the shadow price becomes less negative and approaches zero. Thus, if society was becoming less and less concerned with violence, this might be a possible explanation of Eq. (68).

Nonetheless, for the crime of aggravated assault, where there is no observed deterrence effect and where the relationship between the probability of imprisonment and the offense rate differs from the model for community response [Eq. (54)], it is likely that Eq. (68) represents a behavior different from that postulated in the model of optimal control.

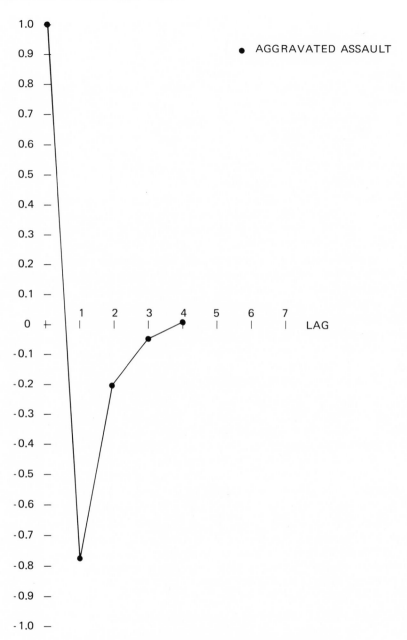

Figure 7. Inferred Transfer Function Weights

VIII. CONCLUSIONS

The empirical estimates for the crimes of homicide, auto theft, robbery, and burglary show that the offense rate for each of these felonies is a negative geometric distributed lag of the probability of imprisonment. There is no evidence that the probability is, in turn, a distributed lag of the offense rate. These findings are consistent with a dynamic model of deterrence, where an increase in the likelihood of sanctions diminishes the flow of new offenders, but where resources allocated to crime control are exogenous. For these crimes there is no evidence the community responds to the crime problem by varying enforcement activity in an attempt to achieve optimal public safety.

The results for aggravated assault are quite different. In contrast to the other crimes, there is no evidence of deterrence. There is evidence that the probability of imprisonment varies with the offense rate, but the pattern differs from the predictions of the model of optimal control.

The dynamic model of deterrence for new offenders and the optimal control model for community response provide insight into the complexity of the relations between crime rates and sanction variables. The empirical results for the five felonies underline the importance of specifying and estimating dynamic relationships between these variables. Static models are inappropriate and could be misleading.

ACKNOWLEDGMENTS

This research was supported under grants No. 79-NI-AX-0069 and No. 81-IJ-CX-0019 from the National Institute of Law Enforcement and Criminal Justice. Points of view are those of the author and do not necessarily reflect the position of the U.S. Department of Justice.

NOTES

1. For example, see Becker (1968), Ehrlich (1973), and Heineke (1978).
2. See Ehrlich (1973) and Hoenack and Weiler (1980).
3. See Phillips and Ray (1982).
4. See Forster (1977).
5. Hoenack et al. (1978) use a similar figure (p. 502) to illustrate the variation of crime with changes in the resources allocated to crime control and to discuss the slope of the supply of offenses, relative to the slope of the probability of arrest function, required for stability (p. 501).
6. It is assumed that for positive consumption and offenses:

$$\frac{\partial U}{\partial C} > 0 \quad \frac{\partial^2 U}{\partial C^2} < 0 \quad \frac{\partial U}{\partial OF} < 0 \quad \frac{\partial^2 U}{\partial OF^2} < 0$$

and

$$\frac{\partial^2 U}{\partial C^2}\frac{\partial^2 U}{\partial OF^2} - \frac{\partial^2 U}{\partial C\,\partial OF} \geq 0 \qquad \frac{\partial^2 U}{\partial C\,\partial OF} < 0.$$

7. The differential equation (13) is implied by the continuous distributed lag,

$$\Omega(t) = \frac{1}{\lambda}\int_0^\infty w(\mu)N(t-\mu)\,d\mu,$$

where the weighting function, $w(\mu)$, is exponential

$$w(\mu) = \lambda e^{-\lambda\mu}$$

with the mean lag equal to $1/\lambda$. To obtain the differential equation, make a change in variables, $q = t - \mu$:

$$\Omega(t) = \frac{1}{\lambda}\int_t^{-\infty} \lambda e^{-\lambda(t-q)}N(q)(-dq)$$

and

$$\Omega(t)e^{\lambda t} = \int_{-\infty}^t e^{\lambda q}N(q)\,dq.$$

Then, differentiating with respect to time, we obtain Eq. (13):

$$\Omega(t)\lambda e^{\lambda t} + e^{\lambda t}\dot\Omega(t) = e^{\lambda t}N(t)$$

8. This can be shown by making the change of variable, $q = t - \mu$, in Eq. (24) and differentiating with respect to time, following the procedure discussed in note 7, above.

9. From Eq. (36),

$$\psi Z'(c) = -\frac{\partial U}{\partial C},$$

and taking derivatives with respect to ψ, we have

$$\psi Z''\frac{\partial C}{\partial \psi} + Z'(C) = -\frac{\partial^2 U}{\partial C^2}\frac{\partial C}{\partial \psi}.$$

Then, solving for $\partial C/\partial\psi$, we have

$$\frac{\partial C}{\partial \psi} = -\frac{Z'(C)}{\psi Z'' + \partial^2 U/\partial C^2} > 0.$$

Alternatively, taking the derivatives with respect to OF, we obtain

$$\psi Z''\frac{\partial C}{\partial OF} = -\frac{\partial^2 U}{\partial C^2}\frac{\partial C}{\partial OF} - \frac{\partial^2 U}{\partial C\,\partial OF}.$$

Then, solving for $\partial C/\partial OF$, we have

$$\frac{\partial C}{\partial OF} = -\frac{\partial^2 U/\partial C\,\partial OF}{\psi Z'' + \partial^2 U/\partial C^2} < 0.$$

10.   Differentiating Eq. (36) with respect to OF, we have

$$\frac{d\psi}{dOF} = \frac{[-Z'\partial^2 U/\partial C^2 + (\partial U/\partial C)Z'']}{(Z')^2} \frac{dC}{dOF} - \frac{Z'(\partial^2 U/\partial C\ \partial OF)}{(Z')^2},$$

and since $dC/dOF > 0$, from Eq. (44), $\partial\psi/dOF > 0$.

11.   From Eq. (36),

$$\psi = \frac{-\partial U/\partial C}{\partial Z/\partial C} \equiv h(C,\ OF)$$

and

$$\frac{d\psi}{dOF} = \frac{\partial h}{\partial C}\frac{\partial C}{dOF} + \frac{\partial h}{\partial OF}.$$

From Eq. (45),

$$\psi = \frac{-\partial U/\partial OF}{\rho + \lambda} \equiv g(C,\ OF)$$

and

$$\frac{d\psi}{dOF} = \frac{\partial g}{\partial C}\frac{dC}{dOF} + \frac{\partial g}{\partial OF}.$$

These two equations can be solved for $d\psi/dOF$, yielding the expression

$$\frac{d\psi}{dOF} = \frac{(\partial^2 U/\partial C^2)(\partial^2 U/\partial OF^2) - (\partial^2 U/\partial C\ \partial OF) + \psi(d^2 Z/dC^2)(\partial^2 U/\partial OF^2)}{[(\partial^2 U/\partial C^2) + \psi(d^2 Z/dC^2)](\rho + \lambda) + (\partial^2 U/\partial OF\ \partial C)(dZ/dC)} < 0.$$

12.   See Box and Jenkins (1970).

13.   The modeling is further complicated because the same error process $\mu_1(t)$ appears in both Eqs. (60) and (61). An attempt was made to include additional variables in the transfer function analysis.

14.   If the cross-correlation function between the residuals was two-sided, a more complex model structure would be indicated:

$$e_1(t) = \alpha_0 e_2(t) + \alpha_1 e_2(t - 1) + \cdots + \mu_1(t)$$

and

$$e_2(t) = \beta_0 e_1(t) + \beta_1 e_1(t - 1) + \cdots + \mu_2(t).$$

An attempt to model the probability of imprisonment as a distributed lag of the homicide rate did not yield significant parameters for the transfer function.

REFERENCES

Becker, Gary S., "Crime and Punishment: An Economic Approach." *Journal of Political Economy* (March/April 1968):526–36.

Box, George, E. P., and Gwilym M. Jenkins, *Time Series Analysis, Forecasting, and Control.* San Francisco: Holden-Day, 1970.

Ehrlich, Isaac, "Participation in Illegitimate Activities: A Theoretical and Empirical Investigation." *Journal of Political Economy* 81, 2(May–June 1973):521–565.

————, "The Deterrent Effect of Capital Punishment: A Question of Life and Death." *American Economic Review* 65, 3(June 1975):397–417.

Forster, Bruce A., "On a One State Variable Optimal Control Problem—Consumption-Pollution Tradeoffs." In John Pitchford and Stephen Turnovsky (eds.), *Applications of Control Theory to Economic Analysis*. Amsterdam: North-Holland, 1977.

Heineke, John M., "Economic Models of Criminal Behavior—An Overview." In J. M. Heineke (ed.), *Economic Models of Criminal Behavior*. Amsterdam: North-Holland, 1978.

Hoenack, Stephen A., R. T. Kudrle, and D. L. Sjoquist, "The Deterrent Effect of Capital Punishment: A Question of Identification," *Policy Analysis* 4 (Fall 1978), pp. 491–527.

Hoenack, Stephen A. and W. C. Weiler, "A Structural Model of Murder Behavior and the Criminal Justice System." *American Economic Review* 70, 3(June 1980):327–341.

Phillips, Llad and Subhash Ray, "Evidence on the Identification and Causality Dispute about the Death Penalty." In O. D. Anderson and M. R. Perryman (eds.), *Applied Time Series Analysis*. North-Holland Publishing Co., 1982.

————, "The Dynamics of Deterrence: Some Contrasting Evidence for Index Felonies." In O. D. Anderson (ed.), *Time Series Analysis: Theory and Practice*. North-Holland Publishing Co. (forthcoming 1983).

Research Annuals in
ECONOMICS

Advances in Applied Micro-Economics
Series Editor: V. Kerry Smith,
University of North Carolina

Advances in Econometrics
Series Editors: R. L. Basmann,
Texas A & M University
and George F. Rhodes, Jr.,
Colorado State University

Advances in the Economics of Energy and Resources
Series Editor: John R. Moroney,
Tulane University

Advances in Health Economics and Health Services Research
(Volume 1 published as Research in Health Economics)
Series Editor: Richard M. Scheffler, *George Washington University* Associate Series Editor:
Louis F. Rossiter, *National Center for Health Services Research*

Applications of Management Science
Series Editor: Randall L. Schultz, *University of Texas at Dallas*

Research in Corporate Social Performance and Policy
Series Editor: Lee E. Preston,
University of Maryland

Research in Domestic and International Agribusiness Management
Series Editor: Ray A. Goldberg,
Harvard University

Research in Economic Anthropology
Series Editor: George Dalton, *Northwestern University*

Research in Economic History
Series Editor: Paul Uselding,
University of Illinois

Research in Experimental Economics
Series Editor: Vernon L. Smith,
University of Arizona

Research in Finance
Series Editor: Haim Levy,
The Hebrew University

Research in Human Capital and Development
Series Editor: Ismail Sirageldin,
The Johns Hopkins University

Research in International Business and Finance
Series Editor: Robert G. Hawkins,
New York University

Research in Labor Economics
Series Editor: Ronald G. Ehrenberg, *Cornell University*

Research in Law and Economics
Series Editor: Richard O. Zerbe, Jr.,
University of Washington

Research in Marketing
Series Editor: Jagdish N. Sheth, *University of Illinois*

Research in Organizational Behavior
Series Editors: Barry M. Staw, *University of California at Berkeley*
and L. L. Cummings, *University of Wisconsin—Madison*

Research in Philosophy and Technology
Series Editor: Paul T. Durbin,
University of Delaware

Research in Political Economy
Series Editor: Paul Zarembka, *State University of New York—Buffalo*

Research in Population Economics
Series Editor: Julian L. Simon,
University of Illinois

Research in Public Policy Analysis and Management
Series Editor: John P. Crecine,
Carnegie-Mellon University

Research in Real Estate
Series Editor: C. F. Sirmans,
University of Georgia

Research in Urban Economics
Series Editor: J. Vernon Henderson, *Brown University*

Please inquire for detailed brochure on each series.

 JAI PRESS INC.